CIMA Exam Practice Kit

Management Accounting Risk and Control Strategy

CIMA Exam Practice Kit

CIMA
PUBLISHING

Management Accounting Risk and Control Strategy

Teddy Foster

ELSEVIER

AMSTERDAM • BOSTON • HEIDELBERG • LONDON • NEW YORK • OXFORD
PARIS • SAN DIEGO • SAN FRANCISCO • SINGAPORE • SYDNEY • TOKYO

CIMA Publishing
An imprint of Elsevier
Linacre House, Jordan Hill, Oxford OX2 8DP
30 Corporate Drive, Burlington, MA 01803

First published 2006

British Library Cataloguing in Publication Data
A catalogue record for this book is available from the British Library

Library of Congress Cataloguing in Publication Data
A catalogue record for this book is available from the Library of Congress

ISBN 10: 0 7506 6937 3
ISBN 13: 978 0 7506 6937 5

Typeset by Integra Software Services Pvt. Ltd, Pondicherry, India
www.integra-india.com
Printed and bound in The Netherlands

Contents

Introduction

Welcome to the CIMA Exam Practice Kit which was launched to coincide with a major change in the syllabus where examinations took place from May 2005.

This Kit has been designed with the needs of home study and distance education candidates in mind and it is also ideal for fully taught courses or for students resitting papers from the old syllabus.

These hints, questions and answers have been produced by some of the best-known freelance tutors in the United Kingdom who have specialised in their respective papers and the questions and topics selected are relevant for the May 2006 and November 2006 examinations.

The exam practice kits will complement CIMA's existing study manuals with the Q&A's from May 2005 published in the 2006 edition of the CIMA study manual and the Q&A's from November 2005 examination published in this edition of the Exam Practice Kit.

Good luck with your studies.

How To Use This Kit

This Practice Kit is an extension of the Study System authored by Paul M. Collier and Sam Agyei-Ampomah. The theory dealt with in the above mentioned Study System is set to questions and answers in this Practice Kit. Where further explanation of a solution is warranted or section of theory in the Study System is relevant, I have included the explanation or reference in [square brackets].

The Study System Takes Precedence

Every set of questions is preceded by reference to the related theory and highlights the key learning in each section. You are advised to study the entire content of each chapter of the Study System so that you are adequately prepared to answer questions from the prescribed material. This Practice Kit is intended to aid your study and does not replace the Study System, change it or limit the examinable content.

Syllabus Guidance, Learning Objectives and Verbs

A The syllabus

The syllabus for the CIMA Professional Chartered Management Accounting qualification 2005 comprises three learning pillars:

- Management Accounting pillar
- Business Management pillar
- Financial Management pillar.

Within each learning pillar there are three syllabus subjects. Two of these subjects are set at the lower 'Managerial' level, with the third subject positioned at the higher 'Strategic' level. All subject examinations have a duration of 3 hours and the pass mark is 50%.

Note: In addition to these 9 examinations, students are required to gain 3 years relevant practical experience and successfully sit the Test of Professional Competence in Management Accounting (TOPCIMA).

B Aims of the syllabus

The aims of the syllabus are

- to provide for the Institute, together with the practical experience requirements, an adequate basis for assuring society that those admitted to membership are competent to act as management accountants for entities, whether in manufacturing, commercial or service organisations, in the public or private sectors of the economy;
- to enable the Institute to examine whether prospective members have an adequate knowledge, understanding and mastery of the stated body of knowledge and skills;
- to complement the Institute's practical experience and skills development requirements.

C Study weightings

A percentage weighting is shown against each topic in the syllabus. This is intended as a guide to the proportion of study time each topic requires.

All topics in the syllabus must be studied, since any single examination question may examine more than one topic, or carry a higher proportion of marks than the percentage study time suggested.

The weightings *do not* specify the number of marks that will be allocated to topics in the examination.

D Learning outcomes

Each topic within the syllabus contains a list of learning outcomes, which should be read in conjunction with the knowledge content for the syllabus. A learning outcome has two main purposes:

1. to define the skill or ability that a well-prepared candidate should be able to exhibit in the examination;
2. to demonstrate the approach likely to be taken by examiners in examination questions.

The learning outcomes are part of a hierarchy of learning objectives. The verbs used at the beginning of each learning outcome relate to a specific learning objective, for example, evaluate alternative approaches to budgeting.

The verb 'evaluate' indicates a high-level learning objective. As learning objectives are hierarchical, it is expected that at this level, students will have knowledge of different budgeting systems and methodologies and be able to apply them.

A list of the learning objectives and the verbs that appear in the syllabus, learning outcomes and examinations follows:

Learning objectives	*Verbs used*	*Definition*
1 Knowledge		
What you are expected to know	List	Make a list of
	State	Express, fully or clearly, the details of/facts of
	Define	Give the exact meaning of
2 Comprehension		
What you are expected to understand	Describe	Communicate the key features of
	Distinguish	Highlight the differences between
	Explain	Make clear or intelligible/State the meaning of
	Identify	Recognise, establish or select after consideration
	Illustrate	Use an example to describe or explain something

3 Application		
How you are expected to apply your knowledge	Apply	To put to practical use
	Calculate/compute	To ascertain or reckon mathematically
	Demonstrate	To prove with certainty or to exhibit by practical means
	Prepare	To make or get ready for use
	Reconcile	To make or prove consistent/compatible
	Solve	Find an answer to
	Tabulate	Arrange in a table
4 Analysis		
How you are expected to analyse the detail of what you have learned	Analyse	Examine in detail the structure of
	Categorise	Place into a defined class or division
	Compare and contrast	Show the similarities and/or differences between
	Construct	To build up or compile
	Discuss	To examine in detail by argument
	Interpret	To translate into intelligible or familiar terms
	Produce	To create or bring into existence
5 Evaluation		
How you are expected to use your learning to evaluate, make decisions or recommendations	Advise	To counsel, inform or notify
	Evaluate	To appraise or assess the value of
	Recommend	To advise on a course of action

Learning Outcomes, Syllabus Content and Examination Format

Paper P3 – Management Accounting Risk and Control Strategy

Syllabus outline

The syllabus comprises:

Topic and study weighting

- A Management Control Systems 15%
- B Risk and Internal Control 20%
- C Review and Audit of Control Systems 15%
- D Management of Financial Risk 30%
- E Risk and Control in Information Systems 20%

Learning aims

Students should be able to

- evaluate and advise on management and internal control systems for a range of risks;
- plan a review process, including an internal audit, of such systems;
- evaluate alternatives and advise on the management of financial risks;
- advise on the development of information systems that support the risk control environment.

Assessment strategy

There will be a written examination paper of 3 hours, with the following sections.

Section A – 50 marks

A maximum of four compulsory questions, totalling 50 marks, all relating to a single scenario.

Section B – 50 marks

Two questions, from a choice of four, each worth 25 marks. Short scenarios will be given, to which some or all questions relate.

A – Management control systems – 15%

Learning outcomes

On completion of their studies students should be able to

1 evaluate and recommend appropriate control systems for the management of organisations;
2 evaluate the control of activities and resources within the organisation;
3 recommend ways in which the problems associated with control systems can be avoided or solved;
4 evaluate the appropriateness of an organisation's management accounting control systems and make recommendations for improvements.

Syllabus content

- The ways in which systems are used to achieve control within the framework of the organisation (e.g. contracts of employment, policies and procedures, discipline and reward, reporting structures, performance appraisal and feedback).
- The application of control systems and related theory to the design of management accounting control systems and information systems in general (i.e. control system components, primary and secondary feedback, positive and negative feedback, open- and closed-loop control).
- Structure and operation of management accounting control systems (e.g. identification of appropriate responsibility and control centres within the organisation, performance target setting, avoiding unintended behavioural consequences of using management accounting controls).
- Variation in control needs and systems dependent on organisational structure (e.g. extent of centralisation versus divisionalisation, management through strategic business units).
- Assessing how lean the management accounting system is (e.g. extent of the need for detailed costing, overhead allocation and budgeting, identification of non-value adding activities in the accounting function).
- Cost of quality applied to the management accounting function and 'getting things right at the first time'.

B – Risk and internal control – 20%

Learning outcomes

On completion of their studies students should be able to

1 define and identify risks facing an organisation;
2 explain ways of measuring and assessing risks facing an organisation, including the organisation's ability to bear such risks;
3 discuss the purposes and importance of internal control and risk management for an organisation;
4 evaluate risk management strategies;

5 evaluate the essential features of internal control systems for identifying, assessing and managing risks;
6 evaluate the costs and benefits of a particular internal control system;
7 discuss the principles of good corporate governance for listed companies, particularly as regards the need for internal controls.

Syllabus content

- Types and sources of risk for business organisations: financial, commodity price, business (e.g. fraud, employee malfeasance, loss of product reputation), technological, external (e.g. economic and political) and corporate reputation (e.g. from environmental and social performance) risks.
- Risks associated with international operations (e.g. from cultural variations and litigation risk, to loss of goods in transit and enhanced credit risk). (*Note*: No specific real country will be tested.)
- Quantification of risk exposures (impact if an adverse event occurs) and their expected values, taking account of likelihood. Minimising the risk of fraud (e.g. fraud policy statements, effective recruitment policies and good internal controls, such as approval procedures and separation of functions, especially over procurement and cash).
- Fraud related to sources of finance (e.g. advance fee fraud and pyramid schemes).
- Minimising political risk (e.g. by gaining government funding, joint ventures, local finance).
- The principle of diversifying risk. (*Note*: Numerical questions will not be set.)
- Purposes of internal control (e.g. safeguarding of shareholders' investment and company assets, facilitation of operational effectiveness and efficiency, contribution to the reliability of reporting).
- Issues to be addressed in defining management's risk policy.
- Elements in internal control systems (e.g. control activities, information and communication processes, processes for ensuring continued effectiveness, etc.).
- Operational features of internal control systems (e.g. embedding in company's operations, responsiveness to evolving risks, timely reporting to management).
- The pervasive nature of internal control and the need for employee training.
- Costs and benefits of maintaining the internal control system.
- The principles of good corporate governance for listed companies (the Combined Code) (e.g. separation of chairman and CEO roles, appointment of non-executive directors, transparency of directors' remuneration policy, relations with shareholders, the audit committee). Examples of recommended good practice may include The King Report on Corporate Governance for South Africa, Sarbanes-Oxley Act in the USA, The Smith and Higgs Reports in the UK, etc.
- Recommendations for internal control (e.g. The Turnbull Report).

C – Review and audit of control system – 15%

Learning outcomes

On completion of their studies students should be able to

1 explain the importance of management review of controls;
2 evaluate the process of internal audit;
3 produce a plan for the audit of various organisational activities including management, accounting and information systems;

4 analyse problems associated with the audit of activities and systems, and recommend action to avoid or solve those problems;
5 recommend action to improve the efficiency, effectiveness and control of activities;
6 discuss the principles of good corporate governance for listed companies, for conducting reviews of internal controls and reporting on compliance;
7 discuss the importance of exercising ethical principles in conducting and reporting on internal reviews.

Syllabus content

- The process of review (e.g. regular reporting to management on the effectiveness of internal controls over significant risks) and audit of internal controls.
- Major tools available to assist with such a process (e.g. audit planning, documenting systems, internal control questionnaires, sampling and testing).
- Detection and investigation of fraud.
- Role of the internal auditor and relationship of the internal audit to the external audit.
- Operation of internal audit, the assessment of audit risk and the process of analytical review, including different types of benchmarking, their use and limitations.
- The principles of good corporate governance for listed companies, for the review of the internal control system and reporting on compliance.
- Relationship of the above to other forms of audit (e.g. value-for-money audit, management audit, social and environmental audit).
- Particular relevance of the fundamental principles in CIMA's Ethical Guidelines to the conduct of an impartial and effective review of internal controls.
- Application of CIMA's Ethical Guidelines on the resolution of ethical conflicts in the context of discoveries made in the course of internal review.

D – Management of financial risk – 30%

Learning outcomes

On completion of their studies students should be able to

1 identify and evaluate financial risks facing an organisation;
2 identify and evaluate appropriate methods for managing financial risks;
3 evaluate the effects of alternative methods of risk management and make recommendations accordingly;
4 calculate the impact of differential inflation rates on forecast exchange rates;
5 explain exchange rate theory;
6 recommend currency risk management strategies.

Syllabus content

- Sources of financial risk, including those associated with international operations (e.g. hedging of foreign investment value) and trading (e.g. purchase prices and sales values).
- Transaction, translation, economic and political risk.
- Minimising political risk (e.g. gaining government funding, joint ventures, obtaining local finance).
- Quantification of risk exposures and their expected values.

- Operation and features of the more common instruments for managing interest rate risk: swaps, forward rate agreements, futures and options. (*Note*: Numerical questions will not be set involving FRAs, futures or options. See the note below relating to the Black Scholes model.)
- Illustration and interpretation of simple graphs depicting cap, collar and floor interest rate options.
- Theory and forecasting of exchange rates (e.g. interest rate parity, purchasing power parity and the Fisher effect).
- Operation and features of the more common instruments for managing currency risk: swaps, forward contracts, money market hedges, futures and options. (*Note*: The Black Scholes option pricing model will not be tested numerically; however, an understanding of the variables which will influence the value of an option should be appreciated.)
- Principles of valuation of financial instruments for management and financial reporting purposes (IAS 39), and controls to ensure that the appropriate accounting method is applied to a given instrument.
- Internal hedging techniques (e.g. netting and matching).

E – Risk and control in information – 20%

Learning outcomes

On completion of their studies students should be able to

1 evaluate and advise managers on the development of IM, IS and IT strategies that support management and internal control requirements;
2 identify and evaluate WIT systems appropriate to an organisation's needs for operational and control information;
3 evaluate benefits and risks in the structuring and organisation of the WIT function and its integration with the rest of the business;
4 evaluate and recommend improvements to the control of information systems;
5 evaluate specific problems and opportunities associated with the audit and control of systems which use information technology.

Syllabus content

- The importance and characteristics of information for organisations and the use of cost–benefit analysis to assess its value.
- The purpose and content of IM, IS and IT strategies, and their role in performance management and internal control.
- Data collection and IT systems that deliver information to different levels in the organisation (e.g. transaction processing, decision support and executive informative systems).
- The potential ways of organising the IT function (e.g. the use of steering committees, support centres for advice and help desk facilities, end-user participation).
- The arguments for and against outsourcing.
- The criteria for selecting outsourcing/Facilities Management partners and for managing ongoing relationships, service level agreements, discontinuation/change of supplier, hand-over considerations.
- Methods for securing systems and data back-up in case of systems failure and/or data loss.
- Minimising the risk of computer-based fraud (e.g. access restriction, password protection, access togging and automatic generation of audit trait).

- Risks in IS/IT systems: erroneous input, unauthorised usage, imported virus infection, unlicensed use of software, theft, corruption of software.
- Risks and benefits of Internet and Intranet use by an organisation.
- Controls which can be designed into an information system, particularly one using information technology (e.g. security, integrity and contingency controls).
- Control and audit of systems development and implementation.
- Techniques available to assist audit in a computerised environment (computer-assisted audit techniques, e.g. audit interrogation software).

Examination Techniques

Essay questions

Your essay should have a clear structure, that is, an introduction, a middle and an end. Think in terms of 1 mark for each relevant point made.

Numerical questions

It is essential to show workings in your answer. If you come up with the wrong answer and no workings, the examiner cannot award any marks. However, if you get the wrong answer but apply the correct technique then you will be given some marks.

Reports and memorandum

Where you are asked to produce an answer in a report type format you will be given easy marks for style and presentation.

- A *report* is a document from an individual or group in one organisation sent to an individual or group in another.
- A *memorandum* is an informal report going from one individual or group to another individual or group in the same organisation.

You should start a report as follows:

To: J. SMITH, CEO, ABC plc

From: M ACCOUNTANT

Date: 31 December 200X

Terms of Reference: Financial Strategy of ABC plc

Management Control Theory

1

> **LEARNING OUTCOMES**
>
> After completing this chapter you should be able to
>
> - evaluate and recommend appropriate control systems for the management of organisations;
> - evaluate the control of activities and resources within the organisation.

Theory

1.1 Organisations are 'social' because they comprise people. They differ from collectives such as families and social groups in that they are goal-oriented and formalised.

1.2 Organisations are characterised as being cybernetic systems based. Cybernetic systems are self-regulating using a feedback mechanism. Systems can be configured into a complex hierarchy of sub-systems.

1.3 Systems can be either open or closed. Closed systems are isolated from the environment meaning that they cannot be changed or influenced. Open systems are influenced by the environment and can be changed. Organisations are configured as open systems facilitating control by management.

1.4 Organisations, as cybernetic systems, contain three levels namely: target-setting level, operations level and control level.

   1.4.1 Typical targets for business are EVA™, ROI and ROCE and these targets which we use will be really reflected in budgets and standard costs.
   1.4.2 Operations is concerned with converting inputs into outputs.
   1.4.3 Control is carried out through a system in which there is provision for corrective action through either a feedback or a feedforward mechanism.

1.5 There are five major standards against which performance can be compared: previous time periods, similar organisations, estimates of future organisational performance *ex ante*, estimates of what might have been achieved *ex post* and the performance necessary to achieve defined goals.

1.6 In this module, we are concerned with selected theories of management and control. The following are key definitions (CIMA *Official Terminology*):

1.6.1 **Control**: The ability to direct the financial and operating policies of an entity with a view to obtaining economic benefits from its activities.

1.6.2 **Management control**: All of the processes used by managers to ensure that organisational goals are achieved and procedures adhered to, and that the organisation responds appropriately to changes in its environment.

1.6.3 **Control environment**: The overall attitude, awareness and actions of directors and management regarding internal controls and their importance to the entity . . . [it] encompasses the management style, and corporate culture and values shared by all employees. It provides a background against which the various other controls are operated.

1.6.4 **Control procedures**: Those policies and procedures in addition to their control environment which are established to achieve that entity's specific objectives.

1.7 Anthony's (1965) classic categorisation of control was at three levels: strategic, management and operational. His work highlighted the interface between strategic planning and operational control such that management control ensured that day-to-day operations were consistent with the overall strategy.

1.8 Otley and Berry (1980) defined management control as monitoring activities and then taking action to ensure that desired ends are attained. (See Figure 1.2 on page 7 of the *Learning System*).

1.9 Central to the cybernetic process is learning. Systems having feedback mechanisms will derive little benefit if learning was not taken place. Fiol and Lyles (1985) defined organisation learning as: "The development of insights, knowledge, and associations between past actions, the effectiveness of those actions, and future actions." They contrasted adaptation, through incremental change, to the environment to other changes. For all purposes, these changes will require creative action (as described by Ford and Ogilvie, 1996) in order to bring about the creation of new knowledge and competitive advantage. (See Figure 1.3 on page 9 of the *Learning System*).

1.10 It is important to understand the differences in typology for management control (Hofstede, 1981). They are divided into two main groups: cybernetic and non-cybernetic. Cybernetic management controls have feedback mechanisms that enable learning and adjustment to the organisational system so that future actions will be different from past actions. Non-cybernetic controls lack feedback mechanisms meaning that these controls relate to specific operations and the organisational system cannot benefit from learning because there is no feedback mechanism.

1.11 Four main organisational structure types are discussed namely: functional structure; divisionalised structure, metrics structures and network structure. Structure is dependent upon the strategy of the organisation. Functional structures are associated with centralised hierarchical organisations; divisionalised structures with multi-national and flat-structured organisations; matrix structures are associated with multi-national or broadly geographically spread organisations but also with project team-oriented organisations; network structures are associated with organisations where collaboration or pooling of resources deliver synergistic advantages.

1.12 Three main responsibilities centre types are: cost centres, profit centres and investment centres.

1.12.1 **Financial control in divisionalised businesses is defined as**: the control of divisional performance by setting a range of targets and monitoring of actual performance towards these targets.

? Questions

1.1 What characteristics distinguish organisations from other collectives such as families and social groups?

1.2 Why would organisations be described as *social*?

1.3 Describe a Cybernetic System.

1.4 Differentiate between an open and a closed system.

1.5 Discuss the three levels of an organisation as a cybernetic system.

1.6 Control can have corrective capabilities. Discuss.

1.7 Differentiate between FEEDFORWARD and FEEDBACK.

1.8 Name the FIVE standards for control.

1.9 Define *control.*

1.10 Define *management control.*

1.11 Define *control environment.*

1.12 Define *control procedures.*

1.13 Discuss Anthony's (1965) classic categorisation of control.

1.14 Name the four conditions of the Otley & Berry management control model.

1.15 What are the limitations of the Otley & Berry management control model?

1.16 Define organisational learning in terms of Fiol & Lyles (1985).

1.17 Why is it creative action important to organisations?

1.18 Describe and contrast the various control types comprising Hofstede's (1981) typology for management control.

1.19 Give two examples of each of the control types in Hofstede's typology.

1.20 Differentiate between the Functional and Divisional structure forms.

1.21 Describe the Matrix structure for an organisation and give two examples.

1.22 Where would a Network structure be appropriate for an organisation?

1.23 Name three forms of responsibility centre.

1.24 What are the most common measures for profit and investment centres?

1.25 Discuss controllability as it relates to the divisionalised organisation.

Solutions

1.1 Goal-orientation and formalisation are two characteristics that distinguish organisations from other collectives such as families and social groups.

1.2 Organisations can be described as social because they comprise people.

1.3 A cybernetic system is a system that has a self-regulating feedback mechanism. It can comprise a complex hierarchy of sub-systems.

1.4 An open system can be influenced by the environment while a closed system is independent from the influences of the environment.

1.5 *Target-setting*: The performance standards and targets set for the organisation;

Operations: The process of converting inputs to outputs that meet market demands;

Control: Comparison of actual performance with targets.

1.6 A system that has corrective action provisions applies to *Closed Loop* systems. *Open loop* systems have no objectives set and cannot be measured objectively.

1.7 *Feedforward* control is the process of forecasting differences between actual and planned outcomes, and implementation of action, before the event, to avoid such differences (CIMA *Official Terminology*). *Feedback* control is the measurement of differences between planned outputs and actual outputs achieved, and the modification of subsequent action and/or plans to achieve future required results (CIMA *Official Terminology*).

1.8
1 Previous time periods
2 Similar organisations
3 *Exante* – estimates of future performance
4 *Expost* – estimates of what might have been achieved
5 The performance necessary to achieve defined goals.

1.9 *Control*: The ability to direct the financial and operationg policies of an entity with a view to gaining economic benefits from its activities (CIMA *Official Terminology*).

1.10 *Management control*: All of the processes used by managers to ensure that organisational goals are achieved and procedures adhered to, and that the organisation responds appropriately to changes in its environment (CIMA *Official Terminology*).

1.11 *Control environment*: The overall attitude, awareness and actions of directors and management regarding internal controls and their importance to the entity . . . [it] encompasses the management style, and corporate culture and values shared by all employees. It provides a background against which the various other controls are operated.

1.12 *Control procedures*: Those policies and procedures in addition to the control environment which are established to achieve the entity's specific objectives.

1.13 Anthony's classic categorisation has three levels:

1 *Strategic control*: Comprising strategic planning, governance procedures, determining the organisation's structure, corporate policies and monitoring. Domain of the Board and CEO.
2 *Management control*: Concerned with implementing strategy and procedures and monitoring performance to ensure it is consistent with strategy and achieves performance targets. Domain of Middle Management.
3 *Operational control*: Takes place at the task level of day-to-day activity where structured and repetitive activities take place. Domain of first-line supervisors.

1.14 1 The existence of an objective that is desired;
2 A means of measuring process outputs in terms of this objective;
3 The ability to predict the effect of potential control actions; and
4 The ability to take actions to reduce deviations from the objective.

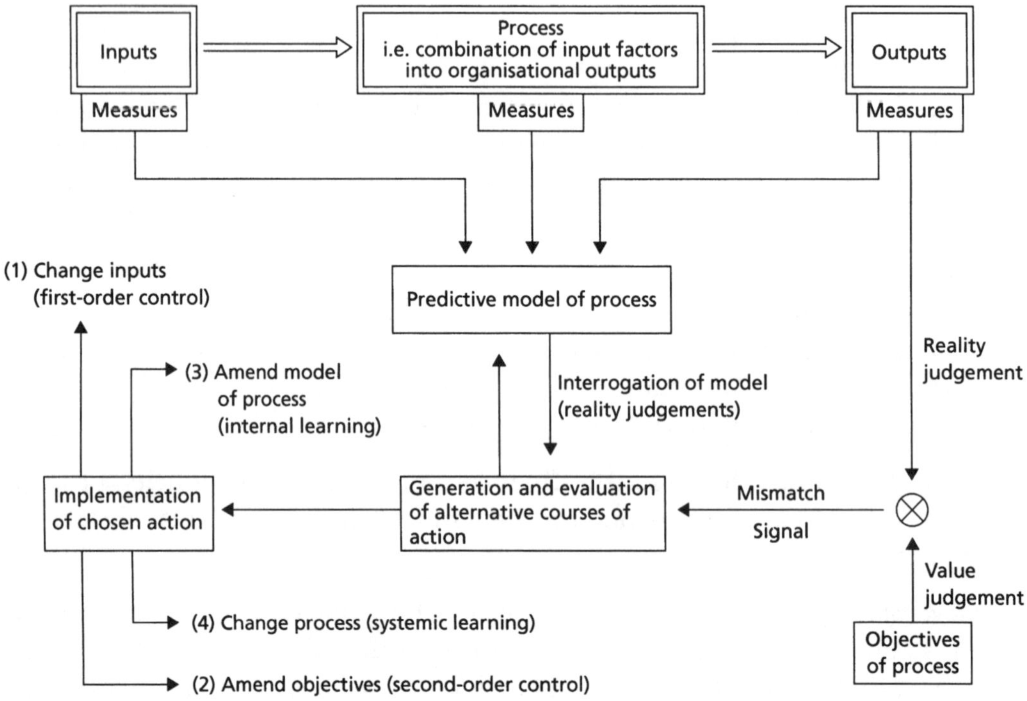

Figure Outline scheme of necessary conditions for a controlled process (Reprinted from Accounting, Organizations and Society, Vol. 5, No. 2, D.T. Otley & A.J. Berry, Control, organization and accounting, pp. 231–44, Copyright 1980, Elsevier Science)

These conditions conform to the concept of a cybernetic control process. The Inputs ⇨ Process ⇨ Outputs model is extended to include a benchmarking element [Predictive Model of Process] that makes it possible to measure performance against a known objective. Depending upon the system being an open system, the management of the organisation can intervene and change the processes to deliver the desired output. The control process is complete when both Reality Judgement and Value Judgement are applied to decision-making.

1.15 According to Otley & Berry (1980), some factors that the model does not cater for are:

(a) Organisational objectives are often vague and ambiguous [unclear]. . . . measures of achievement are possible only in correspondingly vague and often subjective terms . . . [If objectives are unclear and stated in terms that limit objective measurement then clear and accurate feedback will be limited making corrective action difficult];
(b) Change with time. [The effect of this is to make prediction more difficult and increases the risks – something we deal with in greater detail later];
(c) Different models are held by different participants. [The effectiveness of a team is dependant upon the cohesiveness of the participants and if they have differing objectives then the processes will produce differing outputs.]

1.16 Fiol & Lyles (1985) define organisational learning as "The development of insights, knowledge, and associations between past actions, the effectiveness of those actions, and future actions."

[In order to adapt to changes in the environment, the organisation must be able to detect and monitor changes in the environment and adapt (or learn) to deal with those changes. It is therefore critical that organisations understand human learning processes so that they can structure their organisations and processes to accommodate human learning to ensure that they survive and can capitalise on strategic opportunities. Our interest in the process is to devise measurements that enable us to monitor and control the adaptation to the changes. This section deals with elements of that theory.]

1.17 Creative actions are those actions that bring about something new (new knowledge) that enable the management to act or react to the changing environment. ". . . and the lessons learned from taking action are an indispensable source of knowledge creation and competitive advantage." (Extract from Ford & Ogilvie, 1996, p. 58)

1.18 Hofstede (1981) developed a management control typology. Six types were identified of which three are cybernetic in nature [because learning takes place or feedback can be deployed to influence the control system] and the remaining three not.

Cybernetic controls:
Routine control takes place where there are clearly defined objectives, the outputs are measurable, there are known effects of the intervention and the activity is repetitive.

Expert control takes place where objectives are ambiguous, outputs measurable, effects of intervention known but activity is non-repetitive.

Trial-and-error control takes place in an environment where objectives are unambiguous, outputs measurable but effects of interventions *not* known and the control is repetitive.

Non-cybernetic controls:
Intuitive controls take place where objectives are unambiguous, outputs measurable but effects of interventions *not* known and where activity is *non*-repetitive.

Judgemental controls take place where objectives are unambiguous, outputs are *not* measurable, effects of interventions are *not* known and are *non*-repetitive.

Political control takes place where the objectives are ambiguous, outputs are *not* measurable, effects of interventions *not* known and control is *non*-repetitive.

A method for remembering the typology is to construct the following table:

Control Type	Objectives	Outputs	Effects of Interventions	Activity
Cybernetic				
Routine	Unambiguous	Measurable	Known	Repetitive
Expert	Ambiguous	Measurable	Known	Non-repetitive
Trial-and-error	Unambiguous	Measurable	Not known	Repetitive
Non-cybernetic				
Intuitive	Unambiguous	Measurable	Not known	Non-repetitive
Judgemental	Unambiguous	Not measurable	Not known	Non-repetitive
Political	Ambiguous	Not measurable	Not known	Non-repetitive

For a control to meet the requirements to be classified as cybernetic, learning must take place within the organisation.

1.19 [You were required to give *two* examples. I have provided a few more.]

Routine: Banking, letter posting, supermarket checkout, filing, bookkeeping, flight check-in. Control is through predetermined rules and routines.

Expert: Engineering design, medical operation, accounting audit. Control is through an external expert with prior knowledge of the processes.

Trial-and-error: New product launch, launching a prototype rocket, freeing rehabilitated wildlife, sampling an ore body for gold. Control is through learning from failure, through ex-post analysis of the event.

Intuitive: Leading a demoralised football club, selecting staff. Control is an art rather than a science.

Judgemental: A social welfare initiative, a concession to a staff member, resolution of a conflict between two or more parties. Control becomes a matter of subjective judgement.

Political: Public sector organisations, meeting the demands of an influential shareholder, towing the company line. Control is dependant upon power relationships.

1.20 Functional structure is typified by the hierarchy where decision-making is located at the top of the hierarchy and activities grouped according to function (e.g. marketing, finance, production, distribution). Each department executes the functions for all other departments.

Divisional structure is typified by decentralised decision-making devolved to groups based upon major business elements (e.g. Country offices, product line specialists, customer profile groups). Each division has its own functions.

1.21 The matrix structure is a combination of the functional and the divisional structure. Here, the control is shared by the functional manager and the divisional manager.

Examples include control of a sales force in multiple countries. The staff reports to the divisional (country) manager in respect of daily discipline and to the International product manager in respect of the product sales.

1.22 Network structures are best suited to partnerships or collaborations of organisations with different ownerships and objectives exploiting synergy for specialised skill and knowledge. Examples include outsourcing of services or collaborative logistics handling between a client and their supplier.

1.23 The three forms of responsibility centre are:

1 Cost centres
2 Profit centres
3 Investment centres.

1.24 The most common accounting measures of divisional performance are:

- Return on investment (ROI) for profit centres; and
- Residual income (RI) for investment centres.

1.25 Merchant (1987) describes the principle of controllability where individuals are only held accountable for the results that they can control. This highlights one of the limitations of operating profit as a measure of divisional performance. It includes costs over which the divisional manager has no control. When divisions trade within the same group, conflicts arise between the requirement for the group as a whole to make a profit and the profit maximisation objectives of each particular provision. Internal transfer pricing policy can favour or prejudice particular divisions.

Further, objectives and interpretation of performance evaluation between head office and the division will often be quite different and this may result in manipulating of the accounting reports to favour performance measurement of objectives.

Alternative Perspectives and Theoretical Frameworks for Control

2

LEARNING OUTCOMES

After completing this chapter you should be able to

- evaluate and recommend appropriate control systems for the management of organisations;
- evaluate the control of activities and resources within the organisation;
- recommend ways in which the problems associated with control systems can be avoided or solved.

Theory

2.1 Management control cannot rely entirely on cybernetic type control mechanisms. Cybernetic control mechanisms are founded mostly on the economic–rational perspective where behaviour of participants is assumed to be influenced by economically rational behaviour. This assumption relies on the participants, mostly shareholders and organisational managers, being driven by utility maximisation and risk averse motivation.

2.2 When one considers natural and non-rational perspectives, the motivation of participants moves from maximising to *satisficing* behaviour. Under these perspectives, participants' approach to decision-making is driven more by the need to find a suitable all-satisfactory solution rather than the optimal economic solution.

2.3 Then, when considering management control and accounting methodology, one has to factor in the *interpretive or socially constructed reality* perspectives where the meaning of things is distorted by the individual's interpretation of reality.

2.4 A further consideration is the role that the State, regulators, employees, suppliers, customers, competitors and society in general plays in the continued existence and prosperity of the organisation. Here, the radical or critical perspective and stakeholder theory influence management control thinking and accounting practices. These schools of thought highlight the conflicting objectives of shareholders and stakeholders. We are therefore obligated to approach management control from a Pluralist perspective where both the economic–rational and power-based perspectives are synergised resulting in a better understanding of the multiple roles played by both management of the organisation and wider society.

2.5 Agency theory highlights the relationship between shareholders and managers of organisations. In many instances, shareholders (the principal) do not have full access to the organisation's information and therefore run risk that the directors (the agent) could 'shirk' their responsibility. Both the shareholders and the directors, assumed to be risk averse, are dependent upon environmental conditions and the performance of the directors to maximise utility.

2.6 When considering management control, shareholder value remains the dominant influence, and contemporary thinking centers around value based management (VBM). Stakeholder theory, on the other hand, emphasises the role of others in addition to the shareholders, and contemporary practice has seen the rise of corporate social responsibility reporting (CSR) becoming a dominant feature of accounting and financial reporting structures.

2.7 Mayo's Hawthorne experiment highlighted worker behaviour and demonstrated the role of attention seeking in employee behaviour. Seen from a control perspective, it is imperative for the manager to understand human behaviour in order to design control and measurement processes that will shape the behaviour of employees to favourably influence the greater organisational performance.

2.8 Schools of thought including Contingency theorists, the role of culture, power and politics enable us to better understand the decision-making environment in which management must perform their task. The influences of their power, the interpretation of reality, control over the information dissemination process, including the role of accounting practices and reporting, are continually under pressure due to conflicting interests and the process of globalisation and international trade. Our ability to change behaviour, reporting processes and the interpretation of these reporting outputs are constrained by the organisation's historical context, cultural influences of stakeholders, political power within and around the organisation.

2.9 It is, therefore, imperative that we address the role of management control with due consideration of the complexities involved. We are aided in this task when we include paradigms investigated from divergent perspectives. A summary of these perspectives follows:

2.9.1 *Agency theory*: emphasises shareholder value and the manager, as agent, of the shareholder (Principal) being dependent on the environment and their own performance in delivering value (utility) to the shareholder and themselves.

2.9.2 *Stakeholder theory*: addresses the role of participants, other than shareholders and managers, within and related to the organisation and influences the accounting and reporting processes.

2.9.3 *Contingency theory*: highlights the influences of the environment and the uniqueness of individual organisations and the absence of any 'one best way' for management to control organisations.

2.9.4 *Institutional theory*: emphasises the role of institutions outside of the subject organisation and the requirement for complicity with political, social, cultural and value norms in order for the organisation to survive and prosper.

2.9.5 *Cultural theory*: where management control has to factor in the organisation's norms, values and beliefs and the socialisation process is that which exist in organisations.

2.9.6 The picture is not complete unless the role of power, politics and influence are factored into the management control processes and the resulting impact upon accounting and reporting outputs.

? Questions

2.1 Distinguish between the economic-rational perspective and natural/non-rational perspective.

2.2 Explain what Hopwood (1983) was describing when he coined the phrase "accounting in action".

2.3 According to what perspective would management control systems be seen as not being neutral mechanisms but dependent on, and reinforcing of, particular power interests and cross divisions?

2.4 Through which approach are we likely to derive a better understanding of the multiple roles played by management control?

2.5 In the relationship between shareholders and directors, the application of Agency theory can be seen as closely associated with the economic–rational paradigm. Discuss the risks and rewards associated with the agency theory.

2.6 In terms of VBM theory, explain the 'value gap'.

2.7 What is emphasised by VBM?

2.8 List four measurement approaches included in VBM.

2.9 Give an example of stakeholder theory applied to financial reporting.

2.10 What was the key finding of Mayo's Hawthorne experiment?

2.11 Contrast the situation-specific approach of the Contingency theorists with the Universalist approach.

2.12 Why are new entrants to an organisation socialised into the culture of that organisation?

2.13 Discuss the statement "Accounting is a social and institutional practice".

2.14 In the context of Institutional theory, *legitimisation* refers to the dependence of the organisation on support from the environment for its survival. Describe the environment and its influence on the organisation.

2.15 Explain the role of accounting in the context of the diverse theories in relation to management control.

✓ Solutions

2.1 Under the economic-rational perspective, decisions are computed as a result of preferences with economically rational people acting to maximise their own self-interests in pursuit of those things that would bring them utility or benefit.

Under the natural and non-rational perspectives, decision makers would seek to find a solution that would generally attain that goal (satisfying). March and Simon (1958) described satisficing being based on bounded rationality, where actors with general goals search for whatever solution more or less attains these goals.

2.2 Hopwood was describing the effects of socially constructed meaning (the interpretive perspective) two organisational reality. He was describing the "ways in which accounting reflects, reinforces or even constrains the strategic postures adopted by a particular organisation".

[The interpretive perspective describes a situation where "individuals act towards things on the basis of the *meaning* that things that have for them." (Collier and Agyei-Ampomah, 2005). The influence of this perspective on accounting information is to adjust the construct of reporting to reflect meaning that may not be synchronised with economic-rational objectives and, in so doing, present a symbolic representation of reality. Under these conditions, accounting reporting adopts a ceremonial posture that reflects the individual interpretation of the information.]

2.3 The radical or critical perspective sees management control systems not as neutral mechanisms but dependent on, and reinforcing of, particular power interests and class divisions.

2.4 The pluralist applies the interpretive and critical perspectives in addition to the economic–rational approach and, in so doing, gains a better understanding of the multiple roles played by management control both in the organisation and in society as a whole.

2.5 The assumption of the Agency theory is that the Principal and the Agent are risk averse and utility maximisers. The Agent is assumed to maximise utility (or benefit) from reward but disutility from effort expended. The Principal, on the other hand, maximises utility through the effort expended by the Agent and disutility from his 'shirking'. The risk for the Agent depends upon factors in the environment and his own performance and for the Principal upon the above, as well as the quality of accounting information if the Principal cannot observe all of the activities of the Agent.

2.6 'Value gap' is the difference between the market value of the shares and the value of the business.

2.7 Value-based-management (VBM) emphasises value maximisation to shareholders.

2.8 VBM includes the following measurement bases:

1 Total shareholder return
2 Market value added
3 Shareholder value added
4 Economic Value Added (EVA®).

2.9 Corporate responsibility reporting is an example of stakeholder theory.

2.10 Mayo conducted the experiment to research ways to improve worker productivity. He found that workers were motivated more by the attention of the researchers than the actual changes made to their working conditions.

2.11 The Contingency theorists argue that every organisation is unique and control measures should be designed specifically for that organisation while the Universalists argue that there is an optimal control system design that applies at least to some extent across different circumstances and organisations.

2.12 New entrants are socialised into the culture and belief system of an organisation to convey:

1 A sense of identity
2 Generate commitment
3 Enhance social system stability
4 Serve as a sense-making device to shape behaviour.

2.13 Accounting is a process of recording and reporting financial information and can be manipulated to reflect the interpretation of those with political power and influence.

[When we consider the radical changes being undertaken within the International Accounting Standards and, more recently, the International Financial Reporting Standards, we become acutely aware of the influences of the power of groups (the influence of USA reporting standards, for example) on the shaping of the standards. Refer to the IAS and IFRS for more information and look at the update commentary for the discussion that is taking place on key reporting standards. This is discussed by Markus and Pfeffer (1983) in which they argue that "accounting and control systems are related to intra-organisational power because they collect and manipulate information used in decision-making and because they are used to change the performance of individuals".]

2.14 Organisations are dependant upon government or regulatory authority approval for its existence and are dependant upon the acquisition of resources for their operational purposes. Thus, the environment on which the organisation is dependant is comprised of the stakeholders related to the organisation.

[Because the organisation is dependant upon not only the influences of their shareholders but also the political and social power influences of employees, government, regulatory authority, clients, suppliers, consultants, rating agencies, financiers and society at large, they are obligated to structure their controls in such a way as to address these diverse and, often divergent, demands to ensure their continued survival.]

2.15 When constructing an accounting system, the influences of political, social and institutional power should be factored into the design so as to accommodate the culture, norms, ritual and custom of the role players within the organisation and to reflect the needs of the stakeholders in, and associated with, the organisation in such a way that the organisation addresses the intra-organisational influences on the sustained existence and sustained prosperity of the organisation.

Accounting Control and Behavioural Consequences

3

LEARNING OUTCOMES

After completing this chapter you should be able to

- evaluate and recommend appropriate control systems for the management of organisations;
- evaluate the control of activities and resources within the organisation;
- recommend ways in which the problems associated with control systems can be avoided or solved;
- evaluate the appropriateness of an organisation's management accounting control systems and make recommendations for improvements.

Theory

3.1 This section discusses the intended and unintended behavioural consequences of quantitative and qualitative measurement methodologies.

3.2 Standard costing, capital investment appraisal and overhead allocation techniques that make up the traditional measurement methodologies offer the user stability and simplicity on the one hand, but constrained by potential over-simplification and broad approximation leading to the risk of inappropriate decisions on the other. Enhancements, notably activity based costing (ABC), flexed budgets and the addition of strategic cost accounting has extended the use of these instruments to more modern methodologies. Even with these modern advances, indirect cost allocation remains, to a somewhat lesser degree, an approximation.

3.3 Inter-departmental/SBU pricing policies (transfer pricing) remains a contentious issue. Policy is an indicator for performance rewarding, operational success measurement that with behaviour that can be counterproductive for the overall good of the greater organisation. Globalisation is compounding the problem and, with the intervention of governments in respect of counter-tax management strategies, organisations are faced with governance, risk and operational challenges.

3.4 Budgeting has had a long and fruitful role to play in the process of organisational control. However, human behaviour being what it is, in many organisations power, political posturing and gaming take precedence over objective and accurate budgeting linked to strategic objectives. Organisations like the Beyond Budgeting Round Table argue that budgeting is counterproductive, provides for poor value to users, fails to focus on shareholder value, is too rigid and stifle response, protects rather than reduces costs, stifles product and strategy innovation, focuses inappropriately on sales targets rather than customer satisfaction and is often divorced from strategy.

3.5 As with many other aspects of risk management, budgets tend to reinforce a dependency culture that can lead to unethical behaviour or compliance behaviour that exposes the organisation to heightened risk.

3.6 Standard costing provides a platform upon which actual to planned variances can be analysed. With the advent of computerisation, flexed budgets provide a more advanced approach to managing costs and cost variances.

3.7 JIT, TQM, Six Sigma and emergent accounting techniques including strategic management accounting, life-cycle costing, target costing and Kaizen techniques are enhancing the capabilities of organisations' management teams to better manage production, customer-orientated demand with corresponding improvements and rationalisation of accounting (e.g. Backflush accounting used in JIT manufacturing).

3.8 The advantages of JIT, Michael Porter's value chain theory and focused attention on value adding activities, has accelerated the acceptance of a lean manufacturing and lean management accounting.

3.9 In all of the deliberations, we need to be conscious of the fact that controls in general, and accounting controls in particular, could lead to dysfunctional behaviour where measurements and demands made on individuals leave room for self-enrichment or towing-the-line behaviour that is counter to the best interests of the organisation.

3.10 Dysfunctional consequences include tunnel vision, sub-optimisation, myopia, measure fixation, misrepresentation, misinterpretation, gaming and ossification.

3.11 It cannot be overemphasised that close attention to the design of quantitative and qualitative measures is necessary to reinforce desired outcomes and control dysfunctional consequences. The management accountant is well placed, as a result of her professional training and skill, to guide and manage risk controls and measurements to bring about positive valued adding outcomes.

? Questions

3.1 List the main accounting methods through which control is exercised.

3.2 Define *Standard costing*.

3.3 Describe the three main methods of capital investment appraisal.

3.4 What alternative analysis techniques does Shank (1996) argue could provide a better fit (other than DCF modelling) between investment decisions and business strategy implementation?

3.5 Explain how activity based costing improves cost measurement.

3.6 List the three purposes of budgeting according to Emmanuel et al. (1990).

3.7 Describe how feedforward and feedback loops influence budgeting processes.

3.8 Describe three problems in the budgeting process that could influence the validity of a budget as a control mechanism.

3.9 What are the primary difficulties associated with budgeting?

3.10 List the 10 reasons why budgets cause problems according to the Beyond Budgeting Round Table (www.bbrt.co.uk/).

3.11 Discusse the fundamental differences between traditional budgeting and 'beyond budgeting'.

3.12 Describe the role of variance analysis in the budgetary control process.

3.13 How does the Just In Time (JIT) management technique affect the accounting process?

3.14 Why is standard costing seen to be restrictive when TQM techniques are applied?

3.15 Define the cost of quality.

3.16 Describe the two broad categories of cost of quality.

3.17 List four emerging management accounting techniques.

3.18 List Lord's (1996) summary of the characteristics of SMA.

3.19 What are the benefits of life-cycle costing?

3.20 Target costing is concerned with managing whole-of-life costs *during the design phase*. Its aim is to build a product at a cost that could be recovered over the product lifecycle through a price that customers would be willing to pay to obtain the benefits. Describe the stages of target costing that support the above objectives.

3.21 Discuss the difference in focus between Kaizen and target costing in the product life cycle.

3.22 What are the five principles of the lean management accounting?

3.23 Define Backflush costing.

3.24 Discuss dysfunctional consequences of budgeting.

3.25 Describe eight unintended consequences of performance measurement.

Solutions

3.1 Control is exercised through the following main accounting methods:

1 Standard costing
2 Capital investment appraisal
3 Overhead allocation
4 Transfer pricing
5 Budgets and budgetary control.

3.2 *Standard costing* is a control technique which compares standard costs and revenues with actual results to obtain variances which are used to stimulate improved performance (CIMA *Official Terminology*)

3.3 The three main methods of capital investment appraisal are:

1 Accounting rate of return which computes the annual cash flows minus depreciation divided by the initial investment.
2 Payback period computes the time period over which the initial investment is returned.
3 Discounted cash flow (DCF) which requires estimation of future incremental cash flows (additional cash flows based on income net of expenses) that will result from the investment, discounted at a rate of return required from the project.

3.4 Shank (1996) argued that a strategic cost management approach could apply value chain analysis, cost driver analysis and competitive advantage analysis to achieve a better fit between investment decisions and business strategy implementation.

[Strategic cost management is an approach that focuses management attention on external factors that influence market parameters and cost of the organisation. Shank's approach argues, from a more practical perspective, that the application of value chain analysis, which provides an insight into the customer value adding aspects of the organisation, cost driver analysis which links cost determination to decision-making on a cause-and-effect basis, and competitive advantage analysis which informs the sustainable strategic advantage, will provide a more reliable measure of value creation than the output from DCF modelling by addressing the 'richness' of the situation. He argues that a strategic cost management approach will form the basis for decision-making based upon known strengths that the organisation is capable of exploiting. Analysis based upon pre-existing resource and skill provides a link between the organisation's pre-existing competitive advantage and proposed investment. This method measures prospective investments in terms of those advantages. By executing DCF modelling, we are evaluating the potential investment independent from the investing organisation. The key question that Shank raises is whether the investment will have a synergistic fit with the investing organisation's competitive advantage.]

3.5 Activity based costing requires that all costs are allocated to the product or products based upon the consumption by the respective products of activities. Costs of activities, that cannot be traced to the products directly, are arranged in a hierarchy of cost pools. Each cost pool collects costs based upon the influence of a cost driver that best correlates cause-and-effect for that group of activities. While activity based costing methods are based upon approximation, because of the higher degree of correlation between the cost drivers and the consumption of activities, the degree of inaccuracy is reduced and, thereby improving the quality of information for decision-making.

3.6 The three purposes of budgeting, according to Emmanuel et al. (1990) are:

1 A full cost of future events
2 As motivational targets
3 As standards for performance evaluation.

3.7 Feedforward loops enable managers to review budgets before implementation in order to ensure that the budget reflects the organisation's goals and objectives of the strategies. Feedback loops enable management to measure the difference between actual output and planned output of the organisation.

3.8 Three possible problems that could arise in the budgeting process that could limit its performance in its role as a control mechanism are:

1 *Gaming*: Low targets are set because managers believe these will be readily achieved. This has the effect of reducing budgeting to a process of negotiation rather than detailed planning.
2 *Creative accounting*: Manipulating results so that targets are achieved, particularly where these are linked with performance bonuses.
3 *Achievement motive*: Once targets are achieved, managers may no longer be motivated to continue their efforts, particularly as this may result in higher targets being set in the future.

3.9 The primary difficulties related to budgeting are in predicting the volume of sales for the business, especially the sales mix between different products or services and the timing of incomes and expenses.

3.10 The list of 10 reasons why budgets cause problems according to the Beyond Budgeting Round Table (www.bbrt.co.uk/) are listed below:

Budgets:

1 Are time-consuming and expensive
2 Provide poor value to users
3 Fail to focus on shareholder value
4 Are too rigid and prevent fast response
5 Protect rather than reduce costs
6 Stifle product and strategy innovations
7 Focus on sales targets rather than customer satisfaction
8 Are divorced from strategy
9 Reinforce a dependency culture
10 Can lead to unethical behavior.

3.11 The two fundamental differences between traditional budgeting and the 'beyond budgeting' models are:

1 The beyond budgeting model is more adaptive. In place of fixed annual plans and budgets that tie managers to predetermined actions, targets are reviewed regularly and based on stretch goals linked to performance against world-class benchmarks and prior periods.
2 The beyond budgeting model enables a more decentralised way of managing. In place of the traditional hierarchy and centralized leadership, it enables decision-making and performance accountability to be devolved to line managers and creates a self-managed working environment and a culture of personal responsibility.

3.12 Variance analysis involves comparing actual performance against planned, investigating the causes of the variance and taking corrective action to ensure that targets are achieved.

3.13 JIT techniques provide for the reduction in inter-stage manufacturing buffer inventories and reduce cycle times substantially. Work-in-progress inventories are virtually eliminated. These characteristics have the effect of reducing the need for inter-stage accounting due to the minimal amount of inventory in progress at any one time. This has given rise to Backflush costing techniques. Typically, Accounting stages are reduced to raw material, finished goods and cost of goods sold.

3.14 Standard costing techniques can be restrictive when a TQM approach is adopted because there will be a tendency to aim at the more obvious cost reductions (cheaper labour and materials) rather than the aims of TQM which are improvement in quality, reliability, on-time delivery, flexibility etc.

[An important observation is that budgeting, standard costing and variance analysis should not be deployed without taking the wider array of measurement techniques into account and weighing the outputs from the broader measurement array in the decision-making process.]

3.15 The cost of quality is 'the difference between the actual costs of producing, selling and supporting products or services and the equivalent costs if there were no failures during production for usage.' (CIMA *Official Terminology*)

3.16 The two broad categories of cost of quality are:

1 *Conformance costs* which are costs incurred to achieve the specified standard of quality and include prevention costs and costs of appraisal.
2 *Non-conformance* costs are costs which include both internal and external failures.

3.17 Emerging management accounting techniques include:

1 Strategic management accounting
2 Life-cycle costing
3 Target costing
4 Kaizen costing.

3.18 According to Lord (1996), SMA is comprised of:

- The collection of competitor information: pricing, costs, volume and market share;
- Exploitation of cost reduction opportunities: a focus on continuous improvement and on non-financial performance measures;
- Matching the accounting emphasis with the firm's strategic position.

3.19 Life-cycle costing helps to determine whether the profits generated during the production phase cover all the life-cycle costs.

[This is particularly valuable in modern industries where up to 80% of the costs of the product can be incurred during the development phase. With life-cycles for products substantially reduced, particularly in the technology field, it is important for management to be able to predict future product/service development costs associated with new products and to evaluate market conditions and pricing to ensure that the development costs are recovered over the life cycle of the product.]

3.20 Target costing has four stages:

1 Determining the target price which customers will be prepared to pay for the product/service;
2 Deducting a target profit margin to determine the target cost which becomes the cost to which the product/service should be engineered;
3 Estimating the actual cost of the product/service based on the current design;
4 Investigating ways of reducing the estimated cost to the target cost.

3.21 Target costing is a 'before-the-event' process involving the entire products cost evaluation at the design phase. Kaizen costing is applied during the production phase of the life cycle when large innovations may not be possible – hence the name Kaizen (Japanese term for the word 'tightening') where the focus falls on continuous improvement to the production process. The investigation of cost reduction is a cost-to-function analysis that examines the relationship between how much cost is spent on the primary functions of the product/service compared to the secondary functions.

3.22 The five principles of lean management accounting are:

1 *Value provided to customers* is reflected in the price by using a *target costing* the approach;
2 *Value streams management*: Managing the business through processes or value streams rather than traditional departmental structures;
3 Flow of products and services through the value stream while *eliminating waste;*
4 *Pull* to enable flow of products and services based on customer demand *rather than push* through production processes;
5 *Perfection* through quality improvement which is both continuous and breakthrough.

3.23 Backflush costing is a method of costing, associated with a JIT (Just In Time) production system, which applies cost to the output of a process. Costs do not mirror the flow of products through the production process, but are attached to output produced (finished goods stock and cost of sales), on the assumption that such backflushed costs are a realistic measure of the actual cost incurred. (CIMA *Official Terminology*)

3.24 Budgeting dysfunctional behaviour includes:

Smoothing: Shifting revenue or expenses from one accounting period to another to enable smoother increments in profits.

Biasing: The selection of a message that the recipient wants to hear, such as a high forecast (because that is what is wanted) rather than one perceived to be more realistic.

Focusing: Placing emphasis on certain positive aspects of performance rather than other negative ones.

Gaming: Pursuit of a particular performance standard in response to that demanded of the participant even though they know that this is not in the organisation's best interest in terms of its strategy. The creation of 'slack' (asking for more than what is required) to cushion performance requirements and/or to provide padding to counteract budget reduction practices of senior managers; spending budget allocations at the year end whether the expenditure is needed or not.

Filtering: Data are filtered so that desirable aspects of performance are reported by the information system while undesirable aspects of performance are suppressed.

Illegal acts: An action that violates organisational rules.

3.25 Smith (1995), in a public sector study, found the following eight unintended consequences of performance measurement:

1 *Tunnel vision*: The emphasis on quantifiable data at the expense of qualitative data.
2 *Sub-optimisation*: the pursuit of narrow local objectives at the expense of broader organisation-wide ones.
3 *Myopia*: The short-term focus on performance may have a longer-term consequences.
4 *Measure fixation*: An emphasis on measures rather than the underlying objective.
5 *Misrepresentation*: The deliberate manipulation of data so that reported behaviour is different from actual behaviour.
6 *Gaming*: The pursuit of a particular performance standard in response to that demanded of the participant while knowing that this is not in the organisation's best interest in terms of its strategy.
7 *Ossification*: Performance measurement can inhibit innovation and lead to paralysis of action.
8 *Misinterpretation*: The way in which the performance measure is explained.

Corporate Governance and the Audit Committee

4

Learning Outcomes

After completing this chapter you should be able to

- explain the principles of good corporate governance for listed companies (using the UK system as a model), particularly as regards the need for internal controls;
- discuss the principles of good corporate governance for listed companies, for conducting reviews of internal controls and reporting on compliance.

Theory

4.1 The rise of corporate governance is largely in response to the spate of corporate failures across the world. Culminating in the *Combined Code*, the UK reporting requirements for FTSE listed companies has developed over the last decade into robust requirements for boards of directors to demonstrate and disclose their compliance with 'best practice' in respect of corporate governance recommendations.

4.2 Corporate governance models are comprised either of shareholder value/agency models or stakeholder models. The UK corporate governance model is premised in the shareholder value/agency model. The South African corporate governance model, by contrast, is an example of a stakeholder model.

4.3 The *Combined Code* places specific responsibilities upon the board of directors with regards to the composition, structure and defined committee activities of the board. Specific committees, comprised mostly of non-executive directors are charged with the responsibility of determining director remuneration, overseeing audit standards and reviewing board nominations.

4.4 Of these committees, the audit committee fulfils a pivotal role in corporate control. Code C3 of the Combined Code states: *the board should establish an audit committee of at least three, or in the case of smaller companies two members, who should all be independent non-executive directors. The board should satisfy itself that at least one member of the audit committee has a recent and relevant financial experience.*

4.5 CIMA defines an audit committee as: *A formally constituted sub-committee of the main board which should normally meet at least twice a year. Membership of the committee should comprise at least three directors, all non-executive. The majority of the committee members should be independent of the company. The primary function of the audit committee is to assist the board to fulfil its stewardship responsibilities by reviewing the systems of internal control, the external audit process, the work of the internal audit and the financial information which is provided to shareholders* (CIMA *Official Terminology*).

4.6 The combined code guidance on audit committees is referred to as the Smith Guidance. The Smith Guidance emphasises that: . . . a frank, open working relationship and a high level of mutual respect are essential, particularly between the audit committee chairman and the board chairman, the chief executive and the finance director. The audit committee must be prepared to take a robust stand, and all parties must be prepared to make information freely available to the audit committee, to listen to their views and to talk through the issues openly (para. 1.7).

[It is imperative that the participant reviews the roles, responsibilities and structure of the audit committee due to its pivotal role and priority seen from a financial control perspective.]

4.7 The benefits of good corporate governance include risk reduction, performance stimulation, enhanced access to capital markets, improved customer and supplier perception, leadership enhancement and shareholder confidence. Organisation's recognising and the benefits of good corporate governance and stimulating the adaptation of corporate culture towards its acceptance are benefiting from the competitive advantages that it brings through heightened market image and the resultant trust of the organisation.

4.8 Developments within the banking industry, with the advent of the Basel II Accord that is being rolled out internationally at present, brings greater emphasis upon real-time empirical data based credit risk rating and greater emphasis upon operational risk management.

4.9 Corporate governance is clearly here to stay and will grow in prominence and complexity as industry, regulators, governments and auditors get to grips with the processes and society reaps the benefits of the outcomes.

4.10 Corporate governance is a key leadership and functional mechanism that drives policies, procedures and operations that will have an impact on the controls, measurement, auditing and risk responses within the organisation.

? Questions

4.1 List and describe the two models of corporate governance.

4.2 List and briefly describe the chronological development of corporate governance in the UK leading to the *Combined Code* currently in use.

4.3 Discuss the key objectives and implications of the Sarbanes-Oxley Act introduced in the USA in 2002.

4.4 Define corporate governance.

4.5 Elaborate on the approach known as "comply or explain".

4.6 List the principles of the Code relating to directors.

4.7 List the principles of the Code relating to remuneration.

4.8 List the principles of the Code relating to accountability and audit.

4.9 List the principles of the Code relating to relations with shareholders.

4.10 List the principles of the Code relating to institutional shareholders.

4.11 List the principles of Schedule C of the Code relating to disclosure.

4.12 Define Board effectiveness in terms of the *Combined Code*.

4.13 Contrast the roles of chairman and chief executive in terms of the *Combined Code*.

4.14 List and describe Higgs's suggestions for good practice in respect of non-executive directors.

4.15 List the factors that, in terms of Code provision A3, render independence of the director unlikely.

4.16 What is the role of the remuneration committee?

4.17 What is the role of the nomination committee?

4.18 Define 'audit committee' in terms of CIMA *Official Terminology*.

4.19 What are the main roles and responsibilities of the audit committee?

4.20 What are the benefits of good corporate governance?

✓ Solutions

4.1 The corporate governance models are:

1 Shareholder value/agency
2 Stakeholder value

Shareholder value-based corporate governance models single out the shareholder as the affected party and dictates controls and disclosure directed at protecting the shareholders' interests.

Stakeholder value-based corporate governance models recognise interests held by others in addition to the shareholder community and integrates social, environmental and economic aspects of organisational activities for control and disclosure.

4.2 1992 – The Cadbury Report on Financial Aspects of Corporate Governance followed corporate failures including Polly Peck, BCCI, Maxwell Group.

1995 – Greenbury report on Director's Remuneration.

1998 – Hempel report in pursuit of the implementation of the Cadbury report leading to the Corporate Governance *Combined Code.*

1999 – The Institute of Chartered Accountants in England & Wales issued the Turnbull Guidance which was substantially integrated into the *Combined Code.*

2003 – The Higgs report on the role of non-executive directors and, Smith report on the role of audit committees were both issued and integrated into the *Combined Code.*

2004 – The London Stock Exchange and RSM Robinson Rhodes produced a practical guide to corporate governance and the *Combined Code.*

4.3 The core objectives of the Sarbanes-Oxley Act are to promote transparency, integrity and oversight of financial markets. The CEO and CFO are required to certify annual and quarterly financial reports and give assurances regarding effectiveness of internal controls with criminal penalties the consequence of false certifications.

4.4 Corporate governance is the System by which companies are directed and controlled. Boards of directors are responsible for the governance of their companies. The shareholders' role in governance is to appoint the directors and the auditors and to satisfy themselves that an appropriate governance structure is in place. The responsibilities of the board include setting the company's strategic aims, providing the leadership to put them into effect, supervising the management of the business and reporting to shareholders on their stewardship. The board's actions are subject to laws, regulations and their shareholders in general meeting (CIMA *Official Terminology*).

4.5 The "comply or explain" approach adopted by the UK Stock Exchange Listing Rules requires of listed companies to comply with the Combined Code on Corporate Governance or explain in their financial statements all deviations.

4.6 The principles of the Code relating to directors are:

A1 Every Company should be headed by an effective board which is collectively responsible for the success of the company.

A2 There should be a clear division of responsibilities at the head of the company between the running of the board and the executive responsibility for the running of the company's business. No one individual should have unfitted powers of decision-making.

A3 The Board should include a balance of executive and non-executive directors (and in particular independent non-executive directors) such that no individual or small group of individuals can dominate the board's decision-making.

A4 There should be a formal, rigorous and transparent procedure for the appointment of new directors to the board.

A5 The board should be supplied in a timely manner with information in a form and of a quality appropriate to enable it to discharge its duties. All directors should receive induction on joining the board and should regularly update and refresh their skills and knowledge.

A6 The board should undertake a formal and readers annual evaluation of its own performance and that of its committees and individual directors.

A7 All directors should be submitted for re-election at regular intervals, subject to continued satisfactory performance. The board should ensure planned and progressive refreshing of the board.

4.7 The principles of the Code relating to remuneration are:

B1 levels of remuneration should be sufficient to attract, retain and motivate directors of the quality required to run the company successfully, but a company should avoid paying more than is necessary for this purpose. A significant proportion of executive directors' remuneration should be structured so as to link rewards to corporate and individual performance.

B2 There should be a formal and transparent procedure for developing policy on executive remuneration and for fixing remuneration packages of individual directors. No director should be involved in deciding his or her own remuneration.

4.8 The principles of the Code relating to accountability and audit are:

C1 The board should present a balanced and understandable assessment of the company's position and prospects.

C2 The board should maintain a sound system of internal control to safeguard shareholders' investment and the company's assets.

C3 The board should establish formal and transparent arrangements for considering how they should apply the financial reporting and internal control principles and for maintaining an appropriate relationship with the company's auditors.

4.9 The principles of the Code relating to relations with shareholders are:

D1 There should be a dialogue with shareholders based on the mutual understanding of objectives. The board as a whole has responsibility for ensuring that a satisfactory dialogue with shareholders takes place.

D2 The board should use the annual general meeting to communicate with investors and to encourage their participation.

4.10 The principles of the Code relating to institutional shareholders are:

E1 Institutional shareholders should enter into a dialogue with companies based on the mutual understanding of objectives.

E2 When evaluating companies' governance arrangements, particularly those relating to board structure and composition, institutional shareholders should give due weight to all relevant factors drawn to their attention.

E3 Institutional shareholders have a responsibility to make considered use of their votes.

4.11 The principles of the Code relating to Schedule C relating to disclosure state that the following should be included in the annual report:

- A statement of how the board operates, including a high level statement of the types of decisions that are taken by the board and those that are delegated to management.
- The names of the chairman, deputy chairman, chief executive, senior independent director and chairmen and members of the nomination, audit and review and remuneration committees.
- The number of meetings of the board and the committees listed above and individual attendance by directors.
- The names of the non-executive directors who the board determines to be independent, with reasons where necessary.
- Other significant commitments of the chairman.
- Hall performance evaluation of the board, its committees and its directors has been conducted.
- The steps the board has taken to ensure that directors develop an understanding of the views of major shareholders about the company.
- A description of the work of the nomination, remuneration and audit committees.

4.12 The supporting principle for Code A1 states:

The board's role is to provide entrepreneurial leadership of the company within the framework of prudent and effective controls which enables risk to be assessed and managed. The board should set the company's strategic aims, ensure that the necessary financial and human resources are in place for the company to meet its objectives and review management performance. The board should set the company's values and standards and ensure that its obligations to its shareholders and others are understood and met.

4.13 The chairman is responsible for the leadership and effectiveness of the board and effective communication with shareholders. The chairman should be independent. The CEO is responsible for the running of the company's business. Only in exceptional circumstances should a CEO become chairman. The role of chairman and CEO should not vest within one individual.

4.14 Higgs' suggestions for good practice identified the role of non-executive directors in relation to:

- *Strategy*: Non-executive directors are expected to constructively challenge and help to develop proposals on strategy.
- *Performance*: Non-executive directors are required to scrutinise management's performance in meeting agreed goals and monitor performance reporting.

- *Risk*: Non-executive directors should satisfy themselves about the integrity of financial information and that financial controls and systems of risk management are robust and defensible.
- *People*: Non-executive directors are required to determine appropriate levels of remuneration of executive directors, and fulfil the primary role of appointing and removing executive directors, and in succession planning.

4.15 In terms of Code provision A3 independence is unlikely if the director:

- Has been an employee of the company within the last five years;
- Has had a material business relationship with the company within the last three years;
- Has received additional remuneration, participates in share options, performance-related pay or is a member of the company's pension scheme;
- Has close family ties with the company's advisers, directors or senior employees;
- Holds cross-directorships with other directors;
- Represents a significant shareholder;
- Has served on the board for more than nine years.

4.16 The role of the remuneration committee is to determine and agreed with the board the framework for the remuneration of the chief executive, the chairman and other members of the executive management that the board considers should be considered by this committee.

4.17 The role of the nomination committee is to identify and nominate candidates to fill board vacancies when they arise, by evaluating the balance of skills, knowledge and experience on the board and preparing a description of the role and capabilities required for an appointment. (Higgs Suggestions for Good Practice)

4.18 An audit committee, in terms of CIMA *Official Terminology*, is:

A formally constituted sub-committee of the main board which should normally meet at least twice a year. Membership of the committee should comprise at least three directors, all non-executives. The majority of the committee members should be independent of the company. The primary function of the audit committee is to assist the board to fulfil its stewardship responsibilities by reviewing the systems of internal control, the external audit process, the work of the internal audit and the financial information which is provided to shareholders.

4.19 The terms of reference for the audit committee should include at least the following:

- Monitoring the integrity of the company's financial statements, significant judgements made in relation to the financial statements and formal announcements made by the company to the stock exchange.
- Reviewing the company's internal control and risk management systems (although in some cases financial controls may be the responsibility of the audit committee while non-financial controls and risk management may be the responsibility of a separate risk committee of the board, in which case the principals in Code provision C3.1 should also apply to the risk committee).
- Monitoring and reviewing the effectiveness of the internal audit function.
- Making recommendations to the board for the board to place a resolution before shareholders in an annual general meeting for the appointment, re-appointment and removal of the external auditor and to approve the terms of engagement and remuneration of the external auditor.

- Reviewing and monitoring the external auditor's independence and objectivity and the effectiveness of the audit process.
- Developing and implementing policy on the engagement of the external auditors supply non-audit services in order to maintain uditor objectivity and independence.

4.20 The benefits of good corporate governance are:

- Reduced risk
- Stimulated performance
- Improved access to capital markets
- Enhanced marketability of products/services by creating confidence amongst stakeholders
- Improved leadership
- Improved evidence of transparency and accountability.

Risk and Risk Management

5

LEARNING OUTCOMES

After completing this chapter you should be able to

- define and identify risks facing an organisation;
- explain ways of measuring and assessing risks facing an organisation, including the organisation's ability to bear such risks;
- discuss the purposes and importance of risk management for an organisation;
- evaluate risk management strategies.

Theory

5.1 The core of the syllabus for Management Accounting Risk and Control Strategy is dealt with in this chapter. As a consequence this chapter is critical and the theory will be utilised in all other chapters of this course.

5.2 The concept of risk can be defined as 'a chance or possibility of danger, loss, injury or other adverse consequences'. (Typical dictionary definition).

5.3 And the CIMA *Official terminology* defines risk as: *A condition in which there exists a quantifiable despersion in the possible outcomes from any activity.* By contrast, CIMA *Official terminology* defines uncertainty as: *The inability to predict the outcome from an activity due to a lack of information about the required input/output relationships or about the environment within which the activity takes place.*

5.3.1 By definition then, while uncertainty is not measurable, risk is measurable and can be managed. In order to manage risk though we need to disaggregate the generalisation of risk into its different types and then build tools and treatments for them.

5.4 Risk can be classified in various ways. In order to manage and control risk, we need to endeavour to fully understand its component parts and develop tools to measure each of them. The *Learning System* describes various classification methods with which the student should be fully au fait.

5.5 One such classification method is Risk classified by TYPE:

5.5.1 *Business or operational risk* which relates to the activities carried out within an organisation.
5.5.2 *Financial risk* which relates to funding and investment activities.
5.5.3 *Environmental risk* which relates to political, economic, social and the financial environment.
5.5.4 *Reputational risk* which relates to the failure to address other risks.

5.6 Risk can be classified in many other ways including:

5.6.1 According to treatment or measurement
5.6.2 By department or function of the organisation
5.6.3 By severity or impact upon the organisation
5.6.4 There are numerous other possible classifications. However, from a management and control perspective the classifications contained in the Learning System provide adequate disaggregation to facilitate the study of appropriate measurement and treatment.
5.6.5 A key contemporary view of risk is to see it as an opportunity rather than a threat.
5.6.6 Looking at risk then from both a threat and opportunity perspective, management can determine the drivers of both value and risk and devise measurementand treatment accordingly. Accepting that risk is fundamental to the process of operations, management teams that investigate opportunities potentially resulting from risk situations are better empowered to develop strategic positioning advantage.
5.6.7 The impact of societal, national and organisational culture all have a determining impact upon the profile, severity and treatment of the various types of risks. Organisations operating globally are substantially affected by these cultural implications and, therefore, the study of culture, its impact and our ability to determine measurements and treatments become more pronounced.
5.6.8 Social rationalities developed by J. Adams and depicted in Figure 5.2 of the Learning System provides a format for categorising societal orientations. These orientations enable management to gauge community approach to risk management and their most likely reaction to occurrences.
5.6.9 This leads us to focus on managers themselves and their culturally determined orientation towards risk. Adams explains the individual's propensity to take risks and discusses the role of potential rewards in their decision-making and behaviour. 'Accident' losses are the consequence of risk taking. Figure 5.3 in the Learning System depicts the process of Adam's risk thermostat with cultural filters. While this model facilitates understanding of the cultural influences, we require more quantifiable measurements to enable evaluation and selection.

5.6.10 There are numerous definitions for risk management. Relevant definitions for this course include:

5.6.10.1 According to the CIMA *Official Terminology*, risk management is defined as: The process of understanding and managing the risks that the organization is inevitably subject to in attempting to achieve its corporate objectives (CIMA *Official Terminology*).
5.6.10.2 The Institute of Risk Management defines risk management as: "The process by which organizations methodically address the

risks attached to their activities with the goal of achieving sustained benefit within each activity and across the portfolio of these activities. The focus of good risk management is the identification and treatment of these risks. Its objective is to add maximum sustainable value to all the activities of the organization. It marshals the understanding of the potential upside and downside of all those factors which can affect the organization. It increases the probability of success, and reduces both the probability of failure and the uncertainty of achieving the organization's overall objectives."

5.6.10.3 COSO defines risk management as: "A process, effected by an entity's board of directors, management and other personnel, applied in strategy setting and across the enterprise, designed to identify potential events that may affect the entity, and manage risks to be within its risk appetite, to provide reasonable assurance regarding the achievement of entity's objectives."

5.7 For the process of risk management to be successful, management has to address the organisation in terms of its structure, culture, appetite for risk, processes, policies and procedures and the environment(s) in which it operates to establish a comprehensive understanding, set of measurements and appropriate treatments for the risk profile it faces. The systems approach fulfills the action orientation design required to ensure that feedback and feedforward outputs are acted upon to control the impact and direction of the outcomes in terms of the organisation's strategy and objectives.

5.8 Key to the success therefore is the commitment of the board and executive. The elements of risk management that require focused attention include:

5.8.1 Risk strategy
5.8.2 Structuring for risk control
5.8.3 Systems design
5.8.3.1 Risk management cycle
5.8.3.2 Risk management process
5.8.4 Organisational change processes
5.8.5 Resourcing
5.8.6 Communication
5.8.7 Training
5.8.8 Culture development
5.8.9 Measurement and monitoring
5.8.10 Roles and responsibilities
5.8.11 Reporting and disclosure

? Questions

5.1 List four ways in which risk can be classified and briefly describe each one.

5.2 List nine examples of operational risk.

5.3 List four examples of financial risk.

5.4 List eight examples of environmental risk.

5.5 Explain Reputational risk using an example.

5.6 List four examples of economic risk.

5.7 List four examples of political risk.

5.8 Differentiate between risk and uncertainty.

5.9 List four examples of risk as a hazard.

5.10 List four examples of risk as a threat.

5.11 List four examples of risk as opportunity.

5.12 The Institute of Risk Management categorises risk in terms of financial, strategic, operational and hazard. For each of these categories, list the externally driven risks.

5.13 The Institute of Risk Management categorises risk in terms of financial, strategic, operational and hazard. For each of these categories, list the internally driven risks.

5.14 Discuss the role of Culture in risk taking by managers.

5.15 Weber and Hsee proposed a "cushion hypothesis" following a study involving American, German, Polish and Chinese nationals. Explain the effect of this cushion on organisational decision-maker behaviour.

5.16 Discuss the four rationalities together with possible to implications for seeing risk as proposed by Adams (1995).

5.17 Described "risk appetite" in an organisational context.

5.18 Explain the difference between explicit and implicit knowledge.

5.19 In terms of CIMA, risk management in terms of the CIMA definition.

5.20 Discuss enterprise risk management in terms of the COSO definition.

5.21 The shareholders of an organisation are the ultimate risk bearers. Discuss risk management in terms of shareholder value.

5.22 Discuss the four stages of shareholder value creation as defined by Ernst & Young (2001).

5.23 List the benefits of risk management.

5.24 List benefits specific to operational risk management.

5.25 Distinguish between highly integrated and highly dispersed risk management architecture and list eight benefits of the highly integrated option.

5.26 List the elements of a risk management framework.

5.27 In order for risk management to be effective, resourcing has to ensure coverage of a number of functions. List these functions.

5.28 With a specific focus on ensuring the effective functioning of risk management, list the requirements to be considered in the resourcing decision-making process.

5.29 Discuss key human behaviour control measures that are necessary to reinforce an appropriate risk management culture.

5.30 Draw the diagram of the CIMA risk management cycle.

5.31 List twelve methods of identifying risk.

5.32 List twenty methods that can be deployed to measure risk.

5.33 Discuss the key limitations of risk measurement.

5.34 Discuss of the likelihood/consequences matrix in relation to risk evaluation.

5.35 What should risk reporting be comprised of and what should it address?

5.36 List four responses to risk.

Solutions

5.1 Four ways in which risk can be classified are:

1 *Business or operational risk* relates to the activities carried out within an organisation.
2 *financial risk* relates to the financial/investment/funding operations of an organisation.
3 *Environmental risk* relates to changes in the political, economic, social and operating environment.
4 *Reputational risk* relates to the impact upon the image/name/reputation of the organisation and is caused by a failure to adequately address other risks.

5.2 Examples of operational risk include:

Business interruption
Errors of commission or omission by employees
Product failure
Health and safety
Failure of IT or mechanised systems
Fraud
Loss of key people
Litigation
Loss of suppliers.

5.3 Examples of financial risk include:

- *Credit risk*: The risk of not being paid by customers.
- *Liquidity risk*: The risk of running out of money.
- *Currency risk*: The risk of change in the exchange rate when trading internationally.
- *Interest rate risk*: The risk of interest rate change.

5.4 Examples of environmental risk include:

Legislative change
Regulations (Industry and government in many instances)
Climate change
Natural disasters
Loss of business
Competition
Economic slowdown
Stock market fluctuations.

5.5 Numerous instances worldwide of banks experiencing a run on withdrawals is a result of a loss of confidence by the clients of that bank followed by their withdrawal of funds in order to limit their own risk of potential loss.

[In many instances like this, the end result of a run on the bank leads to complete failure of the bank.]

5.6 Examples of economic risk, in terms of international operations, include:

- Loss of business for not dealing with suppliers and customers in the host country currency.
- Loss of income due to exchange rate movements where fixed price contracts are quoted in the currency of the host country.

- Lower than planned return on investment from a foreign direct investment project because of unexpected economic slowdown in that country.
- Investing in the home country, a decision which is subsequently affected by changes in relative exchange rates between the home country and markets in other countries.

5.7 Examples of political risks include:

- Loss of land, plant and equipment due to nationalisation of foreign-owned business interests in a host country after regime change.
- Change in regulation in a foreign country requiring specific use of local materials or labour.
- Cash flow implications as a result of the imposition of exchange controls by a foreign country in which the company trades.
- Loss of profits due to changes in tax rate in a foreign country in which the company trades.

5.8 According to CIMA *Official Terminology*, risk is defined as:

A condition in which there exists a quantifiable dispersion in the possible outcomes of any activity.

By contrast, uncertainty is defined as:

The inability to predict the outcome from any activity due to a lack of information about the required input–output relationships or about the environment within which the activity takes place.

Risk, therefore, describes a situation in which there exists an array of definable and measurable possible outcomes while uncertainty describes those conditions where possible outcomes cannot be predicted.

5.9 Risk as hazard includes:

- The risk of fire
- The risk of failure of an IT system
- The risk of loss of life or injury on a construction site
- The risk of loss of plots and equipment due to flooding.

[NOTE: The examples of risk, in their various classifications in questions 9 to 11, are not exhaustive. There are many more examples of each.]

5.10 Risk as a threat includes:

- Possible entry into a market by a competitor
- Possible loss of customers or market due to a competitor introducing a new technology
- Potential loss of supply of inputs as a result of contractual changes with a supplier
- Potential loss of business due to changes in bilateral agreements between countries in which the organisation trades.

5.11 Risk as an opportunity includes:

- Taking over a competitor that is struggling. The opportunity here is to deploy the company's skills and resources to overcome the weaknesses in the competitors business to increase the earnings of the combined organisation.

- Entering a new market. [Taking a product into a new market could result in failure. It is therefore risky and, where such risk is managed with skill, it could result in a positive outcome and gain for the company. In entering this new market, however, to extract opportunity, the management and measurement of possible negative outcomes is imperative.]
- Investing in a new manufacturing facility.
- Launching a new technology. [The launch of WAP technology was not very successful in the marketplace even though it was groundbreaking at the time. While the returns from WAP itself were small or even negative, it led to the discovery of related market needs and the introduction of MMS etc.]

5.12 The externally driven hazards, according to the Institute of Risk Management, are as follows:

- Financial risks:
  - Interest rates
  - Foreign exchange
  - Credit
- Strategic risks:
  - Competition
  - Customer changes
  - Industry changes
  - Customer demand
- Operational risks:
  - Regulations
  - Culture
  - Board composition
- Hazard risks:
  - Contracts
  - Natural events
  - Suppliers
  - Environment

5.13 The internally driven hazards, according to the Institute of Risk Management, are as follows:

- Financial risks:
  - Liquidity and cash flow
- Strategic risks:
  - M & A integration
  - Research and development
  - Intellectual capital
- Operational risks:
  - Accounting controls
  - Information systems
  - Recruitment
  - Supply chain
- Hazard risks:
  - Public access
  - Employees
  - Properties
  - Products and services.

5.14 "Bettis and Thomas (1990) have shown that researchers have very little knowledge about how managers in organizations perceive and take risks." This statement, taken from the Learning System by Collier and Mgyei-Ampomah (2005), demonstrates the extent to which, in the 21st century, we still have some way to go in understanding risk, risk taking and risk appetite in the decision-making process.

From the work done by Douglas and Wildavsky (1983) it is clear that culture plays a significant role. They found that: "... each culture, each set of shared values in supporting social institutions is biased toward highlighting certain risks and downplaying others.

Weber & Milliman (1997) found that risk taking could be a stable personality trait but that situational variables may be the results of changes in risk perception.

March and Shapira (1987) identified three motivations for risk-taking:

1 Managers saw risk-taking as essential to success in decision-making;
2 Managers associated risk-taking with the expectations of their jobs rather than with any personal preference for risk;
3 Managers recognised the 'emotional pleasures and pain' of risk taking.

When dealing with the human factor, risk management becomes substantially more difficult due to our inability to measure and, therefore, manage the risk decision-making process. Managing the risk-taking decision-making process enters the realm of uncertainty due to this lack of ability to measure or predict likely outcomes and the intuitive (or gut-feel) subjective approach to control becomes the norm.

5.15 The effect of the "cushion hypothesis" proposed by Weber and Hsee (1998) is to cushion members [of the organisation] against the consequences of negatives outcomes. As a result of this cushion effect, decision-makers perception of the riskiness of options is distorted.

5.16 Adams (1995) describes four rationalities that have implications for how people perceive risk. These rationalities, together with possible implications, are detailed as follows:

- *Fatalists*: Have minimal control over their own lives and, therefore, the management of risk is irrelevant to them. The implications of risk will have little meaning for these individuals.
- *Hierarchists*: Organize their world with strong group boundaries and structured relationships in hierarchial fashion. They adopt a bureaucratic risk management style using various risk management techniques. People with this orientation are likely to receive risk as managed through compliance with rules and regulations. The perception of risk will be distorted to a greater or lesser extent depending upon whether or not it is perceived to be addressed by compliance methods contained in the "handbook".
- *Individualists*: Are free thinking individuals who strive to exert control over their environment. Typically, they are self-made people and are an small–medium enterprise entrepreneurs. These individuals are more likely to weigh and understand the possible outcomes of risk. They are, however, less risk averse than people subscribing to other rationalities.
- *Egalitarians*: Have strong group loyalties. They arrived at decisions democratically and have little respect for externally imposed rules. The implications for risk taking and decision-making could be that they respond to slowly and/or disregard the risk implications. They will be most comfortable in a risk-sharing situation (e.g. insurance, hedging or transfer to other organisations).

5.17 Risk appetite describes the amount of risk an organisation is willing to accept in pursuit of value. It is directly related to an organisation's strategy. Risk appetite could be expressed as the acceptable balance between growth, risk and return.

5.18 Explicit knowledge is knowledge which can be recorded and shared while implicit knowledge can be learned and executed by an individual that cannot be recorded or directly shared. (e.g. Learning how to ride a bicycle has to be done directly by each individual and is therefore an implicit knowledge while, once designed, the building of a rocket can be recorded and shared.)

5.19 In terms of CIMA, risk management is defined as:

The process of understanding and managing the risks that the organisation is inevitably subject to in attempting to achieve its corporate objectives. (CIMA *Official Terminology*)

5.20 In terms of COSO, a finance enterprise risk management is defined as:

A process, effected by an entity's board of directors, management and other personnel, applied in strategy setting and across the enterprise, designed to identify potential events that may affect the entity, and manage risks to be within its risk appetite, to provide reasonable assurance regarding the achievement of entity's objectives.

Enterprise risk management (otherwise described as operational risk) is that group of risks that are derived from decisions taken by the management and personnel of an organisation in setting strategy, structuring and resourcing the organisation and operating the system. Enterprise risk should thus be seen as the appetite to undertake risks by an organisation (wittingly or unwittingly) that enable the exploitation of opportunities and, simultaneously, expose the stakeholders to risks associated with those actions.

5.21 Ernst & Young (2001) model shareholder value as being: *the static NPV of existing business model + Value of future growth options.*

The above is more simply described in the Learning System as: "it's the sum of the value of what the company does now and the value of what they could possibly do in the future".

From these definitions we can deduct that shareholders take risks with the view to unlocking value. The risk profile of an organisation for shareholders therefore comprises the perceived present value of the business as it is configured at present plus the value (both positive and negative) of future growth/decline that is undertaken by the directors and management of the organisation.

5.22 Ernst & Young have identified four stages in the process of good risk management to enable business to exploit opportunities for future growth while protecting the value already created. These four stages are as follows:

1 Established what shareholders value about the company – through talking with the investment community and linking value creation processes to key performance indicators.
2 Identify the risks around the key shareholder value drivers – the investment community can identify those factors that will influence the valuation of the company. All other risks will also be considered, even if not known by investors.

3 Determine the preferred treatment for the risks – the investment community can give their views on what actions they would like management to take in relation to the risks. The risk/reward trade-off can be quantified by estimating the change in the company's market valuation if a particular risk treatment was implemented.
4 Communicate risk treatments to shareholders – shareholders need to be well informed, as a shareholder vision is important in relation to the inter-related concepts of risk management and shareholder value.

5.23 The benefits of risk management include:

- Being seen as profitable and successful
- Being seen as predictable (e.g. comply with corporate governance requirements)
- Having fewer exceptional items and profit warnings
- Empowered to manage events proactively (e.g. mergers and acquisitions)
- Intangible assets are less likely to be impaired (e.g. trade names, goodwill and brand reputation)
- Works in favour of good-corporate-citizenship reputation
- Improved supply chain management
- Better credit ratings all possible.

5.24 The benefits of enterprise risk management include:

- Aligning risk appetite with strategic plan
- Balancing growth, risk and return
- Improving response to risk decisions
- Reducing operational surprises and losses
- Improved control of enterprise-wide/cross-enterprise risks
- Improved risk management through decisions and responses based upon integrated multiple risk information
- Improved access to identify and seize opportunities
- Opportunity to improve capital rationing decisions in favour of efficient risk attenuation and opportunity exploitation.

5.25 A highly integrated approach to risk architecture in an organisation would see all business units:

- Sharing a common language
- Sharing tools and techniques
- Executing shared periodic assessment of total risk.

The highly integrated approach to risk is particularly effective when risk factors are common across functional and business units.

By contrast, the highly dispersed approach to risk architecture is more appropriate to organisations way business units differ substantially in terms of their risk profiles and where operations differ substantially.

The integrated approach is generally regarded as best practice and, according to IFAS, includes the following:

1 Organization-wide acceptance of the risk management framework
2 Commitment from executives and the board of directors
3 Has an established risk response strategy
4 Has assigned responsibility for risk management change processes
5 Is adequately resourced

6 Comprises comprehensive communication structures
7 Risk cultures are reinforced through human resource mechanisms
8 The risk management process is monitored.

5.26 The risk management framework can be described as comprising the following elements:

- Risk management policy
- Resourcing risk management
- Implementation of risk management
- Risk management review and reporting.

5.27 In order for risk management to be effective, it should be driven by the board. The board, in turn, should ensure that an appropriate group of executives manage the process. The functions that require management are:

- Primary advocacy for risk management
- Policy, framework and methodology is necessary for each business unit to identify, analyse and manage their risks more effectively
- Development and execution of response processes to risk threat or event
- Assessment and auditing of the adequacy of risk responses
- The facilitation, challenge and leading of risk management
- Control of the risk management process ensuring that policy and strategy are operating effectively
- Trouble-shooting and corrective action functions
- Feedback and reporting requirements within the executive and to the board.

[A key point to note here is that there is a clear message to management: risk management requires specific resourcing that is not subordinated (or appended) to operational line processes. Specific attention should be paid to ensure that effective risk management is implemented and resourced.]

5.28 Management should specifically ensure that they deal with the following with regards to establishing an effective risk management system:

- The cost of providing the resources including additional support required to ensure its correct implementation has to be determined.
- Skills and experience are required to ensure that all aspects of risk exposure are covered adequately.
- Since human resources are the primary source of competitive advantage and, simultaneously a substantial contributor to business risks, career and succession planning is key.
- Provide adequate infrastructure and human resources to ensure constructive relationships are built between business units.
- Knowledge is assembled and managed.

[Without these resources, risk management cannot be effective, leaving the organisation venerable to risk events.]

5.29 In order for people to behave appropriately to ensure the containment and management of risk, careful attention has to be paid to the following key areas:

- Corporate culture influenced, over time, to ensure adoption of formal rules-based and informal values-based practices
- Appropriate job design

- Performance measurement
- Delegation enforcement of accountabilities
- Appropriate incentives and rewards.

5.30

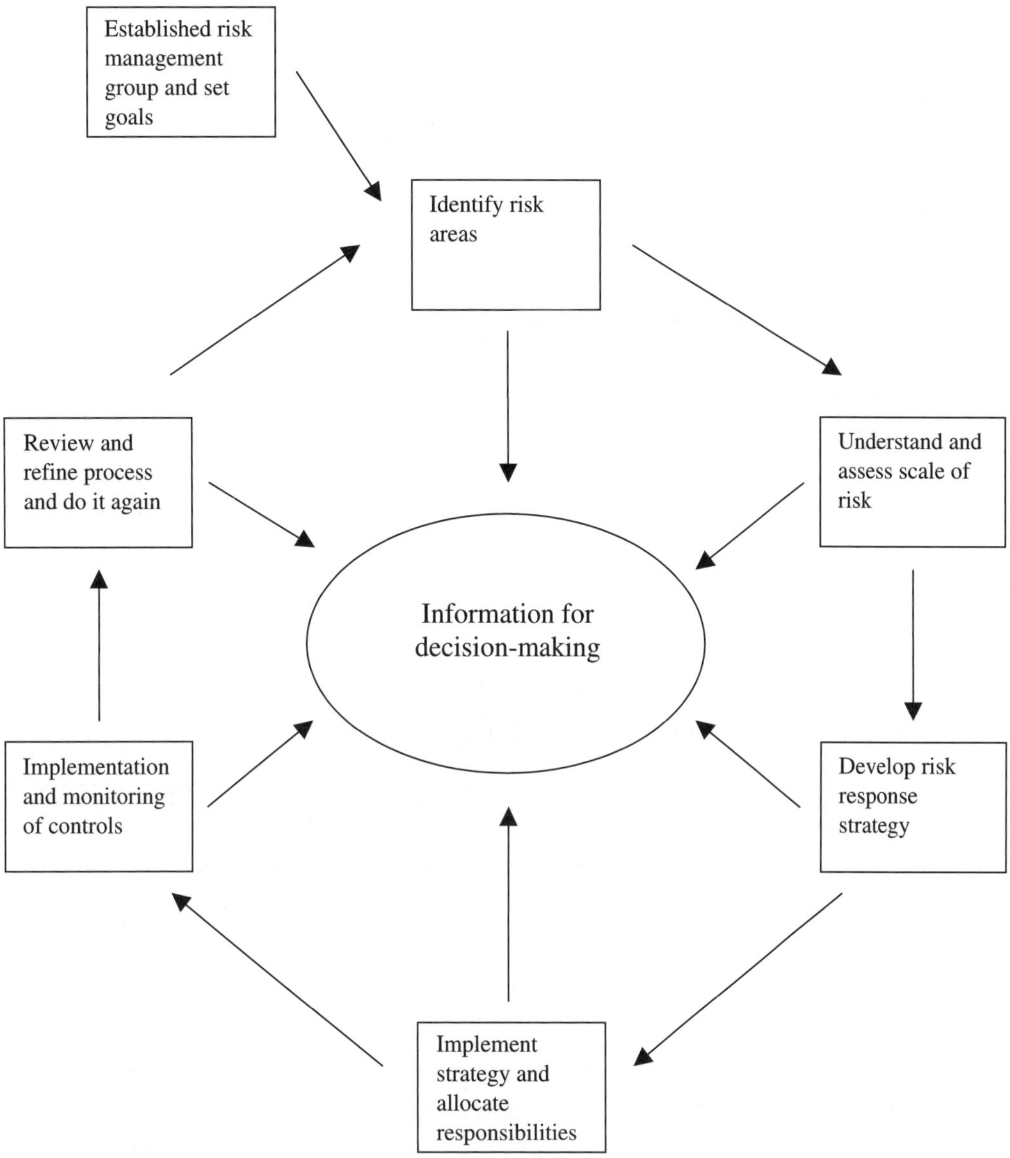

CIMA risk management cycle
Source: Chartered Institute of Management Accountants (2002), *Risk Management: A guide to Good Practice*, CIMA

5.31 Twelve methods of identifying risk include:

1 Brainstorming
2 Workshops
3 Stakeholder consultations
4 Benchmarking
5 Checklists
6 Scenario analysis
7 Incident investigation
8 Auditing and inspection
9 Hazard and operability studies
10 Fishbone analysis

11 Questionnaires/surveys
12 Interviews.

5.32 Risk can be estimated by deploying one or more of the following methods:

1 Information gathering
2 Scenario planning
3 Soft systems analysis
4 Computer simulations (Monte Carlo technique)
5 Decision trees
6 Root cause analysis
7 Fault tree/event tree analysis
8 Dependency modeling
9 Failure mode and effect analysis
10 Human reliability analysis
11 Sensitivity analysis
12 Cost-benefit and risk-benefit analysis
13 Real options modeling
14. Delphi method
15 Risk mapping
16 SWOT
17 PEST
18 HAZOP
19 Statistical inference (Regression analysis)
20 Measures of central tendency and dispersion.

[Each of the above risk measurement methodologies is a comprehensive study in itself. The participant will be required to have a good knowledge of each of these methods. In most cases, these methods will have been developed in quantitative study modules in development phase in proceeding this module. Certain of the techniques will be developed and deployed later in this module.]

5.33 The key limitations of known risk measurements include:

- *Reductionist*: Many of the methods, although formal and structured, rely on assumptions and specific focus or selection for their measurement to be reliable. If the given assumptions are violated, the measure could be inaccurate. They rely on linear cause-and-effect relationships which are not necessarily a true reflection of the prevailing risk condition.
- *Subjectivity*: A number of the methods rely upon individual perceptions which, in themselves, are unreliable when an attempt is made to apply them to generalisation.
- *Combined reductionist and subjectivity*: These methods suffer the effects of both of the abovementioned limitations.

[What we observe here is that there exists an inherent risk in the risk measurement methodology itself, let alone the original risk condition we are attempting to measure. The participant is alerted to be aware of the severity of these shortcomings and to deploy multiple measurement methods wherever possible and to systemise the risk management process in order to build upon past experiences and outcomes so as to develop a comprehensive database to enhance the organisational knowledge surrounding risk and its management.]

5.34 The likelihood/consequence matrix approach to risk evaluation can have varying degrees of ranking dependent upon the approach taken by the organisation. The primary focus of this matrix is to categorise risks according to severity on the one hand and likelihood on the other in order to separate risk conditions along the lines of significance. This has the effect of reducing the number of risk conditions to be considered at each organisational level and promotes the focusing of attention on those risk areas that are the most likely to result in severe loss.

5.35 Risk reporting should include:

- A systematic review of the risk forecast carried out at least annually;
- A review of the management responses to the significant risks and risk strategy;
- A monitoring and feedback loop on action taken and variance in the assessment of the significant risks;
- An early warning system to indicate material change in the risk profile, or circumstances, which could increase exposure or threaten areas of opportunity;
- The inclusion of audit work as part of the communication and reporting process.

Risk reporting should address the following:

- The control systems that have been put in place for risk management;
- The process is used to identify and respond to risks;
- The methods used to manage significant risks;
- A description of the monitoring and review system.

5.36 Risk treatment (or risk response) is the process of selecting and implementing measures to modify risk. Risk responses may include:

- Avoidance
- Reduction
- Sharing
- Acceptance.

Internal Control

6

LEARNING OUTCOMES

After completing this chapter you should be able to

- discuss the purposes and importance of internal control for an organisation;
- evaluate risk management strategies;
- evaluate the essential features of internal control systems for identifying, assessing and managing risks;
- evaluate the costs and benefits of a particular internal control system.

Theory

6.1 Organisations face the external and internal environments of two dimensions namely: controllable and uncontrollable conditions. This chapter discusses the role of internal controls within the organisation that are prescribed on the one hand by legislation and executed by the executive on the other for the purposes of containing risk and managing strategic objectives.

6.2 There are various definitions of internal control systems. In general, the systems approach is applied to internal controls even though various institutions place a greater or lesser emphasis upon quantifiable measurements. In general, internal control is action oriented with board and executive responsibility for achieving the organisation's strategic objectives.

6.3 The US COSO and UK Combined Code are examples of state/industry measures to promote the implementation and maintenance of internal control measures within organisations. These governance documents prescribe processes and disclosure/reporting requirements that compel the organisation to implement and effect control measures.

6.4 Internal controls can be classified as being financial and non-financial quantitative measures on the one hand and qualitative measures on the other. Much more attention is being paid lately to the qualitative aspects of organisations measurement and monitoring environment. Academics, practitioners and executives increasingly place more emphasis upon qualitative and non-financial measures in addition to well-developed financial measures in order to measure and manage organisational activities, resources and environment in order to achieve the objectives of the designed strategy.

6.5 Risks, together with costs, client and supplier relationships, resource management and knowledge of the domain of the board, executive management and general staff. This shift in emphasis on measurement and control is changing the role of management accountants within the organisation. In the past, accounting departments were seen to be responsible for the recording and interpretation of accounting information. Management accounting is now seen as being: *the application of the principles of accounting and financial management to create, protect, preserve and increase value so as to deliver that value to the stakeholders* (CIMA *Official Terminology*). The management accountants role is evolving into a value adding professional activity directed at supporting and empowering stakeholders within the organisation to make informed decisions, based upon sound accounting information, in order to develop, implement and control internal processes in order to achieve strategic objectives.

6.6 This changed role for the management accountant brings about a responsibility to provide up-to-date accounting information and simultaneously factor in non-financial and qualitative aspects and to report these within appropriate time deadlines to internal stakeholders.

6.7 An important characteristic of the new role of management accountants is to monitor the cost-benefit and risk-benefit of collecting data, managing its recording, storage and retrieval process in such a way that value is not destroyed in the process.

6.8 Additional pressures being brought to bear include globalisation, increasing competition, technological change in production and information technology, changing organisational structures, the influences of multi-cultural environments within the workplace and changing perceptions of management with regards to managing change and information needs.

6.9 The management accountant is ideally placed, owing to their professional training that includes analysis of information and systems, to play a significant role in developing and implementing risk management and internal control systems.

? Questions

6.1 Define internal control.

6.2 What constitutes an internal control system?

6.3 Discuss the five elements of the COSO model of internal control.

6.4 How does 'The Turnbull Guidance' influence the Combined Code (Financial Reporting Council, 2003)?

6.5 Controls can be classified as falling into three broad categories namely:

- Financial controls
- Non-financial quantitative controls
- Non-financial qualitative controls.

Discuss each of these controls with reference to Kaplan & Norton's Balanced Scorecard.

6.6 Discuss the influences that are changing the role of management accountants.

6.7 List the elements of cash control that support risk management.

6.8 Describe the elements of debtors control and its impact on risk management.

6.9 What inventory controls should be implemented to manage risk?

6.10 What role does investment practice play in organisational risk?

6.11 What measures can management take to minimise the risk of losses and damage to fixed assets?

6.12 List appropriate measures to control Creditors risk.

6.13 What controls are recommended for revenue and expense risk management?

6.14 What measures can human resources take and what accounting measures can be applied to limit payroll related losses?

6.15 Describe the limitations of internal controls.

Solutions

6.1 Internal control is the whole system of internal controls, financial and otherwise, established in order to provide reasonable assurance of:

(a) Effective and efficient operation
(b) Internal financial control
(c) Compliance with laws and regulations.
(CIMA *Official Terminology*)

6.2 Definitions of internal control systems, deployed by organisations, are varied. Generally speaking though, they comprise the following key elements:

- Their aim is to provide reasonable assurance that the objectives of the organisation are being met;
- They comprise policies and procedures and safeguards to regulate the behaviour of management and internal stakeholders;
- They are based upon acknowledged management style, corporate culture and values that influence the philosophy, operating style and organisational structure;
- Responsibility vests with the board of directors and management to establish, maintain and control the system.
- They meet the requirements of a system based upon measurable objective setting, control of activity and behaviour and evaluation and assessment leading to a review process.

6.3 The COSO model of internal control (applicable in the USA) comprises five elements as follows:

1 *Control environment* which is defined by CIMA as "the overall attitude, awareness and actions of directors and management regarding internal controls and their importance to the entity . . . [it] encompasses the management style, and corporate culture and values shared by a war employees. It provides a background against which the various other controls are operated" (CIMA *Official Terminology*).
2 *Risk assessment* deals with that section of the model directed at identifying the risks of failing to meet financial reporting objectives, failing to meet compliance and failing to meet operational objectives. COSO recommends the identification of external and internal risks to the organisation and its activities.
3 *Monitoring* is concerned with the need for management to monitor the entire control system through specific evaluations.
4 *Information and communication* deals with that area of the model concerned with the capture of relevant internal and external information about the competition, economic and regulatory matters and the potential of strategic and integrated information systems.

6.4 While the Combined Code recognises profit as being the reward for successful risk-taking in business, it seeks to regulate how boards and their management effect internal control to manage risk rather than to eliminate it. The Turnbull Guidance extends the requirement to have boards base their approach on sound risk based systems of internal control coupled with the requirement to review its effectiveness.

[In other words, while the Combined Code required boards to review the effectiveness of risk control systems, the Turnbull Guidance extends the requirement for them having to centre their approach on a risk-based platform.]

6.5 The Balanced Scorecard (Kaplan & Norton) seeks to integrate qualitative measurement with quantitative measurements. Financial controls become a subset of a broader quantitative set of controls. The operative function being measured is evaluated using both quantitative and qualitative controls across four dimensions (Customer, Internal, Financial and Developmental) with a view to ensuring that each is in line with the overall organisational strategic plan.

Financial controls are extended to include quality, customer, supplier, human resource and competition measurement. These quantitative measures are augmented with qualitative controls covering formal structures, informal structures, of rules, policies and procedures, physical controls, strategic plans, incentives and rewards, project management and personnel controls.

Central to the success of models like the Balanced Scorecard is a recognition that corporate culture has a determining effect upon the effectiveness of controls. Marshall et al (1996) argued that an emphasis on internal control systems was insufficient because, while they can provide information, decision-makers need knowledge to interpret that information and, and excessive controls can produce "an illusion of control; hiding the very real risks that lie in those areas where much that is not quantifiable or constant must be factored into a decision (p.90)".

6.6 The role of management accountants is shifting from that of "the application of the principles of accounting and financial management to create, protect, preserve an increase in value so as to deliver that value to the stakeholder" (CIMA *Official Terminology*) to a more business and support-oriented perspective (Scapens et al., 2003).

Scapens et al. identified the following changes that have influenced the shift in focus of the management accountant:

- Globalisation, increasing competition, volatile markets and the emergence of more customer-oriented companies;
- Technological change in production and information technology and the nature of work and information flows as a consequence of enterprise resource planning systems and personal computers;
- Changing organisational structures such as demergers and focusing on core competencies and the outsourcing of non-core activities.
- The feeling in top management that change is necessary and the changing management information needs.

These factors have led to a shift in 'ownership' of the counting reports from accountants to business managers.

CIMA's Fraud and Risk Management Working Group argues that: "Management accountants, whose professional training includes the analysis of information and systems, performance and strategic management, can have a significant role to play in developing and implementing risk management and internal control systems within their organizations." (Chartered Institute of Management Accountants, 2002 p. 3–4).

6.7 Cash control elements that support risk management are:

- Monies received by the organisation are banked;
- Bank accounts exist and a properly safeguarded;
- Bank accounts, especially foreign accounts are properly authorised;
- Signatories for bank accounts are authorised and sufficient
- Payments are properly authorised;
- Transfers between bank accounts are properly accounted for;
- Adequate cash forecasting is carried out to ensure that commitments are recorded and overdraft limits are not exceeded.

6.8 The control over debtors' accounts is crucial to proper risk management.

Debtor controls ensure that:

- Invoicing of customers is properly recorded in debtor accounts;
- Money collected from customers is properly recorded in debtor records;
- Bad debts are written off and adequate provision is made for doubtful debts;
- Debtor accounts are regularly reconciled;
- Appropriate credit checking procedures are in place;
- Collection activity is ongoing and effective;
- Credit notes and write-offs are properly authorised;
- Investigations take place in relation to all disputed amounts with customers;
- Customers verify the balances on their accounts.

6.9 Inventory is a major asset class in many organisations and comprises both potential advantage on the positive side and risk of major loss on the negative side if poorly managed. Control over inventory is essential to ensure that the negative potential is closely managed. Risk management strategies include:

- Periodic physical checks compared with inventory records to ensure that losses are detected and controlled;
- Valuation of inventory is managed in accordance with accounting principles;
- Receipt, dispatch, production and distribution of inventory should be affected the according to robust procedures;
- Security issues with regards to storage and handling all critical if losses and risk of loss are to be contained;
- The suitability of product is determined and obsolete, excess or damaged stock is eliminated according to proper controls and also as a nation;
- Distribution and transit of stock requires stringent procedures including such measures as recipient collaboration audits.

6.10 Treasury activities involving the maintenance of liquidity, investment of idle funds, mergers and acquisitions, interest rate and currency risk strategies all have the potential of enhancing organisational performance or destroying earned profits dependent upon judgement and stringent control measures. Investment on intangibles risks can be contained by deploying the following risk response strategies:

- Audits to verify the physical evidence of ownership of investments and measures to ensure their safe custody;
- Periodic review of all investments to determine their value creation status and to decide upon retention or disposal strategies;

- The establishment and maintenance of acquisition and disposal policies and procedures coupled with appropriate authorisation requirements;
- Amortisation, where appropriate, is applied to ensure correct valuation reporting in accordance with accounting standards.

6.11 With the ever-increasing pace of change, fixed assets designed to unlock future benefits increasingly become liabilities or obsolete. In order to ensure that assets are adequately managed, the following controls should be applied:

- A comprehensive fixed asset register should be maintained and periodically reviewed to ensure that assets are present;
- Acquisitions and disposals are properly authorised;
- Adequate security is provided to prevent theft, damage or misuse;
- Insurance cover exists to compensate for substantial potential losses;
- Assets are adequately depreciated to reflect a reasonable consumption of their value;
- Obsolete and/or worn out assets should be identified and treated appropriately in terms of accounting principles.

6.12 In most organisations, and certainly in trading and manufacturing companies, a large proportion of the company's activities, funds and the resultant acquisition of assets are controlled by staff members dealing with creditors. Control over the risks in this area is maintained through:

- Pre-purchase authorisation policies and procedures followed correctly;
- Purchases properly authorised and issued (in writing);
- Proof-of-delivery procedures implemented and followed to ensure purchased goods are received in good order;
- Procedures are followed to confirm supplier invoice details regarding quantities, price and conditions are checked against the original purchase orders and variances follow policies, procedure and authorisation;
- Invoices are properly recorded in creditors accounts and are reconciled monthly prior to payment requisition processes;
- Payments to suppliers are properly authorised and recorded in creditors accounts;
- Investigations take place, preferably by neutral employees, in situations which arise regarding quality, quantity and pricing issues.

6.13 Revenue, cost of goods sold and expenses constitute the trading and operating activities of an organisation. Controls over these areas to contain risk of loss are required to augment those controls deployed to monitor and control organizational performance. The risk elements can be controlled through:

- Income and expenses are referenced to organisational strategy and objectives through properly maintained budgeting processes.
- Properly documenting sale of goods and services immediately after the transaction occurs.
- Costs are properly recorded and classified.
- Income and expenses are matched and relate to the appropriate accounting period and accruals and prepayments are properly recorded to adjust between periods.
- Authorisation procedures are maintained to ensure that expenses are pre-authorised and that supplier invoices are properly controlled and checked against purchase orders.

6.14 Payroll expenses make up a substantial part of an organisation's expenses and require the following controls to be present to control risk:

- Human resource policies and procedures are established, maintained and followed with regard to recruitment, pre-employment checks and screening processes.
- Proper processes are implemented and followed by departmental managers to ensure that new recruits are properly authorised.
- Rates of pay are in accordance with human resource policies, pay scales and job grades.
- Time worked is properly recorded.
- Annual leave, sick or maternity leave, over time, extras and piecework are properly authorised.
- Employees who terminate employment are removed from the payroll.
- Procedures are established and maintained to verify that employee numbers correlate with the records and that 'ghost' employees are not present.
- Payroll deductions are all properly authorised and accepted by employees and are in compliance with statutory requirements.
- Employee benefits are properly authorised and procedures ensure that payments are regular.

6.15 Internal controls are subject to limitations that should be understood and factored into management behaviour. These limitations include:

1 Management is responsible for the establishment, implementation and maintenance of controls and cannot rely on auditors to review the adequacy of these controls.
2 Robust internal controls can provide a reasonable assurance but are not an absolute guarantee.
3 Independent risk control procedures that are separated from data processing and recordkeeping help enhance reliability. The viability of such an implementation is dependent upon cost–benefit evaluation.
4 There is always the possibility of error or gaps in the accounting system that can be deliberately circumvented or exploited by determined individuals. Management overriding of controls, systems limitations and changed business conditions expose the organisation to risks.

Internal Audit and the Auditing Process

7

LEARNING OUTCOMES

After completing this chapter you should be able to

- explain the importance of management review of controls;
- evaluate the process of internal audit;
- produce a plan for the audit of various organisational activities including, management, accounting and information systems;
- analyse problems associated with the audit of activities and systems, and recommend action to avoid or solve those problems;
- recommend action to improve the efficiency, effectiveness and control of activities;
- discuss the importance of exercising ethical principles in conducting of and reporting on internal reviews.

Theory

7.1 This chapter focuses specifically on the internal audit and the auditing process. It is it important to position auditing in terms of the role and responsibility borne by the directors and management on the one hand and the auditors on the other.

7.2 We start by defining audit: A systematic examination of the activities and status of an entity, based primarily on investigation and analysis of its systems, it controls and records (CIMA *Official Terminology*).

7.3 Auditing thus constitutes a checking and verification process and not a control process in itself. It is therefore completely inappropriate for management to rely upon internal audit processes to control and manage risk. Instead, management should incorporate audit report outputs into the evaluation and feedback mechanisms used to control and manage risk and rely on those outputs as additional information and feedback regarding the competence and performance of their risk management and control system.

7.4 Audits provide an 'opinion', based on a systematic and rigorous benchmarking process involving observation, interviews, reviews of reports, recalculations and analysis, conducted by a trained specialists. Providing this specialist (auditor) is independent of influences within and from external sources to the organisation, their judgement and commentary can provide an invaluable source of feedback to aid in refining the risk and control processes. The audit process is not a replacement for internal control and risk management.

7.5 Depending on the purpose of the audit, they take various forms and their format, scope and output can vary considerably. The participants should be familiar with the following forms of audit:

7.5.1 Financial audit
7.5.2 Compliance audit
7.5.3 Transactions audit
7.5.4 System-based audit
7.5.5 Risk-based audit
7.5.6 Performance audit
7.5.7 Best value audit or value-for-money (VFM) audit
7.5.8 Post-completion audit
7.5.9 Environmental audit
7.5.10 Management audit.

[Each of the above audit types has a specific purpose or focus and knowledge of their definition and purpose is of key importance to the management accountant. The participant is strongly advised to study this section carefully and to memorise these definitions. The general principles of auditing, insofar as it effect this course, apply to all of the above auditing types.]

7.6 From the definitions of internal audit (as detailed in the Learning System) it is apparent that the inclusion of an internal auditing process aids management in evaluating the effectiveness of risk management, control and governance processes.

7.7 In the light of increased pressure and legislation requiring of boards of directors to comply with corporate governance legislation, the role of the internal audit, as an extension or aid to the board in meeting their commitments, has become more acute.

7.8 The scope of the internal audit should be such that it has an unrestricted access to all activities in the organisation. The internal auditor is expected to review and report on a wide range of parameters including:

7.8.1 Adequacy and effectiveness of systems;
7.8.2 Compliance with policies, plans and procedures;
7.8.3 Economical and efficient use of assets and related safeguards of loss;
7.8.4 Suitability, accuracy, reliability and integrity of both financial and non-financial performance information;
7.8.5 Integrity of processes and systems;
7.8.6 Business unit suitability in terms of economical, efficient and effective operation;
7.8.7 Adequacy of follow-up procedures;
7.8.8 Effectiveness of corporate governance policies.

[It is important to note that the responsibility for the planning, implementation and execution of the structure, processes and operations lies with line management and the internal auditor has the responsibility for evaluating and reporting on the suitability, effectiveness and performance of the above elements.

Human nature, organisational politics, corporate and national culture, and power – distance relationships will all have a bearing on the independence of the internal auditor and the scope of influence and access that will be allowed.]

7.9 Emphasis is placed, in this course, on the internal audit, systems-based auditing and risk-based internal auditing.

7.10 Risk-based audit extends the scope beyond financial issues into the broader internal control systems. Audit will pay attention to inherent risks, failure of controls, residual and audit risk.

7.11 Risk assessment in auditing will include:

7.11.1 Intuitive or judgemental assessment
7.11.2 Risk assessment matrix
7.11.3 Risk ranking.

7.12 Audit planning will include resourcing and time to conduct a survey for:

7.12.1 Review of previous internal audit reports and files;
7.12.2 Consideration of changes in the business environment;
7.12.3 Review of external auditors and other control processes;
7.12.4 Obtaining input from an local managers;
7.12.5 Risks identification;
7.12.6 Establishment of audit objectives.

7.13 The plan will set out:

7.13.1 Terms of reference of the audit
7.13.2 Description of the systems and processes
7.13.3 Risks that need special attention
7.13.4 Scope of the work to be carried out
7.13.5 Milestones
7.13.6 Reporting and review procedure
7.13.7 Program and techniques to be applied
7.13.8 Resourcing requirements.

7.14 The internal audit a will deploy methods and models including:

7.14.1 Statistical sampling
7.14.2 Ratio analysis
7.14.3 Benchmarking
7.14.4 Physical inspection
7.14.5 Corroboration
7.14.6 RE-calculation and reconciliation
7.14.7 Surveys and questionnaires;
7.14.8 Narratives describing processes or systems;
7.14.9 Flowcharts
7.14.10 Walk-through, compliance and substantive tests.

7.15 Ethical conduct of an internal auditor is founded in the following principles:

7.15.1 Integrity
7.15.2 Objectivity
7.15.3 Professional competence and due care
7.15.4 Confidentiality
7.15.5 Professional behaviour
7.15.6 Technical standards.

[CIMA Members are required to comply with the ethical guidelines that are published in Chartered Institute of Management Accountants (1992).]

7.16 A key area for consideration is the existence of conflicts of interest. CIMA members are required to manage these conflicts and should:

7.16.1 Follow the organization's grievance policies;
7.16.2 Escalate the issue through successive levels of management, always with the member's superior's knowledge;
7.16.3 Consult an objective adviser or professional body;
7.16.4 When all else fails, the member may have no recourse but to resign and report the matter to the organisation.

7.17 Self-evaluation is a key component to managing one's own effectiveness. The Learning System provides an extensive list of questions that enable judgement of the effectiveness of the internal audit.

? Questions

7.1 Defined the term "audit".

7.2 Differentiate between a financial audit and a compliance audit.

7.3 What it is the purpose of a best-value audit?

7.4 How does the internal audit differ from a financial audit?

7.5 Discuss factors that could have a bearing on the validity and quality of an internal audit.

7.6 And what role does the scope of an internal audit play in its validity?

7.7 List the elements of a 'system-based' audit.

7.8 What are the objectives of risk-based auditing?

7.9 List the characteristics and internal audit approach for different levels of risk maturity.

7.10 Differentiate between *inherent risks* and *residual risk*.

7.11 What factors should be included in a risk assessment matrix?

7.12 What measures can be taken against risk?

7.13 What should an audit plan be comprised of?

7.14 List ten techniques used in internal auditing.

7.15 Describe three test techniques applied in auditing.

7.16 What documents would a set of standardised audit working papers include?

7.17 What should the Head of internal audit expect to report to the audit committee of the board?

7.18 List the fundamental principles that relate to the work of CIMA members.

7.19 What process should a CIMA member follow in the face of a sustained conflict of interest.

7.20 List ten questions that could assist in judging the effectiveness of an internal audit.

✓ Solutions

7.1 Audit is a systematic examination of the activities and status of an entity, based primarily on investigation and analysis of its systems, controls and records (CIMA *Official Terminology*).

7.2 A *financial audit* is typically conducted by external auditors with a view to express an opinion on whether the financial statements present a "true and fair view" and comply with applicable accounting standards.

A *compliance audit* is an audit of specific activities in order to determine whether performance is in conformity with a predetermined contractual, regulatory or statutory requirement (CIMA *Official Terminology*).

7.3 Best-value audits enable an organisation (predominantly organisations not for gain including the public sector) to evaluate the economy, efficiency and effectiveness of operations in the absence of profit measures.

7.4 The objective of an internal audit is: 'to assist members of the organisation in the effective discharge of their responsibilities (CIMA *Official Terminology*).

By contrast, the financial audit is directed at meeting needs of external stakeholders and shareholders by requiring a registered professional to express his opinion as to the 'true and fair' presentation of the company's performance and position as represented in the financial statements.

7.5 The validity and quality of an internal audit is heavily dependent upon the independence and objectivity of the internal auditor. Organisational culture, national culture, power–distance relationships, organisational politics, organisational size and the board's attitude towards the internal audit function all have a pivotal role to play in the objectivity, access, output and prominence accorded to their role.

The internal audit function, to be truly effective, requires an unrestricted access to all activities in the organisation.

7.6 There is a fine line between the role of the internal auditor and the authority and responsibility of line management. Care has to be taken to ensure that an internal audit is properly scoped and that authority and access is given to the auditor to review and report on the following:

- The adequacy and effectiveness of systems of financial, operational and management control;
- The extent of compliance with, and the effect of policies, plans and procedures;
- Safety from loss and economy and efficiency of assets;
- The integrity of processes and systems;
- The suitability of business units' structures and organisation for carrying out its functions economically, efficiently and effectively;
- Follow-up and corrective action weaknesses identified;
- Adequacy and compliance of corporate governance arrangements.

The scope of internal audit is often curtailed with the resultant reduction in objective, reliability and completeness of the process.

7.7 A system-based audit should comprise the following:

- Identification of the objective of the system or process;
- Identification of the prescribed procedures to achieve the system objective and corporate objectives;
- Identification of risks in relation to the achievement of objectives;
- Identification of the management methodology established to determine and manage the risks;
- Evaluates whether the controls in place are appropriate;
- Tests to determine whether the controls are operating effectively in practice;
- Reports covering the findings and monitoring of the implementation of agreed recommendations.

7.8 The objectives of risk-based internal auditing are:

- To determine whether the risk management processes are operating as intended;
- The risk management processes are part of a sound design;
- That risk treatment/responses to risks are adequate and effective in reducing those risks to a level acceptable to the board;
- Effective control signed place to mitigate those risks of which management wishes to treat.

7.9

Risk maturity	**Key characteristics**	**Internal audit approach**
Risk Naive	No formal approach developed for risk management	Promotes risk management and rely on audit risk assessment
Risk Aware	Scattered silo-based approach to risk management	Promote enterprise-wide approach to risk management and rely on audit risk assessment
Risk Defined	Strategy and policies in place and communicated. Risk appetite defined.	Facilitate risk management and/or liaise with risk management and use management assessment of risk where appropriate.
Risk Managed	Enterprise-wide approach to risk management developed and communicated.	Ordered risk management processes and use management assessment of risk as appropriate.
Risk Enabled	Risk management and internal control for the embedded into the operations.	Audit risk management processes and use assessment management of the risk as appropriate.

Source: Institute of Internal Auditors (2003), Risk Based Internal Auditing.

7.10 *Inherent risks* are those risks that follow from the nature of the business and its environment in which it operates while *residual risk* is that risk which remains after controls have been implemented. Residual risk comprises those risks that are not covered by controls and treatment.

7.11 A risk assessment matrix should comprise of the following factors:

- Transaction volume
- Impact on business continuity
- Adequacy of existing controls
- Weather systems are new or long-established
- Quality and experience of staff and management
- Susceptibility to fraud.

7.12 Measures or treatment that can be taken against risk are:

- Transferring the risk through insurance, hedging, use of partners, joint ventures, networks and sharing;
- Reduce the likelihood of risk by the introduction of controls;
- Reducing exposure to risk by avoiding or eliminating activities that are risky generating and/or through the introduction of controls;
- Detecting occurrences through alerts and feedback mechanisms;
- Recovering from occurrences through the provision of redundancy and contingency planning.

7.13 The audit plan should be comprised of the following:

- The terms of reference for the audit;
- Description of the system or process to be audited; identifying its boundaries and connections to other systems and processes;
- Risks that need special attention;
- Scope of work to be carried out, identifying any areas not to be audited;
- Milestone dates for completion and resources allocated to the audit;
- Reporting and review procedure;
- Audit program and techniques to be applied;
- Audit staff allocated to the assignment.

7.14 Techniques used in internal auditing include:

1. Statistical sampling
2. Ratio analysis
3. Benchmarking
4. Physical inspection
5. Corroboration
6. Re-calculation and reconciliation
7. Surveys and questionnaires
8. Narrative descriptions of processes or systems
9. Flowcharting
10. Testing.

7.15 Three test techniques applied in auditing are:

1. *Walk-through tests* which follow several transactions through the system from their origin to the end of the process.
2. *Compliance tests* audit of control which determine whether system controls are operating as intended.
3. *Substantive tests* which aim to establish the validity of the outcome of transactions. These tests are deployed more extensively when compliance tests indicate weak controls or when fraud is suspected.

7.16 A standardized set of audit working papers should include:

- Scope and type of audit
- Report from previous audit and recommendations outstanding
- Timetable for the audit and resources allocated to the audit
- Work programs including analytical methods used
- Evidence collected from ratio analysis, benchmarking, narratives, flowcharts and testing
- Interpretation of the evidence and significant findings
- Conclusions
- Recommendations
- Final report.

7.17 The Head internal audit should expect to report to the Audit Committee of the Board as follows:

- Provide regular assessments of the adequacy and effectiveness of systems of the risk management and internal control processes;
- Report significant internal control issues and potential for improving risk management and control;
- Provide information on the status and results of the annual order to plan and the adequacy of resources for internal audit.

7.18 The fundamental principles that relate to the work of CIMA members are:

- Integrity
- Objectivity
- Professional competence and due care
- Confidentiality
- Professional behaviour
- Technical standards.

[*Ethical Guidelines* for CIMA members are published in the Chartered Institute of Management Accountants (1992). The participant is required to know the contents of these guidelines]

7.19 A CIMA member should escalate according to the following steps when faced with a sustained conflict of interests:

1 Follow the organisation's grievance policy;
2 Discuss the matter with the member's superior and successive levels of management always with the member's superior's knowledge;
3 Seek advice From an objective adviser or the professional body;
4 After exhausting all of the prior levels, the member may have no other option other than to resign and report the matter to the organisation.

7.20 The Institute of Internal Auditors (2003), *Appraising Internal* Audit lists 29 questions that assist in judging the effectiveness of internal audit.

The following ten questions were extracted from this list:

1 Has the purpose, authority and responsibility of the internal audit function been formally defined and approved by the audit committee?
2 Has any consulting activity carried out by internal audit detracted from the primary role?
3 Is internal audit capable of identifying the indicators of fraud?

4 Has the work of the internal audit considered all important business risks?
5 Has there been any significant control breakdown in areas that have been reviewed by internal audit?
6 Does internal audit undertake a program of continuous improvement?
7 Are internal audit practices benchmarked against best practice?
8 Does internal audit carry out its role in accordance with the IIA's International Standards for the Professional Practice of Internal Auditing?
9 Can internal audit respond quickly to organisational change?
10 Does internal audit have the necessary resources and access to information to enable it to carry out its role?

[The participant should be familiar with all of the 29 questions]

Information Systems and Systems Development

8

Learning Outcomes

After completing this chapter you should be able to

- evaluate and advise managers on the development of IM, IS and IT strategies that support management and internal control requirements;
- identify and evaluate IS/IT systems appropriate to an organisation's needs for operational and control information;
- evaluate benefits and risks in the structuring and organisation of the IS/IT function and its integration with the rest of the business;
- evaluate and recommend improvements to the control of information systems.

Theory

8.1 Information is the result of making data usable for decision-making. Organisations require information to manage and control the processes.

8.2 With the advent of computerisation, information management and dissemination has been substantially enhanced in terms of timeliness, accuracy, completeness and the speed with which large volumes of data can be managed and transformed in an automated fashion.

8.3 With globalisation, crumbling national boundaries in terms of business and trade, the ease with which information can be shared and transferred globally via the Internet, organisations are facing ever-increasing opportunities and challenges in the realm of information systems strategy.

8.4 Contemporary knowledge management strategies elevate the debate beyond information management; encompassing formalised methodologies to convert implicit knowledge to explicit knowledge whenever possible; to manage the collection, dissemination and sharing of knowledge on a scale not possible prior to the development of mineable accessible databases.

8.5 Along with the cost–benefit debate of collecting, processing, analysing and dissemination of information, the organisation is now faced with ever-increasing demand for hardware and software to deal with the accelerating flow of data, information and knowledge.

8.6 This course focuses primarily on contemporary information management systems. A large proportion of the focus remains periodic reporting for management including transactions, exception and summarised periodic results. Online, real-time dashboards or briefing books provide managers with key summary information, often in graphical form, to aid with the need for focused attention on critical issues.

8.7 Information systems are concerned with transaction processing, management information, enterprise resource planning, strategic enterprise management, decision support and expert systems. Depending upon the type of organisation, varying degrees of complexity and integration are required. Comprehensive integrated enterprise resource planning systems that extend to decision support, executive information and functional extensions including customer and supplier/supply chain management are available and are becoming accessible even to medium-sized enterprises.

8.8 TCP/IP Technology integrates the movement and sharing of data, images, audio files and real-time video and audio communication over the Internet.

8.9 Internet and extranet technology has enhanced the capability of inter-organisational commerce (E-commerce) and has transformed the banking industry into a global high speed superpower.

8.10 The pace of change, and the escalating level of complexity and scope of IT systems, has sustained the tendency for organisations to outsource this function in whole or in part. Key advantages include greater access to scarce resources and skill, cost savings, improved quality and flexibility to keep up with changing technologies. On the other hand, disadvantages of outsourcing include difficulty in establishing clear service level agreements, risk of unsatisfactory quality and service, higher exposure to information leakage to competitors and hidden complexities and expense relating to unchanged overhead burdens, changeover difficulties and management issues relating to supervision of the outsourced supplier.

8.11 In many organisations, IS development is a key strategic focus requiring organisations to develop competencies in systems design, development and control. This extends the requirement for organisations auditing capabilities to include systems development auditing.

8.12 If not outsourced, the organisation will require skill and competency in terms of systems implementation, post-implementation review and continual improvement projects capability.

8.13 The Information Technology Infrastructure Library (ITIL) is an internationally accepted best practice model that guides business users through the planning, delivery and management of quality IT services. The Service Support processes and goals of the ITIL are:

8.13.1 Configuration management
8.13.2 Incident management
8.13.3 Change management
8.13.4 Problem management
8.13.5 Release management.

8.14 The ITIL Service Delivery processes and goals are:

8.14.1 Service level management
8.14.2 Availability management
8.14.3 Capability management
8.14.4 IT services continuity management
8.14.5 Financial management.

8.15 No organisation can manage and control risk without robust security and integrity management of, and redundancy and contingency infrastructure surrounding, IT systems. The potential for data and information security breaches, hacking, data tampering and the effects of errors of omission and commission by employees renders organisations vulnerable. As a result, ever increasing demand is being placed upon management accountants, auditors and IT professionals to improve and refine financial, non-financial, quantitative and qualitative systems in a highly integrated environment.

? Questions

8.1 What is information?

8.2 What is an information system?

8.3 Name three organisational strategies relating to information.

8.4 Distinguish between electronic point-of-sale (EPOS) and Internet purchasing and discuss the advantages of each of these technologies to the organisation.

8.5 Names six methods of data collection.

8.6 Discuss for methods of presenting information to management.

8.7 Distinguish between transaction processing systems and management information systems.

8.8 Distinguish between enterprise resource planning systems and strategic enterprise management.

8.9 Discuss the roles of decision support systems (DSS) and executive information systems (EIS).

8.10 What roles do expert systems play in an organisation?

8.11 Distinguish between intranets and extranets and list three applications for each.

8.12 What are the major benefits of E-commerce to the organisation?

8.13 List the major advantages and disadvantages of IS outsourcing.

8.14 List the key elements of IS project management.

8.15 List the stages of the Systems Development Life Cycle.

8.16 Describe the key controls of each of the SDLC stages.

8.17 What is the role of internal audit in relation to the development of a new IS system?

8.18 What are the expected outcomes of a post-implementation review?

8.19 What are the functions of an information center?

8.20 What service and support can business organisations expect from the Information Technology Infrastructure Library?

Solutions

8.1 Information is an assembly of raw data that has been converted into a form that informs a user about the data.

8.2 Information system is a system that collects data and transforms it into information and presents it, usually in summarised form, for management.

8.3 Organisations deploy the following three information strategies:

1 *Information systems strategy* focused on the long-term systems required to host information technologies;
2 *Information technology strategy* defines specific information technologies necessary to support the business strategy of the organisation;
3 *Information management strategy* is concerned with methods by which data is stored, converted into information and made available for access.

[The organisation's ability to deploy information technologies is dependent upon the capabilities of the installed computer, networking, telecommunications and other support systems that make up information systems (IS). The high costs and lead times relating to the deployment of IS requires that organisations factory in long range planning to ensure that they have access to the necessary infrastructure to support their planned strategy. Enabled by the installed infrastructure, management can implement those technologies that can be supported by that infrastructure. Constrained by the limitations of a decision not to pursue systems due to perceived cost–benefit considerations could lead to longer-term strategic disadvantage. Therefore, careful cost–-benefit analysis and options decision-making has become a critical strategic activity in respect of information systems deployment.

These decisions have broad ranging implications for information management strategy. A broad range of advantages can be gained from information technology deployment including automation, integration and sharing benefits, dissemination across domestic and global boundaries and standardisation across the organisation. Risks include a loss of control over ownership and access to information, potential tampering and distortion that could affect (parts of or) the entire organisation, unintended uses and outcomes.

A potential cascade of implications resulting from long range, broad decisions not to invest in IS that, in turn, inhibits the deployment of appropriate information technology that may be critical to the achievement of the organisation strategic goals and/or the management of activities and information critical to achieving the objectives of the strategy of the organization.]

8.4 EPOS is an 'in-store' technology that uses barcodes to price goods that, amongst others, enables the organisation to reduce inventory, identify margins by linking the sales price to cost of goods sold, to manage receipts, holding and disposal strategies and manage information regarding customer purchase patterns.

Internet purchasing, on the other hand, enables customers to carry out the doctor processing for themselves remotely from the retailer enabling the retailer to reduce staff, reduce cost of retail space, improved efficiency through automation and trade with clients over a broader geographical spread.

8.5 Six methods of data collection include:

1 Electronic point of sale (EPOS)
2 Electronic funds transfer at point of sale (EFTPOS)
3 Loyalty cards
4 Internet purchasing
5 Electronic data interchange (EDI)
6 Document imaging.

8.6 Four methods of presenting management information include:

1 *Transaction reports*: Detailed reports of transactions conducted over a period;
2 *Exception reports*: Lists exceptions to predetermined rules;
3 Summarized periodic reports: reports produced at regular intervals;
4 *Briefing-book*: Typically comprised of one-page summaries of key financial or non-financial information.

[Contemporary trends include online, real-time dashboards and alerts that enable manages to react and control key aspects of the business with reduced delays resulting in increased successes and performance.]

8.7 *Transaction processing systems* collect source data about each business transaction while *management information systems* convert raw data into usable form and disseminate this information to managers and staff.

8.8 Enterprise resource planning systems help to integrate data flow and access to information from sources throughout the company. This integrated data is then disseminated to users in the organization in accordance with their needs.

Strategic enterprise management systems extended the use of collected data for analysis using computer-based analytical tools and techniques to provide information needed for strategic management decision-making.

8.9 Decision support systems generally contain data analysis models that enable managers to simulate different options. Executive information systems, on the other hand, provide managers with 'drill-down' facilities, giving them access, often in summarised form, to key information based upon actual organisation transactions and data.

8.10 Expert systems store data are gained from experts and often deployed to automate decision-making all provide parameter-driven boundaries within which decisions can be taken.

8.11 Intranets are in-house versions of the Internet, operated by a single organisation. Extranets are systems that link that intranets of related organisations.

Applications for intranets include:

- Telephone lists
- Procedure manuals
- Reference materials (and many more).

Extranets include applications that provided mutual benefit to the organisation's and include:

- Price information
- Delivery schedules
- Stock availability (and many more).

8.12 The major benefits of E-commerce to an organisation include:

- Expanding access to a greater/global marketplace;
- Reduction in transaction costs;
- Extending the reach of related activities including public relations, information dissemination and marketing.

8.13 The major advantages of IS outsourcing include:

- More accurate prediction of costs
- Using only the requisite amount of capacity necessary
- Improved to highly skilled specialists
- Economies of scale access to it through the outsource service provider
- Reduced burden on managing specialist staff
- Improved quality and service.

The major disadvantages of IS outsourcing include:

- Complications with service level agreements that clearly delineate the responsibilities of each party;
- Some loss of flexibility due to the constraints of the contract with the outsource supplier;
- Risk of unsatisfactory quality and service or even failure of the supplier;
- Short-term cost-savings focus at the expense of long-term strategy considerations;
- Sustained overhead burden in addition to outsourcing costs;
- Changeover management complexities;
- Potential management complications with outsource supplier;

8.14 The key elements of IS project management are:

- Project planning and definition
- Senior management commitment
- Project organisation including roles and responsibilities of the steering committee, project board and project manager
- Resource planning and allocation
- Quality control and progress monitoring
- Risk management
- Systems design and approval
- Systems testing and implementation
- User participation and involvement
- Communication and coordination
- User education and training.

8.15 The Systems Development Life Cycle comprises the following stages:

- Feasibility study
- Systems analysis
- Systems designed
- Implementation
- Systems operation and maintenance.

8.16 The key controls at each of the SDLC stages are:

- *Feasibility study stage*: At this stage there should be clear understanding of objectives of the system, deliverables, its cost and time to completion.
- *Systems analysis stage*: At this stage, a high level of expertise and information is required of the problem in order to establish a detailed specification for the system.
- *Systems design stage*: During the design stage, controls are required to ensure that the conversion process meets specification in terms of security, data storage, input layouts, file structure, reports and interfaces with other systems. Comprehensive testing should be conducted on the system and audit is should review the specification, flowcharts, test data and operating instructions.
- *Implementation stage*: Key controls at this stage are verification of staffing competency and supervision.
- *Systems operation and maintenance stage*: Controls include system stability verification, input-conversion-output congruency, staffing competence and systems uptime monitoring.

8.17 The role of internal audit in relation to the development of a new IS system includes:

- Ensure that risks are adequately addressed
- Testing input-conversion-output congruency of financial and non-financial information
- Ensure that an audit trail is present
- Review the scope for possible fraud.

8.18 The expected outcomes of a post-implementation review are:

- The new system satisfies users' needs
- System performance meets the system specification
- Actual costs are within budgeted project costs
- Variations and improvements identified in the development process have been incorporated
- Further recommendations for improvement to the system.

8.19 The functions of an information centre include:

- User problem solving (often through the means of a helpdesk)
- Integration and purchase of hardware and software
- Advice on application development
- Monitoring and maintenance of network system
- Maintaining corporate databases or data warehouses
- System maintenance and testing
- Maintaining IT security.

8.20 Business organisations can expect the following support and service from the ITIL:

- *Configuration management*: To identify, record and report on all IT components.
- *Incident management*: To restore normal service operations as quickly as possible and minimise the adverse impact on business operations.
- *Change management*: To ensure that standardised methods and procedures are used for efficient and prompt handling of all changes to minimise the impact of change-related incidents and improve day-to-day operations.
- *Problem management*: To minimise the adverse impact of incidents and problems on the business that are caused by errors in the IT infrastructure.
- *Release management*: To ensure that both technical and non-technical attributes of a release are considered together.

Information Systems Control and Auditing

9

LEARNING OUTCOMES

After completing this chapter you should be able to

- explain the importance of management review of controls;
- evaluate the process of internal audit;
- produce a plan for the audit of various organisational activities including management, accounting and information systems;
- analyse problems associated with the audit of activities and systems, and recommend action to avoid or solve those problems;
- recommend action to improve the efficiency, effectiveness and control of activities;
- evaluate and recommend improvements to the control of information systems;
- evaluate specific problems and opportunities associated with the audit and control of systems which use information technology.

Theory

9.1 IT systems, as we have seen in the previous chapter, have become a critical strategic competitive tool in the information/globalisation age. As with other business processes, management has to maintain control over its various facets with particular emphasis upon risk management. In order to measure and monitor risk, the board, line management, information systems experts and auditors have to devote resources and attention to the management and monitoring of IT in addition to the remaining financial and non-financial elements of the business.

9.2 Because the IT and enterprise information systems are inextricably bound to the IS system, modern control and management systems tend to be comprehensive and integrated. CobiT, SAC, eSAC and COSO number among the many integrated control models in use.

9.3 Control strategies cover security, integrity and contingencies. These areas are best protected by predictive controls or preventative controls. If those are not available then one has to resort to detective controls and corrective controls.

9.4 These controls can be further categorised as being general, application, software and network control focused.

9.5 In order to undertake auditing of a computer system, specialised skills are required and a thorough understanding of the system is mandatory. Technological developments have seen the evolution of Computer Assisted Audit Techniques (CAATs) that enable automated review of system controls and data. More advanced systems include embedded audit facilities that enable continuous audit review of data, its processing and interrogation, with parallel access to the system for audit purposes.

? Questions

9.1 Reproduce the BS 7799 (ISO 17799) best practice checklist for information security.

9.2 List the risks defined by eSAC.

9.3 Compare the three systems control models: CobiT, eSAC and COSO.

9.4 Name the three broad categories of systems controls.

9.5 Draw a distinction between predictive and preventative controls.

9.6 What logical access controls can be applied to regulate unauthorised access to data?

9.7 List the aspects making up business continuity planning.

9.8 Describe the Application controls.

9.9 List the main risks for which network controls are imperative.

9.10 Explain the function of Firewalls in network controls.

9.11 How can Internet payment transactions be protected?

9.12 Describe three forms of hacking.

9.13 What additional measures can be added to provide increased security against hacking?

9.14 List the basic principles of computer system auditing.

9.15 Discuss the main techniques used to review system controls.

9.16 What is the function of audit interrogation software?

9.17 What is the purpose of a SCARF file?

9.18 What is the function of simulation in the context of data review techniques?

9.19 What is the benefit of systems maintenance auditing?

9.20 What are the implications of software piracy for a user organization?

Solutions

9.1 The BS 7799 (ISO 17799) information system security best practice checklist comprises:

- Security policy
- Security organization
- Asset classification and control
- Personnel security
- Physical and environmental security
- Computer and network management
- Systems access controls
- Systems development and maintenance
- Business continuity and disaster recovery
- Compliance.

9.2 eSAC defines risks as follows:

- Fraud
- Errors of omission and commission
- Business interruptions
- Inefficient use of resources
- Any effective use of resources.

9.3 The comparison between the three models is as follows:

CobiT views internal controls as a process that includes policies, procedures, practices and organisational structures that support business processes and objectives.

eSAC emphasises internal control as a system, a set of functions, sub-systems, people and the interrelationship between all of those.

The COSO model emphasises internal control as a process which is integrated with business activities.

9.4 Systems controls include security, integrity and contingency controls.

9.5 Predictive controls identify likely problems/risks and introduce appropriate controls. Preventative controls minimise the possibility of a risk occurring.

9.6 The following logical access controls can be applied to regulate unauthorised access to data:

- Regular changes to passwords
- Password formats including minimum length requirements and alphanumeric character combinations
- Prevention of screen display of password during typing
- Encryption
- Lock-out after multiple unsuccessful log-in attempts
- Time-outs after disuse for a predetermined period
- Logging of access.

9.7 Business continuity planning includes:

- Making a risk assessment
- Developing a contingency it plan to address those risks
- The roles and responsibility of key individuals should be defined
- Backup facilities for all data

- Alternative sites for data processing established
- Equipment providers identified
- Stuffing and succession planning
- Processes necessary to restore business-critical information to enable the organisation to continue operating;
- Determine the time involved to restore computer systems and business-critical information.

9.8 Application controls include input controls, processing controls and output controls. Import controls involve a authorisation of transactions prior to data entry, and password and access control, data entry screens prescribing the format for data entry online verification codes, limits, reasonableness checks and adjustment controls.

Processing controls include standardization, control totals and balancing techniques.

Output controls include transaction listing, exception reports, forms control, suspense accounts and distribution lists.

9.9 The main risks for which network controls are imperative are:

- Hacking via the Internet
- Computer virus or worm
- Electronic eavesdropping into confidential information
- Credit card payments via the Internet rejected fraudulently
- Accidental or deliberate alteration of data transferred over the network
- Human error of omission or commission
- Computer system malfunction
- Natural disasters.

9.10 Firewalls are a combination of hardware and software that are located between that set of the organisation's computer system requiring screening and those accessible from outside. Firewalls enable an organisation to restrict access to selected systems and data through a single gateway, enabling password controlled access to define it users.

9.11 Transactions, for example Internet payments, are protected using a process of data encryption. Encryption is a process whereby data is converted into a non-readable format before transmission and then re-converted after transmission.

9.12 Hacking could comprise the following three forms:

- Traffic escalation that overloads a website resulting in it going offline;
- Access obtained through password security breach;
- Insertion of viruses.

9.13 Methods that can be deployed to provide additional security against hacking are:

- Vulnerability testing through deliberate attempts to breach security;
- Regular monitoring, alerts and vigilance of staff to detect intrusion;
- Virus scanning of all emails received.

9.14 The basic principles of auditing a computer system are:

- Understanding the system
- Identifying how the system can be tested
- Reviewing security
- Data encryption validation
- Information accuracy generated by the system

- Validation of transaction and amendment authorization
- Transaction acknowledgement/confirmation systems
- Data validity checking
- Recovery procedures validation.

9.15 The main techniques used to review system controls are:

- *Test data*. A set of data that is processed by a computer and compared with expected results based upon manual processing;
- *Embedded audit facilities*. Functionality incorporated into the system that allows for continuous audit review of data and its processing. The verification of embedded audit facilities is executed by introducing a known false entry. Other examples of embedded audit facilities are code comparison programs and logical path analysis programs.

9.16 Audit interrogation software enables auditors to:

- Extract data from files for further audit work
- Interrogate computer files and extract required information
- Performs statistical analysis quickly and accurately
- Verify management reports with system data
- Detect items that are not system rule compliant.

9.17 A SCARF (systems control and review file) is used to collect selected data items extracted from financial records to enable their investigation by an auditor at a later time.

9.18 Simulation, as a data review technique, involves the preparation of a separate program that simulates the operation of the organisation's real system.

9.19 Systems maintenance auditing verifies that change control, documentation and authorisation procedures have been followed.

9.20 User organisations deploying pirated software face the following disadvantages:

- Higher propensity for failure
- Absence of warranties and support
- Increased risk of viruses and negative impacts on systems
- Significant exposure to financial penalties and/or criminal prosecution
- Reputation risk.

Fraud

10

LEARNING OUTCOMES

After completing this chapter you should be able to

- define and identify risks facing an organisation;
- explain ways of measuring and assessing risks facing an organisation, including the organisation's ability to bear such risks;
- evaluate the essential features of internal control systems for identifying, assessing and managing risks;
- recommend action to improve the efficiency, effectiveness and control of activities;
- evaluate and recommend improvements to the control of information systems.

Theory

10.1 Fraud represents one of the highest incidence of white collar crime. Recent high-profile corporate failures, particularly those in the USA, have brought about the introduction by governments of corporate governance legislation that is enforcing upon boards of directors to assume responsibility that, in some cases, can result in personal criminal prosecution and/or substantial personal and corporate financial penalties.

10.2 The Sarbanes-Oxley statute in the USA and the Combined Code in the UK are prominent corporate governance measures that aim to provide safeguards against fraud and senior executives/director behaviour.

10.3 Internally, management has the responsibility of providing controls to guard against crimes against customers, against employees, financial institutions, suppliers, the government and internationally.

10.4 For fraud to be perpetrated, both opportunity and motive must pre-exist. Management has the responsibility of monitoring for and implementing controls to counter or mitigate the effects that fraud could have upon the organisation and its stakeholders.

10.5 Factors that play a determining role in fraud prevention are the establishment of an anti-fraud culture, cultivating risk awareness, implementing and supporting whistle blowing and the installation of sound internal controls.

10.6 It is important for management of organisations to be aware that external auditors do not have the responsibility for detecting fraud. Management has the task of structuring, leading, culture creation and installation of systems and methods to identify and respond to fraud.

10.7 Computer systems create an additional avenue through which fraud can be perpetrated and often provides a vehicle where fraud detection is more difficult to detect.

10.8 Management fraud constitutes a high proportion of corporate frauds. Their detection is made more difficult due to their position of power and their influence over others fortunes that renders whistle blowing ineffective.

10.9 Organised crime and syndicated fraud has become an even greater threat due to the increased volume of international trade and globalisation.

10.10 Fraud management strategy is a critical component of corporate risk management. In addition to implementing detection and monitoring systems and procedures, organisations act proactively by participating in industry and national crime prevention structures that enable them to leverage specialist skills including forensic, investigative and analysis techniques that are normally beyond the scope of commercial operations.

? Questions

10.1 How is reward defined?

10.2 Name the three prerequisites for fraud to occur.

10.3 What techniques can be deployed to counter dishonesty?

10.4 What measures can an organisation deploy to limit opportunity for fraud?

10.5 How can organisations manage motive?

10.6 List warning signs that may indicate the presence of fraud risk.

10.7 How can an organisation achieve fraud prevention?

10.8 Developing an anti-fraud culture is acknowledged as a sound contributor to fraud risk management. What should management focus on in order to develop an anti-fraud culture?

10.9 How can risk awareness be cultivated with employees?

10.10 Why are employees reluctant to blow the whistle on fraud?

10.11 How should organisations respond to fraud?

10.12 What particular set of controls should be deployed to counter computer fraud?

10.13 Management fraud has led to the collapse of many organisations. What specific indicators could alert the management accountant of the possibility of management fraud being present?

10.14 What is the impact of identity fraud on the individual and the organisation?

10.15 List three other forms of fraud that organisations should be vigilant for.

✓ Solutions

10.1 Fraud can be defined as that conduct that results in someone obtaining an advantage, avoiding an obligation or courting a loss to another party dishonestly.

10.2 The three prerequisites necessary for fraud to be perpetrated are:

1 Dishonesty
2 Opportunity
3 Motive.

10.3 Techniques that can be deployed to counter dishonesty include:

- Pre-employment checks on all new staff
- Lifestyle monitoring of staff
- Severe discipline for offenders
- Proactive and effective moral leadership.

[The New York Police Department pursued a policy of prosecuting even the most minor of offences and, over a reasonably short time frame, found that all crime levels showed a declining tendency. This approach has subsequently been implemented in many other parts of the world with similar success profiles. Where organisations adopt a firm approach to deviant behaviour, however small, they will build knowledge and expertise in the handling of crime and fraud.]

10.4 The measures an organisation can deploy to limit opportunity for fraud include:

- Separation of duties where possible
- Controls over inputs
- Controls over processing
- Controls over outputs
- Physical security of assets
- Job and duty rotation
- Routine auditing
- Enforcing leave to be taken regularly
- Requiring control/authorisation by more than one individual.

10.5 Organizations can manage motives through:

- The establishment of good employment conditions
- A policy of instant dismissals where fraud is perpetrated
- Maintain sympathetic complaints procedures
- Provide support structures to alleviate employee distress
- Monitor behaviour and characteristics indicative of being motive indicators.

10.6 Warning signs that could indicate the presence of fraud risk include:

- Absence of anti-fraud culture
- Absence of sound system of internal controls
- Low levels of financial management expertise
- A history of legal or regulatory violations
- Strained relationships
- Lack of supervision staff
- Inadequate recruitment processes
- Redundancies

- Employee dissatisfaction
- Unusual staff behaviour
- Discrepancies between earnings and lifestyle
- Low salary levels of key staff
- Employees working unsocial hours unsupervised
- Lack of job segregation and independent checking of key transactions
- Poor management accountability and reporting
- Alteration of documents and records
- Photocopies documents replacing originals
- Missing authorisations
- Poor physical security of assets
- Poor access controls to physical assets and IT systems
- In adequacy of internal controls
- Poor documentation of internal controls
- Poor documentary support for transactions, especially credit notes
- Large cash transactions
- Management compensation highly dependent on meeting aggressive performance targets
- Significant pressure on management to obtain additional finance
- Extensive use of tax havens without clear business justification
- Complex transactions
- Complex legal ownership and/or organisational structure
- Rapid changes in profitability
- Existence of personal or corporate guarantees
- Highly competitive market conditions and decreasing profitability levels within the organisation
- The organisation operating in a declining business sector and facing possible business failure
- Rapid technological change which may increase potential for product obsolescence
- New accounting or regulatory requirements which could significantly alter reported results.

10.7 Fraud risk management prevention strategy includes:

- Anti-fraud culture
- Risk awareness
- Whistle blowing
- Sound internal control systems
- The fact that a fraud strategy exists also serves as a deterrent.

10.8 In order for management to develop an anti-fraud culture within the organisation, high ethical standards have to be cultivated. In order to cultivate these standards, management could follow the following guiding principles:

- Not acting in a way that could bring the organisation into disrepute;
- Acting with integrity towards colleagues, customers, suppliers and the public;
- Ensuring that business objectives are clearly stated and communicated:
- Ensuring that benefits are distributed fairly and impartially;
- Safeguarding the confidentiality of personal data;
- Complying with legal requirements.

10.9 Risk awareness can be cultivated through training, publicity of past events and ensuring that the possibility of fraud is kept top-of-mind with personnel in key positions.

10.10 Employees are reluctant to blow the whistle on fraud because of:

- Loyalties among workers
- Fear of the consequences
- Having unsubstantiated suspicions.

[The Public Interest Disclosure Act of 1999 provides some protection for whistle-blowers and guidance to management.]

10.11 Organisations should respond to fraud by:

- Applying internal disciplinary action in accordance with personnel policies;
- Pursuing a policy of civil litigation for recovery of the loss;
- Enforcing criminal prosecution through the police whenever possible.

10.12 The following particular set of controls could be deployed to counter computer fraud:

- Control and testing of program changes
- Physical security of computer systems
- Password controls
- Control over the issue of output forms including company orders, cheques and credits notes.

10.13 The management accountant should be vigilant for signs of management fraud by observing the following behaviour:

- Deliberate distortion of cut-off procedures to shift profits between years
- Capitalisation of expenses
- Under-provisions
- Over-valuation of inventory
- Manipulation of records to hide management incompetence
- Paying inflated prices to suppliers in return for bribes
- Employment of family members
- Charging personal expenses to the organisation.

10.14 The impact of identity fraud on the individual is that, once criminals have copied someone's identity, they can embark on criminal activity in that person's name with the knowledge that any follow-up investigations will not lead back to the criminals. This makes it difficult for organisations to know who they are really dealing with.

10.15 Organisations should be vigilant for the following additional forms of fraud:

- The so-called "419 fraud" where victims are asked to help move large sums of money with the promise of a substantial share of the cash in return
- High Yield Investment fraud and Prime Bank fraud
- Pyramid schemes.

Introduction to Risk Management and Derivatives

11

LEARNING OUTCOMES

After completing this chapter you should be able to

- interpret the risks facing an organisation that arise from movements in interest rates;
- appreciate the purpose and functions of a treasury department;
- understand the different reasons for corporate hedging;
- explain the various steps in the financial risk management process;
- understand basic derivatives and their uses.

Theory

11.1 The focus of this course is on risk management in the organisation. The following four chapters deal with the role of financial instruments as a measure of risk management. The participants should note that financial market instruments can be approached in three ways namely:

11.1.1 From a risk management or hedging perspective
11.1.2 From an arbitrager perspective (the process of buying and selling a financial instrument simultaneously in two markets)
11.1.3 Speculation.

11.2 The key learning over these four chapters will be to develop an understanding of the mechanisms involved in interest rate and currency derivatives and to distinguish between activities involving risk-averse market instrument management or hedging techniques and the opposite speculative and risk-taking behaviour. In order for the participant to have a good understanding, it will be necessary to practice simulation examples.

11.3 Financial risk management processes involve identifying the risk exposure, quantifying the exposure using either regression analysis, simulation or value-at-risk techniques.

11.4 *Regression method*. easy to implement, familiar and easy to understand but based on historical data and not necessarily a predictor of future events.

11.5 *Simulation method.* complex and difficult to implement, conceptually complex and thus difficult to explain to non-specialists but is dynamic and can be adapted to different assumptions and circumstances.

11.6 *Value-at-risk method.* can be complex with difficult statistical assumptions to implement; it easier to understand and communicate to non-specialists and the outcome is dependent upon underlying assumptions.

11.7 We will be exercising interest rate and currency derivatives including:

11.7.1 Forward contracts
11.7.2 Futures contracts
11.7.3 Swaps
11.7.4 Options.

Questions

11.1 Describe the four main functions of the treasury.

11.2 Describe the key focus for each of the strategic, tactical and operational levels of treasury management.

11.3 What are the benefits of hedging financial risks?

11.4 When could hedging be considered counterproductive?

11.5 Blok-Foster Plc exports blue widgets from England to South Africa. Based upon prominent economists' predictions of economic growth, interest rates and currency movements, B-F Plc estimate that the profit equivalent in GBP from the South African market will range between a high of £25 m, £20 m and a low of £15 m with probabilities of 0.25, 0 and 4, 0.35 respectively.

Calculate the expected value and standard deviation of the profits from the South African market.

11.6 Differentiate between forward contracts and futures contracts.

11.7 For what reason would a major motor manufacturer and a steel mill enter into a forward contract?

11.8 Briefly explain the mechanism of a swap and an option and describe their benefit to the contracting parties.

11.9 What is the difference between hedging and speculative trading in financial instruments?

11.10 Explain how arbitrage trading is conducted.

✓ Solutions

11.1 The main functions of the treasury include:

- Banking
- Liquidity management
- Funding management
- Currency management.

11.2 Treasury activities involved at each of the three levels include:

1 *Strategic*: Long-term capital structure of the organisation including cost of capital considerations, balancing equity, debentures, loan capital and investment.
2 *Tactical*: Includes the management of investments and liquidity and involves decisions on hedging of currency and/or interest rate risk.
3 *Operational*: Daily cash banking and surplus cash placement with banks.

11.3 Financial risk hedging includes the following potential benefits:

- Reduces the probability and cost of financial distress
- Has the potential to reduce taxes
- Reduces volatility of cash flows and can increase the value of the company
- Reduce its contracting costs because it reduces the risks faced by managers.

11.4 In certain instances, hedging could be considered counterproductive where:

- Shareholders hold diversified portfolios, hedging could harm rather than enhance shareholders returns.
- Transaction costs, brokerage fees and commissions consume all possible benefits.
- Hesitancy by senior managers due to lack of expertise.
- Complexities associated with tax avoidance and disclosure requirements outweigh the benefits.

11.5 The expected income from the South African market is calculated as follows:

$$E(X) = \Sigma P_i X_i$$

$$E(X) = (25 \times 0.25) + (20 \times 0.4) + (15 \times 0.35)$$

$$= £19.5M$$

$$\sigma = \sqrt{\Sigma P_i[X_i - E(X)]^2}$$

$$= \sqrt{0.25(25 - 19.5)^2 + 0.4(20 - 19.5)^2 + 0.35(15 - 19.5)^2}$$

$$= \sqrt{7.5625 + 0.1 + 7.0875}$$

$$= \sqrt{14.75}$$

$$= £3.84M$$

Profits from the South African market are expected to be £19.5M with a standard deviation of £3.84M.

11.6 Forward contracts are legally binding agreements between two parties to buy or sell an asset at a given time in the future for a given price agreed today. These contracts are generally concluded between the two parties with, possibly a trader intermediary facilitating the process.

Futures contracts, on the other hand, are similar contracts concluded via standardised trading agreements listed on futures/commodity markets like NYMEX or CME.

11.7 The motor manufacturer may wish to fix the price of steel in order to better predict the cost of producing motor vehicles for a specific market. The benefit the motor manufacturer will enjoy will be the knowledge today of the price of steel and for production to be executed in the future.

From the steel mill's point of view, they will know the price and hence their revenue stream that will flow in the future as a result of the fixed price computed with the motor manufacturer. The steel mill will enjoy the benefit of knowing what their future revenue stream will look like today.

Both the steel mill and the motor manufacturer will have negated the risk or foregone the benefit of the commodity steel price at that future date. The benefit to both parties is the knowledge today of the future cost/price they will pay/receive for that volume of the commodity (steel). This facilitates planning and removes uncertainty.

11.8 A swap is a contract between two parties requiring of both parties to deliver, at specified intervals, payments based upon differing rates for a common underlying notional principal. Both parties gain from the swap by participating in the differential between the underlying interest or exchange rates to which the parties are exposed/contracted. The intermediary (bank or brokerage) normally arranges the swap for portion of the shared differential.

An option is a contract that gives the holder the right, but not the obligation, to purchase or sell an underlying commodity on a predetermined future date in exchange for a premium paid today. This enables the purchaser to either cap the cost of a commodity or receive a minimum price, depending upon whether a call or put option is purchased.

11.9 A party, trading for the purposes of hedging, enters the market with a pre-existing exposure to an interest rate or exchange rate. All international business transactions will, in the event of change in market prices/rates, result in a loss to the organisation. Under these conditions, the party enters the marketplace and takes a position with a financial instrument to soften the impact of potential changes, thus reducing the impact of the loss.

A speculator, on the other hand, is a party that enters the marketplace for financial instruments based upon a notion or hunch that a particular commodity, interest or exchange rate will move in a particular direction. This party does not necessarily have a pre-existing exposure and will, therefore, be exposed to the full effect of the rate or price of the underlying principal.

11.10 Arbitrage is the process of trading in a common financial instrument in two markets for a common underlying commodity or principal. The arbitrageur thus simultaneously purchases a commodity or principal in one market and sells it in another at the same time.

Arbitrageurs thus have access and knowledge to multiple markets and are able to exploit price differences at a given time. Arbitrage is risk neutral because the benefit to the arbitrageur accrues without time or further trading risk.

Interest Rate Management

12

Learning Outcomes

After completing this chapter you should be able to

- interpret the risks facing an organisation that arise from movements in interest rates;
- identify and evaluate appropriate methods for managing interest rate risk;
- demonstrate how and when to convert fixed rate interest to floating rate interest;
- illustrate the effect of interest rate risk management techniques such as swaps, forward rate agreements, futures, options and swaptions.

Theory

12.1 This chapter focuses on the organisation's exposure to interest rate risk. Every organisation is exposed to capital cost dependent upon their equity structure and sources and availability of debt in the markets in which they raise capital.

12.2 In this highly competitive world, businesses cannot allow cash reserves to lie idle. Treasury will have the task of maximising the earnings from investments while critically balancing operational and project cash requirements.

12.3 To a large extent, interest rate risk arises out of timing differences between cash commitments and cash receipts. In order to ensure adequate capital availability, organisations have to maintain reserves on the one hand and negotiate borrowings on the other.

12.4 Our task is to identify instances and periods of exposure to interest rate risk and, being risk averse and therefore not speculative in terms of interest rate, would seek to minimise those risks.

12.5 The impact of interest rates on the business therefore depends upon the choice or availability of funding. The exposures arise due to:

12.5.1 The mix between capital and debt
12.5.2 The mix between fixed and floating rate debt
12.5.3 The mix between short-term and long-term debt.

12.6 The instruments are available to us for this purpose includes:

12.6.1 Internal hedging techniques which comprise:

12.6.1.1 *Smoothing*: Fixed and variable interest rates debt is negotiated or deployed in equal amounts and thus balancing the exposure which naturally provides a hedge, one against the other.

12.6.1.2 *Matching*: Funding investments with debt instruments that have a similar interest exposure – e.g.: fixed interest rate income funded by fixed interest rate debt.

12.6.1.3 *Netting*: Both assets and liability positions are aggregated to determine the net exposure.

12.6.2 External hedging includes:

12.6.2.1 Interest rate swaps

12.6.2.2 And forward rate agreements

12.6.2.3 Interest rate futures

12.6.2.4 Interest rate options

12.6.2.5 And hybrid techniques such as swaptions.

12.7 The choice of instrument to use is dependent upon availability in the market, cost–benefit considerations, risk appetite and timescale.

? Questions

12.1 What is the difference between credit and market risk?

12.2 What is meant by matching in the hedging context?

12.3 Companies X and Y wish to negotiate a swap based on a notional £50 million, 5-year loan. Their credit profiles enable them to offers from lenders as follows:

	Fixed Rate	Floating Rate
Company X:	5.5%	LIBOR + 0.1%
Company Y:	6.5%	LIBOR + 0.4%

Company X requires a floating rate loan and company Y requires a fixed rate loan. Design a swap that will net the bank, acting as intermediary, 0.1% per annum and that will appear equally attractive to both companies.

12.4 Forward rate agreements applied

JD & Co Plc has a covenant with its lenders of EBITDA/interest <4 times cover. The total outstanding loan balance is £230 million and is all variable interest bearing. Market expectation is that interest rates are set to rise in the UK due to inflationary pressures from 6% to 7% p.a. GDP growth is expected to fall and market conditions are likely to harden. Indications from marketing are that sales are expected to fall sharply and EBITDA returns for this financial year will drop to £60 million. Planning for the next 3 years has also revealed that market conditions were expected to remain suppressed or recover to current conditions if the oil price dropped.

Janet Henry, the CFO, has investigated the market and established that Euros denominated loans can be secured at 6.2% subject to identical conditions applicable to existing loans and attracts a 1% raising fee. A £ denominated FRA is available at 6.5%. Fixed interest rate loans in £ are available at 7%.

Janet has approached you for advice. What would you recommend her to do?

12.5 Interest-futures applied

This question extends the discussion in question 4.

Your investigations suggest that interest futures are available at a price of 93.7. The IRF covers the period to 1 month past the financial year end.

The market for interest rate options suggest a strike price of 6.35% at the identical close-out date as the IRF. The premium is £2000.

How would this additional information affect your recommendation to Janet?

12.6 Interest rate options applied – cap

This question extends the discussion in questions 4 and 5.

Janet was about to implement your advice (question 5 continued) when she mentioned that the loan was, in fact, for a 5-year period of which 4 years would be remaining at the financial year end.

Further investigation, in the light of this additional information revealed that a 4-year 6.5% cap on a £230 million loan limit will attract a premium of £2300 and if the cap is combined with a floor of 6.2%, the premium will be £1100.

How does this new knowledge affect your recommendation?

Solutions

12.1 Credit risk is the risk that party A assumes when contracting with party B that relates to party B failing to meet its obligations. Credit risk is thus transaction-specific and relates to the contracting parties only.

Market risk is risk that all parties in a particular market will be exposed to. Market risk is therefore, not party-specific that translates to external changes that have an impact on the contracting parties.

[Market risk could, however, be a forerunner/indicator of credit risk in the sense that, if party B defaulted on the contract (credit risk) as a result of a steep rise interest rates (market risk) then credit risk considerations should be evaluated in terms of market risk.]

12.2 Matching, in the hedging sense, is an internal hedging technique deployed where the organisation is in a position to negotiate funding arrangements that match their market conditions. For example, should an organisation have fixed price contracts, funding should be arranged on a fixed rate basis to avoid interest rate risk.

12.3 The structure of an interest rate swap, leaving both parties equally satisfied and arranging bank loan with 0.1% commission, could be effected as follows:

	Company X	Company Y	Quality Spread
Fixed Rate:	5.5%	6.5%	1.0
Floating Rate:	LIBOR + 0.1	LIBOR + 0.4	0.3
Differential			0.7

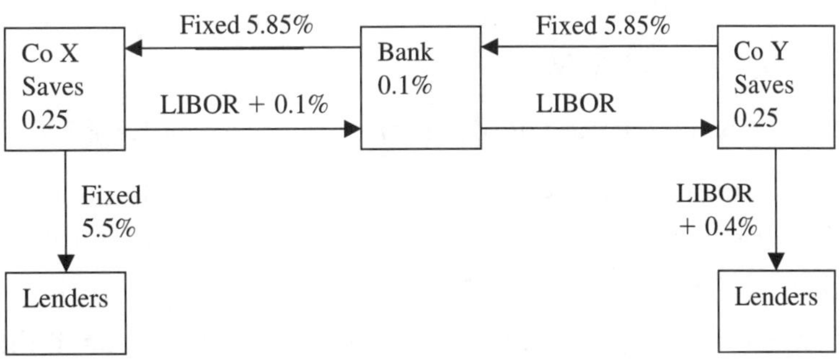

Company X: Acquires variable rate and saves 0.25%;
Company Y: Acquires fixed rate and saves 0.25%
Bank: Assumes credit risk and receives 0.1% commission

12.4 In preparation for my advice to you Janet, I have presented the following analysis:

The covenant with the lenders will require that you keep interest repayments below £15 M (£60 M/4) based upon projected EBITDA.

Variable Loan (assume rise to 7%) (£230 M × 7%)	£16.10 M p.a.
Euro Loan (£230 M in Euro equivalent × 6.2%)	£14.26 M p.a.
Hedged (£16.10 M − (£230 M × (7% − FRA £230 × 6.5%)))	£14.95 M p.a.

The most favourable option would be to accept the Euro-based loan provided that you are prepared to accept the related currency risk.

Fixed rates fall outside of the covenant range and are not advisable.

The FRA hedged option results in a cost adjustment of £0.69 M and offers the most cost-effective option under conditions of fully hedged market risk.

My recommendation is to accept the FRA.

12.5 Given the additional information, I have considered your position and recommend that you consider another solution.

Additional findings:

Option: Variable Loan (assume 7%) (£230M × 7%)	£16.10M p.a
Less: Option pay-out (7 − 6.35%)	£1.4605M p.a.
Add: Fee	£0.001M p.a.
Cost	£14.6405M p.a.

The option should be selected when there is fair certainty that the interest 'rate will exceed 6.36%.

This option provided more freedom and leaves you free to pay lower interest should the rate not rise as high as expected and provides cover for the covenant limit.

12.6 Covering the covenant limit at year end is part of the solution required. The loan is for 4 future years and therefore, if market conditions do not improve, future covenant exposure is likely.

Covering the full loan period is required.

The negotiation of a cap would result in the following:

Cap (£230 M × 6.5%)	14.95 M
Fee	0.02 M
Cost	14.97 M

The cap satisfies the covenant, should interest rates rise above 6.5%.

The floor will result in a saving of £1000 but could preclude the company from paying interest at 6%, should the conditions return to current status. Assuming 6% in any future year, the company will lose £3600 p.a.

The better choice is a cap without a floor which provides flexibility to follow the lower market and cover the covenant in all future years.

Foreign Exchange: Relationships and Risks 13

LEARNING OUTCOMES

After completing this chapter you should be able to

- interpret the impact of currency risk;
- calculate the impact of differential national inflation rates on forecasting exchange rates;
- explain exchange rate theory.

Theory

13.1 In a globalising world, foreign exchange risk has become a prominent feature of business life. The majority of countries now operated floating exchange rates with the result that international trade is subject to exchange rate uncertainty and risk.

13.2 The hedging instruments available for exchange rate management are similar to interest rate instruments. The complexity lies in establishing expected exchange rate movements based on economic dynamics in the marketplace.

13.3 Theoretical Forex relationships include speculation, balance of payments, government policy, and interest rate differentials and inflation rate differentials. Numerous modelling tools are available and we concern ourselves with the following:

13.3.1 Interest rate parity model
13.3.2 And purchasing power parity model
13.3.3 The Fisher effect
13.3.4 Expectation theory.

13.4 Deriving its rational from monetary economic mechanisms, exchange rates correlate with money market rates. International investment money follows markets where high interest rates prevail. Because arbitrage will move markets closer and close opportunity gaps, we can assume a reasonably efficient market. The relationship between the interest rates and the spot and forward exchange rates enables us to calculate the expected exchange rate one period ahead.

13.5 The purchasing power model is premised upon the assumption that, where a country has a higher rate of inflation than its trading partners, that country's exchange rate will fall to realign the purchasing power parity.

13.6 The Fisher effect explains the exchange rates moving in reverse relationship with interest rate movement linked to inflation rate rise/fall.

13.7 Interest rate parity and purchasing power parity assume active arbitrage with a blind spot when investors agree that one currency is riskier than others.

13.8 The risk profile faced, when international trade and investment are undertaken, extends to exchange rate transaction and translation risks, political and economic risk.

13.9 Transaction risk impacts on the organisation's cash flow as well as its performance as measured from its home currency.

13.10 Translation risk relates to the impact on the valuation of foreign assets and liabilities when valued in the reporting currency. The impact is mainly on the funding and valuation issues and can have the effect of influencing credit ratings and borrowing power.

13.11 Political risk has few objective determinants and can often be exaggerated by rumour and contagion rather than being based upon events on the ground. The actions of governments do have substantial shift effect when there is a risk of expropriation, discrimination or the imposition of specific rules regarding ownership, labour or materials.

13.12 The existence of risk deters most and that creates opportunity for others to exploit gaps and structures to their advantage. Knowledge becomes the critical success factor.

? Questions

13.1 Distinguish between spot and forward rates.

13.2 What is the difference between interest rate parity and purchasing power parity?

13.3 What does the Fisher effect endeavour to explain?

13.4 What is the effect of exchange rate movements on transactional risk?

13.5 What is the effect of exchange rate movements on translational risk?

Solutions

13.1 The spot rate is the exchange rate for a transaction that is due for immediate delivery, while the forward rate applies to a transaction to be conducted sometime in the future.

13.2 Where a country has interest rates higher than those applicable in other countries, they will attract foreign investment which, in turn, will result in a rise in that country's currency exchange rate.

The purchasing power parity model is premised upon currencies being dependent upon/moving in response to differential inflation rates. According to this model, country's experiencing a higher inflation rate than others will be subject to currency devaluation to restore purchasing power equilibrium.

Both the interest rate parity model and the purchasing power parity model rely upon a high level of arbitrage activity to bring about quick adjustments to market rates resulting in an efficient market. Both of these models negate the effects/potential for political or country risks.

13.3 The Fisher effect derives a monetary interest rate from the product of real interest and the country's inflation rate. This mechanism is premised upon monetary economic policy where countries endeavour to limit inflationary pressures through interest rate mechanisms. Higher interest rates have the effect of cooling economic growth and, thereby containing inflation. In the absence of political or country risk considerations, the anticipated effect of an increase in inflation will result in increased interest rates. Increased interest rates will attract foreign investors that, in turn, will purchase the currency driving its rate up.

13.4 The effect of exchange rate movements on transaction risk is to reduce/increase earnings in the home country as a result of the change in exchange rate of a foreign country in which the organisation trades. Cash flow and profitability are both affected.

13.5 Translation risk is the effect of disclosing the value of foreign held assets in home currency terms. A decline in exchange rates will diminish the asset value reported by the organisation with corresponding negative borrowing power as a result of a weekend balance sheet.

Foreign Exchange Risk Management 14

LEARNING OUTCOMES

After completing this chapter you should be able to

- recommend foreign exchange risk management strategies;
- identify the different types of internal hedging techniques;
- calculate the optimum hedging technique, giving consideration to the forward market, the money market, futures and options;
- illustrate the use of currency swaps.

Theory

14.1 Foreign exchange risk, as with interest rate risk, can be internally and externally managed.

14.2 Internal management techniques include home currency invoicing, bilateral and multilateral netting, leading and lagging techniques, matching and restructuring.

14.3 External hedging techniques include forward contracts, futures, options and swaps.

14.4 The theory relating to these techniques was dealt with in Chapters 11,12 and 13 and will, therefore, not be repeated here.

14.5 The international accounting standards and the international financial reporting standards have brought about substantial additional disclosure requirements. IAS21 has been adapted, requiring transactions to be recognised at the exchange rate on the date of the original transaction, non-cash assets to be reported at the date of acquisition or revaluation and cash or near-cash instruments to be translated at the reporting date. IFRS3 requires that intangible assets be disclosed at transaction value and be subjected to impairment adjustments annually.

14.6 The implications of these disclosure requirements for the organisation are:

14.6.1 Substantially increased costs of record-keeping.
14.6.2 Disclosure parameters that could expose strategic detail to competitors.
14.6.3 Management choices that try to avoid the complexity and, in so doing, unwittingly leave the organisation open to risk.
14.6.4 The subjectivity of country and political risk leaves the organisation vulnerable and, therefore careful and comprehensive hedging of currency risk is important.

? Questions

14.1 Explain the internal hedging technique: bilateral netting.

14.2 How does an organisation deploy a lead or lag measure to hedge a currency exposure?

14.3 What steps can an organisation take to restructure so as to reduce their long-term exposure to exchange rate fluctuations?

14.4 What problems could an organisation encounter with currency forward contracts?

14.5 What is meant by the term 'in the money' and how does that affect the premium of an option?

Solutions

14.1 Bilateral netting is a technique employed by subsidiaries within an organisation. These subsidiaries net-off their debit and credit positions leaving the residual exposed to currency risk that then has to be hedged externally.

[Multilateral netting applies where an organisation nets off between subsidiaries from a central office.]

14.2 Lead and lag techniques involve the organisation in practices where transactions are rescheduled to take advantage of a currency change or anticipated change. A lead measure would be applied where payment is required early for performance to take place later. Lag measures could involve arranging for payment to be delayed to capitalise on anticipated currency strengthening.

14.3 Restructuring an organisation is normally a long-term solution to a problem. Where sustained advantage or disadvantage is perceived in multi-currency markets, the organisation should take measures to capitalise on opportunities and avoid deteriorating conditions. Specific measures include:

- Increasing sales where opportunities abound and reduce sales in deteriorating currency markets;
- Increased dependency upon foreign suppliers where currency deterioration favours cost cutting and vice versa where currency depreciation makes pricing unfavourable;
- Establishing manufacturing facilities in weak currency markets and closing/selling production facilities in markets where currency appreciation reduces competitiveness;
- Incurring new debt facilities denominated in a foreign currency where that currency is weakening; making it cheaper when seen from the home currency perspective and liquidating debt denominated in a foreign currency where it is appreciating.

14.4 Forward exchange contracts are binding. As a result, when conditions change making the contract unfavourable, the organisation is bound by the contract and will incur the negative effects imposed. The rationale for these products is to bring about certainty. The price (opportunity cost) that the organisation pays for certainty is the loss of access to changes in the opposite direction that would otherwise result in a benefit.

Where availability or needs change, the organisation will be required to top-up any shortfall or over-pay where forward cover arrangements exceed the final requirements.

In extreme cases, where the supplier defaults or political circumstances substantially alter trading conditions, the organisation remains obligated to proceed with the contract is respectively.

14.5 The term 'in the money' refers to a condition where the strike price is more favourable to the clients than is currently available. Under these conditions, the premium payable will likely be higher.

Long Questions and Answers 15

Scenario 1

E Ltd, a long-established, medium-sized manufacturing company, designs and manufactures electrical generating units for customers all over the world. These electrical generating units are designed to provide effective stand-by electricity wherever continuous power is critical, such as for hospitals, offices, hotels, airports and banks. E Ltd uses the latest computer technology to design and manufacture the generating units (including CAD and CAM systems) to meet the demands of a variety of customers. E Ltd operates in a highly competitive market, both at home and overseas.

Its factory operates to the highest quality standards, including ISO9001. However, as a result of increasing product complexity, and customer demands for unique product specifications, the Board of Directors recognised that their existing production planning system was unable to cope with these increased demands. In addition, the organisation had encountered problems of obsolete stock, materials booked to wrong jobs, and problems in measuring the cost of work completed. The Board of Directors considered that the optimum solution would be to introduce an integrated production planning and management reporting system.

Integrated system requirements

The Managing Director of E Ltd set up a steering committee to ascertain the requirements of the new system. The steering committee consisted of the Managing Director, the Finance Director and the Manufacturing Director. The steering committee, having considered the current problems, decided that the initial systems requirements would need to include a stock control facility, production planning, product costing and a financial reporting system.

The steering committee very quickly recognised that E Ltd did not have the internal expertise to design and develop such an information system. A brief document was subsequently produced by the steering committee, outlining the systems requirements as highlighted above. Six national systems design and development organisations were invited to submit tenders for either bespoke or off-the-shelf systems. No definite systems specifications were presented in the Invitation to Tender, as the MD pointed out: 'We are not the experts – we'll let them tell us what we need, after all they should know.'

Supplier selection

Four suppliers responded to the Invitation to Tender document. Two of these were subsequently rejected on the grounds of being too expensive, despite both having numerous years of project experience in this type of systems development. The remaining two suppliers were invited to present to the steering committee a project implementation plan, detailing their system specifications, product features and functions as well as a plan of the implementation procedures, time-scales and costs. Having reviewed the two proposals, the steering committee decided to award the contract to Z Ltd, a systems software design company which had been in business for 2 years. Z Ltd had built its reputation on designing *to order* systems (i.e. bespoke software designed and built from a number of standard business modules, which can be re-designed and integrated to order). However, Z Ltd did not have prior experience in developing large integrated production systems; but it was the least expensive provider.

The Z Ltd Integrated Production System (ZIPS)

The main features of the new system as proposed by Z Ltd are as follows:

- material management (including the potential for supplier systems integration using ISDN);
- stock control;
- production planning (including capacity planning);
- project planning and management;
- product costing;
- financial reporting.

(These features are those provided as standard in Z Ltd's pre-written standard business modules as used in previously-designed Z Ltd systems, and are known as 'Systems modules'. These will be amended to suit the needs of E Ltd.)

Technical features

The proposed system will operate from an NT operating system, using a client-server architecture, and is built around a relational database management system. It contains in-built report-writing facilities for complete user manipulation and also has an in-built executive information system (EIS). The management of E Ltd believes that the real-time online processing facilities will have major benefits for the company. In order to run the new integrated software, E Ltd must invest in more up-to-date hardware – including 15 new Pentium computers, 5 laser printers and additional communications facilities (a Local Area Network). Z Ltd planned for an approximately 12-month development life cycle to complete the project, from initial systems analysis to full operation.

The project

The first task was to set up a project team. This consisted of a senior consultant from Z Ltd who was assigned the role of Project Manager, six systems analysts from Z Ltd (each of whom would lead a module design team), along with the IT Manager, the Internal Audit Manager, the Management Accountant and the Production Manager of E Ltd. The Project Manager was also currently working on completion of another Z Ltd project for another organisation, which he assured E Ltd would be finished by week 8 of the Z Ltd Integrated Production System (ZIPS) project. The Project Manager had stated to the steering committee: 'the analysts don't need me to tell them what to do'.

The Project Manager and the systems analysts produced the following plan for the project.

Project phases

Systems analysis and design (including systems development)	24 weeks	(Weeks 1–24)
Module integration	12 weeks	(Weeks 25–36)
Systems testing*	5 weeks	(Weeks 37–41)
File conversion	8 weeks	(Weeks 42–49)
Changeover (direct)	1 week	(Week 50)

* In addition, 2 weeks of training were built into the programme to be carried out at the same time as systems testing and file conversion (weeks 41 and 42), and this training phase was for senior managers only. All other staff would be trained once the system went live.

Analysis and design teams, consisting of analysts and programmers from Z Ltd, were set up to build the individual systems modules. The analysts did not anticipate that the individual module teams would need to meet before integration began in week 25. Two weeks' floating contingency was built into the overall programme.

Project progression

The project commenced on schedule, and the systems analysis and design phase progressed as expected. However, there was some concern from the project team members from within E Ltd that there was very little co-ordination between the end-users of the existing system and the module design teams. It was also noted that the Project Manager was rarely available in the first 10–12 weeks, as he was busy dealing with problems on other Z Ltd jobs. In fact, he did not take over full-time responsibility for the ZIPS project until week 16, at which point the first official project team meeting took place.

At this meeting, the IT manager of E Ltd voiced his considerable concern that the module teams had not yet met to co-ordinate and discuss the design considerations prior to integration of the individual systems modules. However, the Project Manager was unconcerned: 'What's the problem? The project's on time and you've got 12 weeks built into the schedule for integration. Plenty of time.'

Module integration began early, in week 22. Problems began to occur soon after, as it became obvious that the individual systems modules were not integrating as expected. In particular, it was apparent that the financial reporting module was not integrating effectively with the stock control system or the product costing module. The Internal Auditor was particularly concerned with the lack of effective data controls within the financial reporting module, and the evident lack of data security and compatibility between all modules.

Over the next 8 weeks the module design teams continued to re-design the modules to overcome the integration problems, but most changes were not to the satisfaction of the project team members from E Ltd.

The project is now in week 30, and most of the integration phase remains incomplete. Following a crisis meeting between the project team and the steering committee, it has been decided that the IT Manager of E Ltd should become the ZIPS Project Manager and that a new project plan be drawn up immediately. As the Management Accountant, you will continue to work with the project team for the remainder of the project.

Question 1

As the Management Accountant and project team member, write an **internal memorandum to the other members of the project team**, which

(a) recommends the data controls that need to be considered within the financial reporting module of the new ZIPS system. Include an analysis of

  (i) input controls;
  (ii) processing controls;
  (iii) output controls.

(10 marks)

(b) explains the aims and purposes of the internal audit function as compared with the external audit function, and their differing roles in a computerised systems audit.

(7 marks)

(c) explains the potential internal and external audit problems faced by E Ltd, as a result of

  (i) moving to an integrated information system, and
  (ii) the use of a real-time processing system.

(8 marks)
(Total = 25 marks)

Answer 1

INTERNAL MEMORANDUM

Fao: The Project Team Members

From: The Management Accountant
Date: 24 May 2001

(a)

Internal control requirements of the ZIPS

Most controls within an IT environment can be split into general and application controls. General controls focus on the environment within which computerised financial reporting systems work, whereas application controls are concerned with preventing, detecting and correcting errors and irregularities in transactions that are processed within an IT environment, and are designed to be application specific.

The three major stages of data processing work are: accumulating input data; processing; and the consolidation of the data into some form of output. Therefore, controls need to be implemented within all three stages of the financial reporting systems processing.

(i) *Input controls*

The main aims of input controls are to ensure accuracy, completeness and validity of the financial data. The use of written procedures and user manuals for all of the individual modules should encourage correct usage of the system, together with user-friendly screen design and user tools (e.g. use of WIMP – Windows, Icons, Mouse and Pointer facilities) and the use of on-screen dialogue prompts and help facilities. It is important that these in-built tools are standard throughout the modules to ensure consistency and assist in ensuring standards of input and subsequent control. There is a need for strict password controls for entry into the different ZIPS modules to ensure only authorised access within the system. Also, as a result of the real-time processing environment, it is important to have strict authorisation and supervisory controls, for example dual input of transaction data wherever possible. This would involve two people being required to complete a transactions' final input to the master file (i.e. supervisory authorisation controls).

A further data input control would be to use pre-printed data entry and transaction-recording forms, for example standard order forms used in the materials management module and invoice stationery used by the accounting department in the financial reporting module. Pre-formatted, standardised data entry screens, together with error correction procedures, would also provide assurance of control over data entering the financial reporting module. Within each ZIPS module, input validation routines (edit tests) would provide assurance of data validity and standardisation of entry procedures.

For example, supplier account codes within the stock control module must be entered in a predetermined format, and the system will not allow further data entry until the correct format is used.

(ii) *Processing controls*

Processing controls focus on the manipulation of accounting data after input to the computer system. Batch control totals may be used to ensure that entry of multiple documents in batches can be cross-checked by the computer for accuracy of entry. E Ltd may enter supplier invoices or receipts from customers using batches and batch totals may be effective in this case. However, the real-time processing facility of the new ZIPS system may remove the need for batch input.

Access controls within the ZIPS database management system can also be utilised in order to protect sensitive parts of the system (i.e. some parts of the system may be protected to be 'read only'). For example, in the ZIPS system, only the accounting department staff would be allowed to access the financial reporting module, and within the accounting department only specified users would be given the authority to amend data.

Detection of data errors could be achieved by using in-built sequence checks, detection of data processing errors could be achieved by field size checks and systems balancing checks could be achieved by run-to-run totals.

Within the ZIPS system, the output from one module will become the input to another. Thus, systems testing is an important processing control for the system, because it tests not only the processing capabilities of individual programs, but also the linkages between the programs and system modules. Also, within the ZIPS system, only the senior executives would be allowed access to the Executive Information System.

(iii) *Output controls*

Once data has been processed internally by the computer system, it is usually transferred to some form of output medium for storage, or in the case of printed output, prepared as reports. The objective of output controls is to ensure the output's validity, accuracy and completeness.

One form of output control is the activity listings (proof listings), which provide complete, detailed information about all changes to master-files (and provide a good audit trail). Sample listings can be produced so that incomplete or incorrect output can be identified. These need to be available on demand for all of the ZIPS modules.

Pre-numbered output documents/forms may also be used when issuing multiple forms or documents such as cheques. The numbers on these pre-numbered forms advance sequentially together with the computer-generated cheque-writing procedures that print a computer-generated number upon the cheque during the output procedure. These numbers can then be reconciled and any discrepancies checked prior to issue.

Authorised distribution lists may also be utilised in order to protect sensitive computer-generated information. For example, in the ZIPS system, only the senior managers would receive sensitive payroll reports.

(b)

The main job of the internal audit function is to analyse the financial and operational information of the organisation in order to assess whether control exists and if it is working correctly. The internal audit function acts as an internal control. Internal audits are likely to review the economy, efficiency and effectiveness of operations and make subsequent recommendations for improvement. The internal audit function also reviews compliance with law and regulations and undertakes one-off investigations of operations, for example fraud investigations. The primary responsibility of internal audit is to monitor all aspects of the business in order to ensure that internal control exists and is adhered to.

The primary role of the external audit function is to provide an external, independent opinion as to the validity and accuracy of the organisation's financial position. Appointed by the shareholders, external auditors have a responsibility to the owners (shareholders) to report their opinion as to the true and fair view of the organisations' financial statements. It is also their responsibility to ensure the reliability of the internal audit work on controlling the financial position of the business.

Within the computer environment, the internal audit function would mainly be concerned with the existence of the controls highlighted in *requirement (a)* of this memo. It would test for the existence of such controls, by means of compliance testing in order to assess:

- How good are the controls?
- What weaknesses may exist?
- Can managers rely on the internal controls and the integrity of the information from the information system, that is, is the information from the system accurate?

If the answer is unclear, or if the internal auditor is not satisfied with the current internal controls, then he/she will carry out further detailed substantive testing on individual transactions and balances.

The external auditor is likely to concentrate on the existence of controls within the financial system. In the case of ZIPS, this is likely to be more complex, as the modules are integrated and share information using a relational database structure, therefore the external auditor will have to ensure a thorough audit of all module interfaces with the financial reporting system.

(c)

(i) *Audit problems of moving to an integrated information system*

Moving to one integrated database means that new master files for the ZIPS system as a whole need to be established, tested and monitored and one common coding system for all individual ZIPS modules set up. The current individual systems will need to be re-coded to fit the new structure, therefore data may be lost or corrupted. It is vital that the auditor follows a rigorous testing procedure throughout the integration stage of development and afterwards to ensure that all data has been correctly coded and transferred into the new master files.

The new integrated system will also rely heavily upon the accurate transfer of information between the stock control, product costing and financial reporting modules, thus the auditor must ensure that the system is fully and correctly integrated and that information from one system is correctly transferred to another. However, this is a problem for the auditor of the ZIPS system, because of the way the development has proceeded to date, with little attempt to integrate the modules prior to week 24. As can be seen from the ZIPS project, directly after integration it became clear that information transferred between the stock control system and the financial reporting system was incorrect.

There may also be problems of initial data entry error due to unfamiliarity within the first few weeks with the new system (such as new file structures and screen layouts). The new sales order processing screen may be slightly different for example, which may mean that data entry errors occur initially. As the current plan for the ZIPS project is to train the users after going live, this problem is highly likely to occur and the auditor must be aware of it.

A further problem for the auditor, evident in the ZIPS project, is the lack of data security between modules and lack of compatibility. It is critical that the auditor ensures that sufficient security measures are built in at the design stage.

(ii) *Audit problems of real-time processing systems*

As a result of real-time processing, it is possible that primary records such as material orders and GRNs are no longer received and kept in hard copy format. This will present problems for the auditor in terms of establishing a clear audit trail. The new system also has the potential for supplier integration using ISDN, which although it may improve efficiency, could in fact result in security and audit problems. The auditor must therefore ensure that strict security measures and adequate firewalls are built in to this part of the system. A lack of batch controls on data entry and the possibility of the lack of primary records may make it difficult to ensure and verify the completeness and accuracy of input and processing, as many transactions are likely to be input to the master file directly on receipt. Ensuring segregation of duties is a further concern for the auditor in real-time processing systems, as data input, processing and verification are likely to occur in one stage and be carried out by one person. For example, vulnerability of master files to immediate update and tampering/errors requires strict access and security controls, and security arrangements need to be audited regularly.

In summary, the auditors must ensure that thorough systems testing be done in order to ensure the new integrated system can cope with the type and volume of transactions that the new system will process. Also, there is a need to test that there are adequate audit trails.

Scenario 2

You are a management accountant working for B plc, a company which is based in northern Europe and which manufactures and sells a range of eye and dental care products.

In 1998, B plc established a $25 million joint venture manufacturing plant in Asiana, a country in northern Asia. The objective was to produce a range of high-quality eye care and optical merchandise in Asiana, and to sell the products in Asiana and its neighbouring countries. The joint venture partner, C Corporation, was a leading and highly reputable eye-care institute, with a worldwide reputation for research and development in optical products.

The Board of Directors of B plc considered the Asiana market particularly as an opportunity to service the needs of a large and increasingly affluent population. Asiana has a total population of over 500 million people. In recent years, the central government of Asiana reduced import duties imposed on imported materials in order to attract foreign investment.

The project scope

Approved in August 1998, the project to construct the new manufacturing plant began with the selection and formation of a multi-national project team. For the project objectives to be met, production of eye-care products needed to start in October 2000 and total project costs needed to be within $25 million. All manufacturing and design processes must meet ISO9001 (1994) quality standards. The project team selected an Asianan architectural and engineering firm, V, a long-established and highly reputable firm, to prepare detailed construction drawings and performance specifications from B plc's concept designs.

Project background

It was necessary to overcome major obstacles to complete the manufacturing plant, including highly bureaucratic paperwork, different management styles, lack of available basic utilities such as electricity, water and sewage and limited communication networks. B plc's style of management is democratic and participatory, with a strong emphasis on teamwork. This contrasted with the more autocratic style of management practised in Asiana.

Project team management

The main project team was divided into sub-teams, each responsible for a product line. Reporting of cost, schedule and technical performance occurred on a weekly basis, by each product line manager to the Project Manager.

The Project Manager, an experienced senior manager from B plc, selected the team members on the basis of their expertise, flexibility, and ability to work under pressure within a team environment. The team included members from various departments of B plc (see p. xx). The team members were mainly based at the European HQ (with the exception of the product line managers who were based on site in Asiana).

The project team also contained staff from C Corporation who were based on the Asianan site. The on-site manager in Asiana was responsible for all activities on site, and reported directly to the Project Manager.

The project team structure is shown in the diagram below.

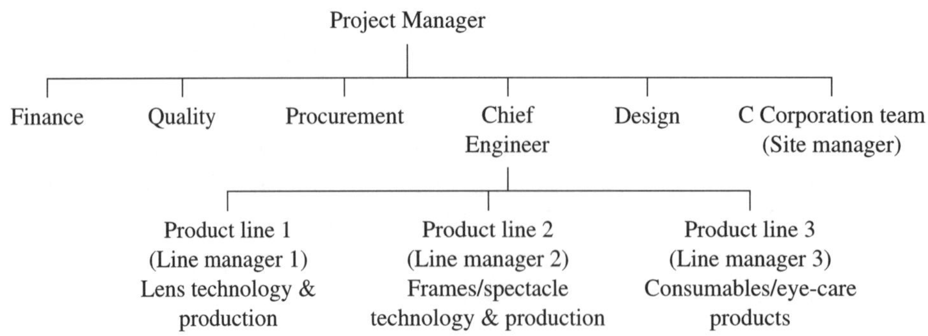

At the first project team meeting, held in late August 1998, the basic facility parameters were established, including all utility requirements (i.e. water, sewage and electricity), space requirements and production workflow. B plc used feedback from other multi-national firms and from their own previous project experience in order to ensure all aspects of the project were considered.

Cost management

The project had its own system for controlling and monitoring project costs and achievements. The budget was set at $25 million at the start of the project, and was formulated using a bottom-up approach. Costs were divided into numerous work breakdown packages for each phase of construction, and then subsequently split into budgets for each product line.

Each product line manager was responsible to the Chief Engineer (see team structure diagram above) for his/her own work breakdown packages and each phase of work. Regular cost reporting and cost variance analysis was carried out by the finance team, and it was the responsibility of each product line manager to explain significant variance from budget to the Chief Engineer, who then reported to the Project Manager. The Project Manager was responsible for reporting the financial results of the project to the Board of Directors on a weekly basis.

This financial reporting system was designed to report the cost of work performed to date and the value earned from it. Also, on a monthly basis, the finance team produced an Expected Final Cost report (EFC), which highlighted costs to date by key category for each product line, and expected final project cost. This was reported to all project team members and the Board of Directors at the end of each month. The product line managers kept their own cost records using the project management software on the on-site computers.

Quality management

It was essential to import high-precision, special-purpose technology from Europe and America. A key part of the project was specifying manufacturing and design procedures so that manufacturing processes would produce consistent products in accordance with ISO9001(1994). Six government inspections are required annually for the plant once it is fully operational. All project team members and staff working on the joint venture site had to undertake a 6-week quality training programme.

Prior to production, each process was validated and each product subjected to internal product quality testing to ensure that perfect standards were met. Once these internal validations were completed, an external compliance audit was conducted, and approval then given from the Corporate Quality Assurance department at B plc HQ to begin production. Quarterly internal production and process quality audits are to be carried out every year.

Risk management

The risks of managing and controlling such a complex multi-national project were recognised by B plc as falling into two key categories – internal and external. Internal risks were monitored and controlled by means of regular financial reporting, clear project structure, clearly-defined project roles and clear levels of authority and reporting responsibilities. External risks included changes in government regulations (fluctuating duty tariffs, import restrictions), unavailability of basic resources, lack of skilled manpower and bureaucratic slowness. B plc considered that these were out of the control of the project team and therefore only needed to be monitored.

Information management

Communication to and from the site was difficult, and each product line manager had to spend at least 1 day each week at C Corporation offices, using the e-mail or telephone facilities. This, together with the very structured reporting procedures set up by B plc, meant that management of information flow in the project was often complex and lengthy. For example, when the product line manager for each product line was required to present his weekly cost reports (called Form 1) to the Chief Engineer, these then had to be collated by the Chief Engineer for presentation to the Project Manager into another Form (called Form 2). Form 2 included the cost data from Form 1 plus additional commentary and graphics. The process was as represented in the Data Flow Diagram (DFD) in Appendix 1 (see page 7). The whole process shown in the DFD normally took in excess of 10 days. This kind of information and reporting procedure was common elsewhere in the project.

Project outcome

The Asiana plant began production on 1 November 2000, 26 months after project approval. The project was only 2 weeks late, completed only marginally over budget ($70,000) and met all of the original quality deliverables. The Board of Directors of B plc considered the project to be a complete success. However, it has been agreed that within the next 6 months a detailed post-completion review must be carried out to evaluate the real impact of this project and the future developments required.

You have been asked to continue working with the joint venture team until November 2002.

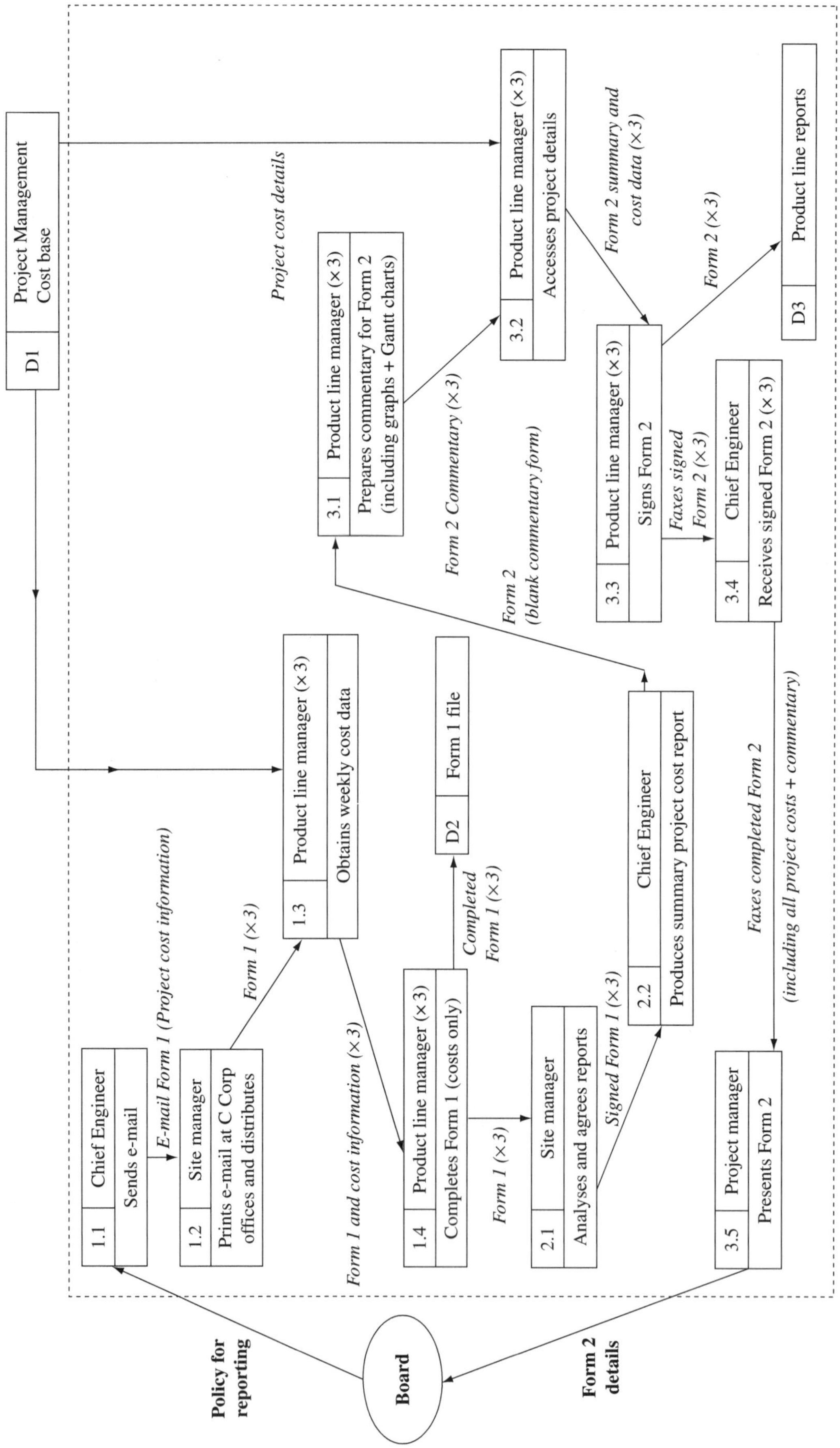
D1 Project Management Cost base
Project cost details
D2 Form 1 file
D3 Product line reports
Board
Policy for reporting
Form 2 details
1.1 Chief Engineer Sends e-mail
E-mail Form 1 (Project cost information)
1.2 Site manager Prints e-mail at C Corp offices and distributes
Form 1 (×3)
1.3 Product line manager (×3) Obtains weekly cost data
Form 1 and cost information (×3)
1.4 Product line manager (×3) Completes Form 1 (costs only)
Completed Form 1 (×3)
Form 1 (×3)
2.1 Site manager Analyses and agrees reports
Signed Form 1 (×3)
2.2 Chief Engineer Produces summary project cost report
Form 2 (blank commentary form)
3.1 Product line manager (×3) Prepares commentary for Form 2 (including graphs + Gantt charts)
Form 2 Commentary (×3)
3.2 Product line manager (×3) Accesses project details
Form 2 summary and cost data (×3)
3.3 Product line manager (×3) Signs Form 2
Form 2 (×3)
Faxes signed Form 2 (×3)
3.4 Chief Engineer Receives signed Form 2 (×3)
Faxes completed Form 2 (including all project costs + commentary)
3.5 Project manager Presents Form 2

Question 2

Before undertaking the post-completion review, the Board of Directors wants to ensure that the company learns from the risks encountered in this project. The Financial Director has asked the finance department to **put together a report**, for which you will **prepare the first draft**, to all other departments in the organisation. In your report,

(a) evaluate the cost management activities used by B plc for this project;

(10 marks)

(b) analyse the non-financial internal and external risks of this project, including in your answer an evaluation of B plc's management of external risks. Recommend ways to ensure the successful control of these risks (both internal and external) in future projects.

(12 marks)
(Total = 22 marks)

Answer 2

DRAFT REPORT

To: All B plc Staff
From: The Finance Department

Re: Project risk management and control
Date: 22 November 2001

Introduction

The following report will discuss the management of risk in project environments and how B plc manages risk in the Asiana project. First, the report will consider the activities undertaken to ensure effective cost management.

(a)

Cost management activities undertaken by B plc

Budgeting procedure

To begin, the project budget was formulated using a bottom-up approach, which focuses on tracking all cost elements associated with the project. This was achieved by splitting costs into numerous work breakdown packages for each phase of construction. This was subsequently split into budgets for each department and each product line. Although this approach to budgeting is time consuming and often difficult, on large complex projects such as this there is too much at stake to leave to chance or vague guesswork.

Responsibility

Ensuring responsibility for costs and cost management is an important aspect of financial control. Each product line team manager was responsible to the Chief Engineer for his/her own work breakdown packages and each phase. If this is to be successful then the product line team manager must have had a say in the formulation of the budget he/she was responsible for.

Cost reporting

Making project cost a visible and important aspect of the project management process is a further important aspect of financial control. Regular cost reporting and variance analysis was carried out by the finance team, with each product line manager being responsible for explaining significant variance from budget to the Project Manager. Again, responsibility for cost control is passed to the line managers and not finance, thus helping to engender a cost control awareness throughout the project. Also, the financial results were reported regularly to managers outside the project, thus widening the cost control function.

Also, on a monthly basis, the finance team produced an expected final cost report (EFC), which highlighted costs to date by key category per product line and expected final project cost. This was reported to all project team members and the Board. Again, regular and focused cost reporting on final project cost will help to ensure that all team members are constantly aware of the final target and that any costs spent are done so with this target in mind.

(b)

Internal risks

Internal risks are those originating from inside the organisation, and should be largely controllable. Sources of internal risk could include the unreliability of worker performance, poor internal communications or unchecked expenditure, and human risk whereby people are very unpredictable. Projects are often plagued by problems concerning human resource reliability, competence and availability.

External risks

These are risks coming from outside our organisation and include changes in government regulations (e.g. fluctuating duty tariffs, import restrictions), unavailability of basic resources, lack of skilled manpower and bureaucratic slowness. Further risks for the Asiana project could have included the introduction of competitive products or new technological breakthroughs, and the risk that the products may fail in the market place. Often external risks are not directly controllable, but it is possible to minimise these risks by adequate planning and monitoring activities.

An evaluation of the management of external risk

B plc used feedback from other multi-national firms and from their own previous project experience in order to ensure all aspects of the project were considered, evidence that the company did adequately plan for external risks. B plc could have maintained regular contact with government officials within Asiana in order to ensure a good working relationship and to improve their knowledge of planned government actions which may affect them.

Recommendations for success in controlling these risks in the future

- Good pre-project risk evaluation. This will require:
  - analysis of previous project experience or information from other organisations (as was done in this project);
  - modelling techniques (such as Monte Carlo simulation) to assess risks and returns;
  - carry out thorough feasibility studies and cost–benefit analysis.
- There is a need to provide training programmes for workers in production techniques and quality standards, and to maintain this training after completion of a project.
- Appropriate team selection methods must be used, ensuring a well-balanced team including experts from all functional areas, who also have the skills to work within a project environment.
- Good internal procedures and documentation are essential for future project success – again training is required to ensure that all team members understand the importance of standardisation of procedures and documents.
- Clear reporting structure and procedures must be in place before a project begins, to reduce bureaucratic delays.
- Monitoring of economic trends and government actions prior to project selection, in order to test and evaluate the external risks involved;
- Analysis of potential customer and competitive actions is required to provide evidence of the likely impact any new project will have on the important stakeholders and competitors;

- Analysis of recent technological breakthroughs developments in order to ensure that the most appropriate and latest techniques and technology have been considered and their feasibility and suitability evaluated.

Conclusion

All projects, whatever their size or nature, will involve some degree of risk, and it is therefore important to ensure that all risks are considered, evaluated and appropriately monitored and controlled. These risks may be financial or non-financial, internal or external. Importantly, any organisation must establish where risks exist and establish methods to either eliminate or reduce them prior to undertaking a project.

Signed: Management Accountant.

Scenario 3

Background

Total learning experience (TLE) is a training organisation set up 20 years ago by the current owners, Jack and Linda Grey. TLE provides a wide range of training courses both locally and nationally. These courses include professional tuition for trainee accountants, business management training (including presentation skills, communication techniques and negotiation skills) and specialist training courses (e.g. insurance, banking and law). It is a financially successful business and very highly regarded as a national training organisation.

For the last 8 years, TLE has held the 'Quality Attainment' certificate awarded by the professional accounting institute for which it provides accounting courses. This is awarded to training providers who demonstrate the attainment of high standards in teaching and course management. Since 1990, TLE has operated from a city centre premises with six training rooms, a student common room and three administrative offices (currently one for administration staff and tutors, one for accounts and one for the two owners).

The organisation

Teaching staff

TLE employs 10 full-time tutors. TLE also uses 8 freelance tutors who are hired mainly to undertake the specialist training courses. Seven of the 10 full-time tutors and all the freelance tutors are based at home, and only come into the offices if teaching, or to pick up timetables or course materials. Most of the tutors have their own computers at home.

Administration and accounting staff

All administration staff are based permanently in the TLE offices. This includes the office manager, Wendy White, who has been with TLE since 1990. She is responsible for course management, timetabling and course materials management (including responsibility for the management of examination papers). Wendy has an administration assistant to help in the day-to-day running of the administrative functions, including management of course bookings. Course bookings refers to all activities relating to students/clients enrolling on their chosen training course (see *Course booking system* on page 4).

Also based in the offices is the finance manager, John Brown. He started working for TLE 3 years ago and is responsible for all financial and management accounting activities and general IT issues. There is also an accounts clerk who is responsible for data entry to the accounting system used by TLE. This includes invoicing, payments and payroll.

Information technology position 1995 to 2000

Before moving to the city centre offices, Jack and Linda kept all business records (including the accounts) and course materials manually. When Wendy White joined TLE in 1990, she took responsibility for the manual system and she believed that computers were 'totally unnecessary'. Between 1990 and 1995, she re-designed many of the filing systems and hand-written records kept by TLE and developed her own very well-organised manual record-keeping system. However, as the number and range of courses developed and the business grew, it became clear to Jack and Linda that this system was no longer sufficient. A number of billing errors had occurred, timetables were sometimes incorrect and both business clients and students had complained about poor/late course information. In 1995, TLE invested in an IBM minicomputer to be used for all administrative functions carried out by Wendy and a standalone desktop PC for use by the tutors (there were five tutors in 1995) to prepare course materials. In addition, a black-and-white ink-jet printer was purchased and shared between the two computers. Both the minicomputer and the PC were equipped with a basic applications software package, including word processing, spreadsheet and desktop publishing facilities. Wendy transferred all of her manual student records into a 'student file', the business client data into a 'client file' and course data into a 'courses file'. (*Note*: all of these were separate word processing documents.) Wendy transferred the timetabling information onto a number of spreadsheet files.

Information technology position 2000–2003

On his arrival in June 2000, John Brown's first task was to upgrade the existing computers. The most up-to-date operating system was installed and the latest versions of the application packages were also purchased. John also purchased three additional PCs: one for the administration assistant, one for the accounts clerk and one for his own use. He also introduced an off-the-shelf accounting package, which was installed onto the accounts PC, to carry out the basic accounting and financial reporting functions. An off-the-shelf database software package was also installed on all of the computers, but it is rarely used as the staff have not been trained in how to use it. Additional purchases included one fax machine and one photocopier. All of the computers were standalone.

The three office-based tutors share the use of the original office PC bought in 1995 to prepare course material but often complain about the lack of computer availability. They often resort to using the administration and accounts computers early in the morning or at the end of the teaching day. There are no password systems currently in use on any of the administrative or accounts computers. Both accounts and administration information is backed up on CD at the end of every month. These discs are then stored in Jack and Linda's office.

Timetable management

All of the professional accounting courses are delivered in the six TLE training rooms. The usage of the rooms is planned and timetabled several months in advance by Wendy. This information is kept on a large whiteboard in Wendy's office and highlights the rooms in use, by which course, at what time and by which tutor. Wendy uses this information to produce a weekly usage forecast spreadsheet for each room, which is produced each Friday and posted on the door of each room on Monday morning. (*Note*: a timetabling software package is available, but Wendy considers that her own whiteboard system and spreadsheets are perfectly sufficient.)

Timetabling of staff is done by means of a diary system. Each tutor has his or her own diary which is kept by the administration assistant. She is responsible for filling in the diary for each tutor and then sending this monthly (1 month in advance, so the teaching diary for January is sent out in December) to each home-based tutor by post or fax. It is the responsibility of all tutors to let the administration assistant know which days they are unavailable (such as holiday commitments) at least 6 weeks in advance. Ideally, the administration assistant should call all tutors at least once a week, but often (due to pressures of time) she does not achieve this. When an off-site course enquiry for business management training is received, the administration assistant provisionally books out the appropriate day in the tutor's diary and then informs the tutor the month before the course is due to be delivered.

Course booking system

Professional courses

Six weeks prior to the start of a professional course, standard pre-printed booking forms (produced by a local firm of printers) are sent to all students currently listed on the student file held by Wendy. Other booking forms are sent as and when requested (by phone or by a posted tear-off slip included in local newspaper advertisements or leaflets posted to all registered students in the local area).

On receipt of completed booking forms, new and updated student details are entered onto the student file which is then used to update the course file and produce the course register. The administration assistant prints and copies the updated student file and passes it to the accounts clerk who enters the details into the accounts customer file to provide information for billing.

When students arrive on the first day of the course, they are required to bring with them a cheque for payment of the course fees. These cheques are put into a safety deposit box in the main administration office and collected at the end of each week before they are put into the bank. There is no current security code or lock on any of the office doors.

Business management skills and specialist courses

Business management training courses are normally delivered at the specific request of the client organisation. Many of these courses are repeat work for large companies and much work is generated by word-of-mouth recommendations, due to the high standards of course delivery. Course details are discussed between the client organisation and TLE, using the tutor diaries kept by the administration assistant to check tutor availability. On agreement, tutor diaries are updated, client files are updated and the information is passed to the accounts clerk for invoicing.

During the weeks when the training rooms are not being used by professional accounting courses, TLE utilises the time by offering a range of specialist training courses. These are timetabled and agreed with the freelance tutors some months in advance of delivery. They are advertised in specialist journals and magazines, in the local and national press and by advertising mail shots sent to organisations such as banks, solicitors, consultants and insurance companies. Booking forms are issued when a client rings the advertised telephone number or returns a tear-off slip from the mail shot.

Recent problems

Although TLE has maintained a strong reputation for high-quality course delivery, in the last year there have been a number of problems.

- A presentation skills course due to be delivered to a new client at their premises had to be cancelled at short notice because of double booking of the tutor. The client has refused to use TLE again.
- A number of mock examination papers went missing as the filing cabinet in which they were kept (in the administration office) was left unlocked one lunchtime. The professional body has expressed its dissatisfaction with this lack of care and intends to review TLE's quality accreditation status.
- A number of past students were sent invoices for courses which they did not attend. Their details were entered onto the sales ledger incorrectly after the student file was copied by the administration assistant to the accounts clerk. There have been a number of billing queries, mainly due to the difference in the information held by accounts and administration about clients and students.

Staff meeting – March 2003

Jack and Linda held a staff meeting for all tutors and office staff in order to review the current position and to suggest ways to improve. They also wished to discuss with the team the news that a national training organisation had just opened nearby. This organisation is promoting its courses heavily and has its own website (something which TLE does not currently have) offering on-line booking facilities. During the meeting the staff raised a number of issues which included the following:

Administration staff issues:

- difficulties in managing tutor diaries;
- inefficiencies in course bookings;
- too much paperwork and time spent copying and printing files;
- open access to administration offices.

Tutor issues:

- lack of facilities for material preparation;
- poor communication between office and home;
- difficulties in contacting the office if teaching off-site;
- duplication of materials on different courses.

Accounting issues:

- duplication of records kept in accounting and administration systems;
- security of both cash and computerised information.

John Brown suggested that many of the problems raised during the meeting could be solved by introducing a more appropriate information system. He particularly emphasised the need for the introduction of an office network and a facility to allow on-line booking procedures. Jack and Linda admit to knowing little about information systems or how to proceed with such a project. John himself does not think that he has the necessary skills and experience to manage such a project and suggests that an outside firm of consultants should be used.

You are a project manager, working for a local firm of consultants. You recently received a phone call from John Brown asking for your organisation's assistance in the project.

Question 3

(a) Discuss the advantages and disadvantages of:

(i) in-house developed information systems;
(ii) externally developed information systems with reference to the preceding information regarding the company.

(Assume that the information systems are bespoke, that is, that they are being developed specifically to match the requirements of the organisation.)

(12 marks)

(b) Prepare an outline plan for the audit of a systems development project with reference to the preceding information regarding the company.

(8 marks)
(Total = 20 marks)

Question 4

(a) Explain **four** features of networked computerised environments which cause problems when auditing networked computerised systems with reference to the preceding information regarding the company.

(12 marks)

(b) Explain the importance of a quality plan in order to maintain appropriate quality standards during the systems development process with reference to the preceding information regarding the company.

(8 marks)
(Total = 20 marks)

Answer 3

(a)

(i) *Advantages of in-house developed information systems*

1 The system developed is likely to match the needs of the users more closely. This is likely to mean that staff are more likely to accept the system and are more likely to want to be involved. An in-house developed system should meet user needs more effectively.
2 An in-house development team will always be on-site and available to work on the project if required. Therefore, they are more likely to be focused upon the project's progress and success.
3 An in-house development team is more likely to gain user acceptance more quickly rather than an unknown external team.

Disadvantages of in-house developed information systems

1 It is unlikely that the in-house development team will work 100% on the project as they will have their own day-to-day tasks to get on with. This may hinder project progress and reduce focus on the overall goal.
2 The in-house team is unlikely to have sufficient experience and technical knowledge, unless they have specific IT/IS training. This could add extra time and may result in increased errors and costs.
3 Users may expect a system which satisfies every need and this could cause dissatisfaction and increased costs.

(ii) *Advantages of externally developed information systems*

1 The team is likely to contain developers who have a vast wealth of experience and knowledge to build a system which is suitable for the organisation.
2 An external developer is likely to be more cost-conscious as they will have prepared a tender to a specific budget. They will have a clear profit figure to maintain and will endeavour to ensure that this is achieved.
3 They will have greater experience in on-going maintenance and support of systems and are likely to provide ongoing support and maintenance as part of the contract.

Disadvantages of externally developed information systems

1 They do not have the internal knowledge of the organisation's business goals and operations and therefore it will take more time for them to understand the exact needs of the users.
2 This may cause additional time in the analysis stage which may increase costs.
3 They may use your ideas for competitor or rival systems. As they are likely to understand the system as well as the client, they could use this knowledge to win business developing even better system for competitors.
4 They may go out of business or decide to no longer support your system.

(b)

The first stage of the systems development audit would be to appoint an audit team who have sufficient knowledge and experience of systems development projects and IT. Roles and responsibilities for the team need to be agreed. The main tasks of that audit team will be as follows:

- It is important to establish that a senior manager has been appointed to lead the systems development project, who has an appropriate understanding of systems and IT. Ensure that either the senior IT manager (if in-house development) or the external project manager is fully experienced and reports at an appropriate level in the organisation.
- Establish a project team, representing all areas affected by the system and at all levels of the organisation set up.
- Check that a project initiation document has been produced.
- Check that all suitable alternative systems approaches have been investigated adequately.
- Ensure that a thorough feasibility study has been carried out and the findings evaluated at the appropriate level of the organisation. The project must be clearly justified on financial and technical grounds and all concerned must understand the project objectives.
- Check that reputable suppliers and contractors have been selected by appropriate methods.
- Carry out adequate review of methods and progress checking regularly.
- Review and approve the adequacy of reporting on project progress at an appropriate level.
- Put in place adequate change control mechanisms.
- Check all documentation is kept logically and clearly.
- Review all of the above procedures as part of post-completion audit.

Answer 4

(a)

Network environments

Networks allow remote access from numerous locations and multi-user access. This may result in unauthorised internal use (as a result of user error, misuse of passwords or fraud) and unauthorised external users (hackers). Networks require the security of effective password systems which must be regularly audited.

External links

Electronic data interchange (EDI), electronic payment systems (EPOS), intranets/Internet and e-mails are all examples of the ways in which organisations are now open to external entities due to computerisation. Again all of these are open to abuse and error as a result of misuse of passwords, hacking and viruses. Data needs to be encrypted and accuracy checks needs to be maintained regularly. Tracking external access and entry to the system is complex for the auditor.

Databases

These require continual maintenance and specialist database management systems and clear definitions of authority and access rights. Database management systems must ensure that access is limited and levels of access authority are maintained.

Complexity and rapid technological changes

Computerised environments are often complex, as outlined above, with many organisations having complex network systems, business links to external entities and data stored within large database systems. In addition, most systems operate using real-time data processing and real-time data access which is likely to result in much less documentation and listing of balances and batch totals. All of these issues and the rapid change in technological development mean that auditors have difficulty following the same audit procedures as previous audits and that they must keep up to date with hardware and software innovations.

(b)

- A quality plan provides a formal definition of how the project is to be accomplished. It will define the goals of the project and will highlight the quality standards required at each stage of the systems development process.
- It also provides a definition of the duties and responsibilities of the project manager and team in terms of achieving quality standards, by setting out the quality expectations of each activity in the development process.
- A quality plan helps to define the expectations of the customer and encourages team co-operation and shared goals of the team members.
- It provides a clear framework for project quality issues to be discussed and addressed. It ensures that everyone involved in the project has a reference point for quality issues and it therefore avoids ambiguity and confusion over what is expected from all team members.
- It outlines the quality expectations of the project so that all involved know what is expected of them.
- It demonstrates to external customers and clients the importance of quality to the organisation.
- It will be used by the quality control staff, and any external quality standard bodies, to measure achievements of quality and to recommend further improvements.
- It could be used as evidence for solving problems or disputes and it will be a vital tool to assess project achievement at the end of the project's life.

Question 5

Requirements

(a) Discuss the benefits and limitations of using cost–benefit analysis to assess the value of information.

(10 marks)

Eagle Inc manufactures sports shoes used for playing sports such as tennis, squash, and badminton and for running. It has a unique brand name and logo, and promotes its shoes with the slogan 'Wear Eagles to Win'. The company successfully sold 3.5 million pairs of shoes worldwide last year with a net profit of $20 million.

Although the company is successful, the Board of Eagle Inc is always looking for methods of gaining additional competitive advantage. The market research department has identified a small but growing demand for sports shoes which are personalised to the individual wearer. Customers would like the facility to change certain aspects of the shoes such as sole and trim colour, depth of the sole and pattern on the top of the shoe.

The manufacturing system at Eagle Inc can be amended relatively easily to provide this degree of tailoring to individual shoes. The Board has therefore decided to conduct a trial to determine whether or not the facility for customers to order shoes via the company's existing web site should be introduced. This trial will initially be limited to a central European country of 20 million people, and will offer both standard and personalised shoes. 275,000 pairs of Eagle Inc shoes are currently sold in that country each year.

(b) Discuss the information that will be required to determine the success, or otherwise, of the new web-based ordering system.

(15 marks)
(Total = 25 marks)

Answer 5

(a) Traditional CBA tends to be focused on accounting costs and benefits. With many of the costs and benefits of information being intangible, this analysis may not form a suitable way of assessing the value of information.

Various benefits and limitations of CBA are explained below:

Costs – tangible

The costs of establishing an information system are relatively easy to determine in relation to the hardware and software to purchase. This provides a distinct benefit of CBA in that the amount of money to be spent on establishing a new system from the point-of-view of hardware and software is relatively easy to determine.

The main limitation with the technique is identifying which costs are actually attributable to producing the new information. For example, most organisations already have a network of some description; so distributing any additional information should not be a problem. However, increase in network traffic will result from the new information, along with growth in information transfer from other applications. When the network bandwidth needs upgrading, which application pays for this? CBA may have some difficulty in allocating costs over a number of projects where the boundaries for that allocation are unclear.

Costs – intangible

Many of the intangible costs of information relate to not having that information available, for example, lack of information about competitors may result in incorrect decision-making within the organisation. The issue is how to measure the cost of not having information. These are intangible costs, which traditional accounting systems cannot capture so they may be excluded from the CBA.

Traditional information economics also suggests that the expected value of information is equal to the value to the business of having that information less the value of the business gained without having to amend information systems. In other words, the existing information system may be able to provide some of the new information required, at little or no additional expense. A more realistic measure of cost is not simply the tangible cost involved, but the business benefit lost from not providing some information. However, there is no clear system for actually measuring business benefit compared to the cost of providing information.

CBA is therefore particularly weak when it comes to measuring the intangible costs of new systems.

Benefits – tangible

Some of the benefits of enhanced information systems can be seen in terms of the improvement in quality of information being provided. For example, if information is provided in 2 seconds rather than 20 seconds, then the information is probably timelier. Placing some value on this benefit may be difficult, although it could be included in the CBA under a heading of other benefits and a guess made as to the value.

However, there will be significant diminishing returns to this provision, for example, providing information in 0.2 of a second rather than 2 seconds will attract a much smaller amount of benefit. Humans cannot necessarily react to information this quickly.

There are limits to benefits from automation, so the benefits of improving the quality of information should not be overstated. Determining the exact amount of benefit will be difficult, because the extent of time savings and whether those time savings can actually be used may not be known.

Benefits – intangible

While providing information more quickly has a benefit in that staff are not waiting for the information to arrive, placing a value on how well they use that information is more difficult. The benefits of having additional information can be measured in terms of improved customer service, competitive advantage gained and so on. Where CBA looks at the actual money being spent and tangible savings, then the problems of measuring these intangible benefits means that they may not be included in the CBA, or not included at an appropriate value.

For example, if investment in producing some new information is required, simply to stay in business, then that investment must be made. However, the focus may be on the cost of providing that information and so, at the extreme, the organisation may lose competitive advantage simply because it cannot afford the system when judged by CBA.

Benefits from providing more or better information may also take a long time to accrue. Information systems have to be accepted by staff and time will be taken for historical analysis to build up to any meaningful level. Traditional measures of CBA such as Payback or ROI may be inappropriate, because they provide too short a time-frame for assessing the benefits of information.

(b) The information required to determine the success or otherwise of the new web-based ordering system is discussed below. The additional information relates to the additional costs and income resulting from the trial as well as non-financial information on evaluating the results of the trial.

Website

The website will need amendment to provide not only the basic information about shoes, but also the on-line design of shoes and purchase via the Internet. Information will therefore need to show:

- costs of updating the existing site to allow design of individual shoes;
- costs of updating and running a purchasing system over the Internet, including secure transfer of credit card and order details; and
- any costs relating to the enhancement of the computers needed to host the website.

Information will be available from the IT department, or from a third-party supplier, where the company contracts out the maintenance and hosting of the website.

Manufacturing system

Although the scenario states that the manufacturing system can be amended easily to provide for the manufacture of tailored shoes, this amendment will still need to be carried out. In particular, there will be costs involved with:

- re-tooling to allow for the customer-specific shoes to be manufactured;
- linking orders from the website into the existing manufacturing system, although this may be a manual or a computer link;
- possible purchase of CAD/CAM equipment to manufacture the shoes;

- improved communication to suppliers to enable appropriate raw materials to be supplied as required. This may mean linking suppliers directly into the shoe ordering system so that when a purchase is made, the supplier can send appropriate raw materials direct to Eagle Inc on a daily basis;
- possibly hiring of additional workers to oversee the new production line, or training costs for existing workers.

Information on these costs will be obtained from:

- quotes from equipment suppliers;
- the IT department or outsourcing company if the website is hosted externally; and
- personnel department in respect of additional staff to be hired, or current staff to be trained.

Advertising

The new service will have to be advertised in an appropriate way. Possible options include:

- links from search engines, news services and other Internet sites;
- posters;
- direct mailing to existing customers; and
- possibly information at existing shops, although potential loss of business for those shops will limit this opportunity.

The marketing director should set an advertising budget. Alternatively, quotes for an appropriate campaign can be obtained from the company's normal advertising agency.

Evaluating results

Part of the trial will mean evaluating the actual results obtained. Providing an appropriate data collection method with the purchase of shoes (such as an Internet-based questionnaire immediately on purchasing with a follow-up e-mail request after delivery of the shoes) will be necessary. The e-mail option is attractive as this will be the purchasing method for the shoes.

Analysing the results and presentation of a report to the Board will also be required. Capturing the data electronically in the first place will limit analysis costs. Preparation of a Board report may not incur any additional costs if the management accountant carries this out or a junior accountant already employed by the company.

Possible lost margin

Selling the shoes on the Internet will normally mean obtaining a smaller margin for each pair of shoes sold. This will result in a cost where the customer would otherwise still have used the existing purchasing systems.

Information regarding customer preferences will be obtained from questionnaires, when a calculation of any lost revenue can be made.

The success of the trial can be determined on a variety of indicators including:

- The profit or contribution generated from the sale of each pair of shoes. Some care is necessary only to include those costs normally relating to selling on the Internet rather than try and discount all set-up costs against a relatively small sales sample.
- Change in customer satisfaction regarding Eagle Inc and the products being manufactured. A positive result will indicate that the trial is a success and so it should be

expanded. Information on customer satisfaction will be available from the Internet questionnaires.

- Change in employee satisfaction. Some employees may find it more rewarding to manufacture exactly the shoes required by a customer. However, potential loss of contact either via the telephone or fewer people in the shops is likely to provide negative impacts on employee satisfaction.
- Additional revenue generated from advertising space on Eagle Inc's website.
- Increased awareness of Eagle Inc as a company, particularly in respect of being innovative and shoe sales possibly reaching a wider customer base from the use of a different selling medium.

A detailed financial report will be necessary, outlining changes in contribution and profit with a recommendation to the Board on whether the new system should be implemented.

Question 6

The Q Company ('Q') is an information provider. It has been in existence for 3 years and has grown relatively rapidly, but in response to customer demand rather than following any specific strategy.

Companies and individuals approach Q and ask it to research and provide information on a wide variety of topics. Topics range from weather forecasts for specific regions or cities to complete case histories of individuals including their names, directorships, addresses, telephone numbers, family and any other details that can be obtained legally on the Internet.

To provide this service, Q employs a team of 20 staff: 4 receptionists/administrators, 6 software engineers and 10 information managers. The information managers use Q's specialist software to search the Internet to obtain the information requested by clients. Information is returned to the client within 48 hours, normally by an encrypted attachment to an e-mail.

The cost incurred and revenue received per customer by Q for this service are shown graphically below. To encourage new business, Q tends to offer an initial consultation and the first 500 words of information free to any customer. Revenues increase steeply after this, although most customers specify a maximum amount of information required, and therefore the revenue curve becomes horizontal.

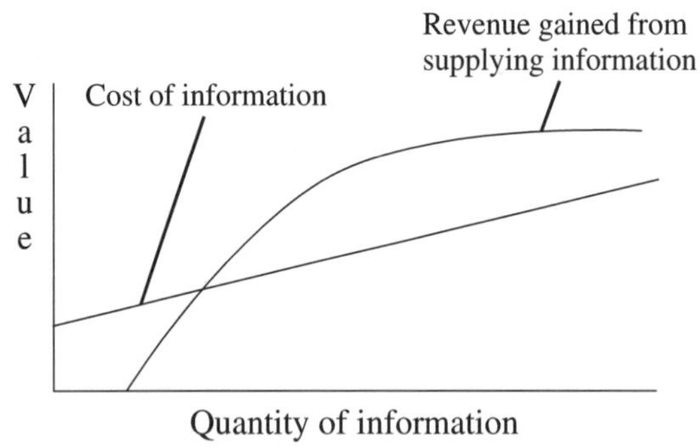

After considerable discussion within Q, various suggestions were put forward to try and increase the company's profits.

- Decrease fixed costs by decreasing the number of software engineers and administration staff.
- Make Q's specialist software available to third parties under a licence agreement by an annual fee or one-off payment.
- Provide information in graphical format, not just text, and make this available to customers.
- Upgrade Q's Internet connection to 'state of the art' to allow more rapid searches of the Internet, significantly decreasing the amount of time spent waiting for information.

No agreement was reached on a course of action, so an independent Management Accountant has been asked to provide a recommendation.

Requirements

(a) Prepare a report for Q, evaluating the four suggestions, with a recommendation on which suggestions, if any, to follow.

(16 marks)

(b) Advise Q on how to develop an IS/IT/IM strategy.

(9 marks)
(Total = 25 marks)

Answer 6

(a)

REPORT

To: Managers at Q

From: Management Accountant

Date: 20 November 2003

Subject: Strategy to maximise profit/IT strategy

In accordance with your instructions, I give below a report on the four different strategies to try and increase profit, along with my recommended course of action.

1 *Decrease fixed costs by decreasing the number of software engineers and administration staff*

In the short-term, this will have the effect of increasing profit, simply because the fixed costs in the company will fall. The cost curve will therefore start from the Y axis on your graph at a lower point, providing increased profit at most levels of information provision.

However, this strategy has some disadvantages.

- First, it assumes that revenues will remain the same; this may not be the case if the level of service given by the company falls.
- Secondly, it assumes that the specialist software provided by Q can be maintained and updated in the medium to long-term. Providing fewer software engineers runs the risk of competitors producing their own software that is 'better' than Q's. This will result in loss of business for Q.

This strategy is therefore not recommended.

2 *Making Q's specialist software available under a licence agreement to third parties*

This strategy has the distinct benefit that it appears not to affect the cost structure of the company. Assuming that the administration staff or information managers can sell the software, then this strategy allows for additional revenue to be generated on existing resources.

There will be some costs involved in producing an acceptable licensing agreement. Recent attempts at selling a licence to use software rather than selling it outright have proved difficult and specialist legal advice will be necessary.

There may also be additional revenue generated from selling training services to clients.

On the negative side, letting third parties use the software may decrease revenues either because Internet searches are carried out by third parties rather than Q, or because third parties attempt to sell their services using the software. A comprehensive licence agreement will guard against the second danger, but the first is to be expected given the nature of the sale.

This appears to be a feasible option.

3 *Providing information in graphical format, not just text*

Enhancing the format of reports provided to clients may help Q obtain some competitive advantage, as well as making the reports more readable. However, this strategy will work only if potential clients are aware of the additional service being provided. Q must therefore incur some advertising expense before additional revenue can be obtained.

Staff must also consider how much additional work is required to incorporate appropriate graphics into the report. If this increases the time taken to provide information, then some value may be lost; presumably some information is only valuable (such as weather forecasts) simply because it is provided in a short timeframe.

Additional graphics will also increase the file size, which may be an issue where the client does not have a fast Internet connection.

Q would be advised to find out what competitors are providing before making a decision on this strategy. If graphical output is standard, then this must almost certainly be adopted. However, if text output is normal, then graphics may earn some competitive advantage, but only if time and costs are not compromised.

4 *Upgrading Q's Internet connection to 'state of the art' to allow more rapid searches of the Internet*

Providing a faster Internet link will obviously incur additional costs – these will have to be ascertained prior to making any final decision.

However, there is a query concerning whether the faster link will actually enable faster report production. If it does, and revenues can be increased to offset the increased cost, then this is a viable option. However, it may be that report generation is not going to be significantly improved by a quicker Internet link. In this case the option can be discounted.

Recommendation

The strategy of licensing Q's software for use by third parties appears to be the easiest and quickest method of raising additional income without incurring more costs. This strategy is therefore recommended.

(b) An IS/IT/IM strategy is important for any organisation. In overview, this strategy helps to control the use of information within a company, and provides guidelines to the development of information and information systems. It also allows the company to be more pro-active in the implementation and use of systems, an area which Q does not appear to have considered in any detail in the last few years.

In overview, the three strategies can be explained as follows:

1 Information Technology strategy refers to the hardware configuration that an organisation requires to transfer information.
2 Information Systems strategy relates to the long-term plan concerning the use of IT within the organisation.
3 Information Management strategy refers to the approach to managing data and information within the organisation, specifically how data and information are stored and accessed.

All three strategies are normally set at the same time, with the IS strategy determining the IT and IM strategies to a large extent.

However, a general framework for setting these strategies is outlined below:

1 *Determine business strategy*

Initially, the business strategy of the organisation must be determined. Checking this strategy is essential because the IS strategy must support this strategy and not drive it. It is not 100% clear what the overall business strategy of Q is at present. Clarification of this strategy and what Q needs to do right (i.e. what the critical success factors are) will help establish Q's purpose.

Just because new IT systems may be available (such as the fast Internet connection), it does not mean that they have to be used in the organisation. Also, any new IT systems may not be compatible with other software or hardware used in the organisation. Additional checks will be necessary to confirm compatibility.

Q needs to decide what the overall business strategy is.

2 *Set up or amend IS strategy in line with business strategy*

The IS strategy must support the overall business strategy. For example, the business strategy may be to provide a differentiated service at a high margin. In this case, the IS strategy will ensure that the support systems are in place to help the information managers provide that client service. These systems may be expensive, but necessary to meet the strategy.

Alternatively, the strategy may be to provide a low-cost product. In this case, the IS strategy may recommend different systems. However, this does not appear to be the case at Q.

If Q is trying for market differentiation, then strategies like selling the software or enhancing reports appear to be appropriate. However, if costs are to be decreased, then reducing staff numbers or providing faster Internet connections possibly to obtain data more quickly would be expected.

Q needs to decide how the IS will be changed to support the overall business strategy.

3 *Procedure for change*

Having decided to amend the IS strategy in some way, a plan for developing and implementing the system will have to be developed. As well as setting out the plan in an appropriate manner (SSDAM for example, may be useful here) alternative hardware and software as well as development methods may need to be considered. Development in-house or outsourcing will be the basic choice. A full Cost–Benefit Analysis may also be used now, or earlier in the change process, to check that the change will provide the necessary benefits to the organisation at an acceptable cost.

Having determined the overall strategy for change, this can be implemented and systems amended. Checks may also be required to ensure that staff and customers are kept fully informed. This is especially relevant where reports will be produced more quickly or different report formats are planned. This will help to ensure that any competitive advantage from the change is obtained.

Q needs to implement a procedure to manage IS change.

4 *Ensure objectives have been met*

Finally, a review will be necessary to ensure that the initial objectives of the change have been met. If this is not the case, then further review may be required to determine why, and confirm what additional changes are actually required.

Question 7

Background to Erehwon – country and people

Erehwon is an island in the Caribbean with a population of approximately 1.25 million people and a land area of 50,000 square kilometres. It has four major towns, including the capital Carterville, all located on the coast, with a large number of smaller villages inland.

The majority of the citizens of Erehwon are employed in manual jobs, although most have cars and basic consumer goods such as television sets and video players. The main medium of exchange is cash. Credit cards are advertised widely on radio and television as being fun and easy-to-use, but relatively few people have applied for them and even fewer use them as a means of payment. There is an inherent mistrust of credit card technology.

The economy is split fairly equally between industrial production in the main towns and farming inland. Industry within Erehwon includes soft drink manufacture and bottling, textile and clothing manufacture and provision of specialist financial services to other islands in the Caribbean. Farming concentrates on two main crops of bananas and coffee. A wide variety of holiday hotels and other resort-based holiday attractions are also available. However, most people on vacation do not travel extensively within Erehwon as the country does not have many holiday attractions outside of the resorts.

Background to Erehwon – transport infrastructure

The transport infrastructure is extremely limited. There are no railways and only one public bus service operates along one route in the capital. Personal transport is almost exclusively by car. Unfortunately, roads within Erehwon are not well maintained with most government expenditure being allocated to maintaining the runway on the island's international airport.

While roads may be poorly maintained, the citizens of Erehwon have no choice but to use their cars for transport. Traffic congestion is increasing to the extent that government statistics show that, on average, each individual spends over an hour each day sitting in his/her car.

The government recognises that personal transport does have distinct benefits for individuals but it is not necessarily economically or environmentally efficient. The government of Erehwon is particularly concerned about environmental damage from motor vehicle exhausts and the island's dependence on Venezuela for oil. Alternative transport solutions have been investigated in the past, and are likely to be considered again in the future.

Proposed amendments to transport infrastructure

Within the government of Erehwon, the Strategic Government Communications Committee (SGCC) develops and implements government policy regarding transport alternatives.

Recently, the SGCC has been considering the implementation of a tram system (i.e. buses running on railway tracks). This would link the four towns and provide links in the rural economy. Passengers will be expected to pay a flat fee to travel on the trams, which will be collected using credit or debit cards at the entrance to the tram. Passengers will simply swipe their card through a reader allowing access gates to open to provide entry to the tram. Potential passengers without a debit or credit card will be able to purchase 'tram cards' from many major stores. The tram card will be swiped in the same way to credit cards, and will be purchased with a specific number of tram journeys credited to the card.

The system would necessitate building of tram lines (similar to railway lines) throughout Erehwon for the trams to run on. Similar systems have been implemented successfully in other major cities in the world. However, Erehwon would need to import all the infrastructure and the trams due to lack of appropriate industry on the island.

While the capital expenditure would be significant, the system would provide specific benefits in terms of:

- decreased pollution as the trams would run on electricity;
- decreased congestion on roads as there would be fewer journeys in private cars;
- decreased dependence on oil as electricity can be generated from many different sources including wave power (a pilot project is being run near Carterville).

The system is also thought to be a vote-winner because it will start to address the issue of traffic congestion, one of the key factors politicians are attempting to remedy at this time. Elections for the national government will be held in 5 months time.

Requirements

(a) Advise the SGCC what sources of information are relevant to determining the costs and benefits of the proposed tram system, explaining what type of information can be derived from each source.

(16 marks)

(b) Identify and explain two Critical Success Factors and their associated Performance Indicators, which can be used to evaluate the success or otherwise of the tram system after implementation.

Discuss where information will be obtained for each of the Performance Indicators.

(14 marks)

(c) Evaluate the different communication systems which can be used to inform the general public on Erehwon of the benefits of the tram system, and recommend which system is most suitable for the island.

(10 marks)

(d) Discuss the potential benefits and problems of using credit card technology to pay for tram fees.

(10 marks)
(Total = 50 marks)

Question 8

Requirements

For your own organisation or one you are familiar with:

(a) Explain the role of an information centre and evaluate its suitability as a means of integrating technical and business staff.

(15 marks)

(b) Explain the ways in which an information centre might contribute to the development and modification of Information Systems, Information Technology and Information Management strategies.

(10 marks)
(Total = 25 marks)

Answer 7

(a) Costs

Overall costs of setting up and running the tram system can be obtained from the government or similar organisations in other countries where the tram systems have been implemented. However, cost estimates must take into account transport costs of all materials to Erehwon and possible lack of skilled labour on the island to actually build the system.

Costs will include:

Capital costs of the trams and the tram network – rails, signalling systems and so on. Ongoing running costs of the tram system split between fixed and variable costs. Fixed costs are likely to include maintenance of the trams and rails, tram drivers (unless overtime is worked), administration and so on. The variable costs will be minimal and include simply the electricity used and possibly increased maintenance and overtime payments if more trams are run than originally expected. Other one-off costs that must be budgeted for include land purchase and possible compensation payments to citizens where houses are purchased to provide sufficient room for the tram system in towns. This information is relevant because the total cost of building the tram system must be known in advance. If the cost is too great for the government to fund by itself, then the system may not be built or other sources of finance may need to be investigated.

Before the above costs are incurred, a feasibility study will have to be produced showing whether or not the tram system is viable and fits in with the overall strategy of decreasing environmental impacts and decreasing reliance on oil.

Costs will obviously be decreased by income generated from running the tram system. Obtaining forecasts of passenger numbers will be difficult, as this type of system has not been used in Erehwon before. Obtaining passenger figures from other locations may therefore not be appropriate because they will not cater for the specific situation in Erewhon. Estimated numbers may be available from surveys of citizens in Erehwon. Passenger numbers will also depend on the price charged for each journey.

The relevance of obtaining information on income is to try and see whether the costs of running the tram system will be covered by the income generated from using it. If this does not happen, then the SGCC may need to recommend some subsidy to keep the system running.

Potential benefits of the tram system are fairly clear, although they will be difficult to quantify.

Information on existing pollution levels may be obtained from any government monitoring services or meteorological departments on the island. Given the lack of money to maintain roads, it is likely that very little money is available to determine actual pollution levels. However, if fall in pollution is one of the aims of the tram system, then the SGCC could obtain information on carbon monoxide and other pollutant levels and compare this to other parts of Erehwon or similar island without such a heavy use of cars. This information will help to show what levels of pollution are achievable and provide a target to work towards should the tram system be implemented.

Information on traffic congestion may also be difficult to obtain. A lot of non-structured information such as traffic reports on local radio stations, or possibly automobile accidents will be indicative of heavy road usage. However, lost journey time will be difficult to quantify unless individual citizens note how long journeys take with different volumes of traffic on the roads. Savings in terms of time will also be almost impossible to determine.

The last benefit regarding decreased dependence on oil will be achievable if the tram system is implemented, simply because electricity can be generated from other energy sources than oil. How far Erehwon manages to implement alternative energy generation may also be a function of whether the tram system is implemented warranting alternative methods of generating electricity.

(b) Critical Success Factors (CSF) relate to those things which an organisation must do right in order for it to be a success. Performance Indicators (PI) provide a method of measuring the CSFs to check whether or not those CSFs have been achieved. In the situation of the tram system in Erehwon, the following CSFs and Pls could be used:

- CSF – Overall investment budget not exceeded.
- PI – Comparison of budget against actual amount spent.

This CSF and its PI ensure that the project does not exceed the overall budget. The CSF is appropriate to a government department where the amount of money allocated to a project will be finite and additional money may not be available to meet excess expenditure.

- CSF Customer satisfaction with the Tram system.
- PI Number of complaints per 10,000 passenger journeys.

PI Number of tram journeys made each week. This CSF and its PI focus on the external success of the tram system. A lack of complaints will show that customers are satisfied with the system. Similarly, an increase in tram journeys will indicate acceptance and increased use of the system.

Sources of information for the Pls will include:

PI – Comparison of budget against actual expenditure

The budget will be obtained from the steering committee for the project. It should include all relevant costs broken down into appropriate categories.

Actual expenditure should be obtainable from the accounts department of the government. Costs should be allocated to the same categories as the budget and then totalled to show percentage of budget spent and expected costs to completion. This information will help the project manager identify potential cost overruns early, rather than simply tracking expenditure against budget.

PI – Customer complaints

Customer complaints will presumably be made in writing or e-mailed to the appropriate government department. Capturing the information will be difficult where there is no set location to send complaints. Provision of complaint cards on the trams, or even specifying an address or department within the government will help to ensure completeness of information.

Having obtained details of complaints, these will need to be categorised by type and totals of complaints per week or month obtained.

Total passenger journeys should be available from the tram information systems because all passengers are recorded entering each tram. Total passenger journeys can therefore be derived by uploading information from each tram onto a central computer at the end of each day.

The number of complaints per 10,000 journeys can then be obtained by dividing number of journeys by number of complaints.

PI – Number of tram journeys made each week

Total number of passenger journeys can be obtained from the central information systems, as already noted above. Journeys made each week can be monitored by amalgamating journeys for each day, and then displaying this as a graph to help identify trends in number of journeys made.

(c) Communications methods available to communicate benefits of the tram system to the citizens of Erehwon include:

- TV
- Radio
- Newspaper/flyers/other printed material
- E-mail

The choice of the most appropriate method depends partly on the cost of each method as well as whether potential users of the tram system actually use that communication system.

TV tends to be relatively expensive due partly from the cost of producing advertisements and then purchase of airtime to show the adverts. Airtime cost varies depending on the popularity of the television programme being shown and the time of day. However, most citizens appear to own a TV, hence the medium should reach the target audience. TV also has the benefit of being able to show the trams in use and therefore attracts customers to the hopefully clean and efficient system.

Radio advertising will be cheaper than TV, given that no visual images are required to make the advert. Given that many citizens currently drive to work in their cars, they presumably listen to the radio during this journey. Placing radio adverts during the morning and evening rush hours could be a particularly effective form of advertising. The main drawback with this system is lack of pictures to show what the trams are like. However, after the system becomes operational, this will become less of a problem.

Leaflets and flyers are relatively cheap to produce and can provide Information in terms of pictures and text regarding the tram system. They can also be referred to as required, compared to TV and radio adverts which are transient. Leaflets can be made available by distribution to individual homes making the information accessible to potential tram customers. The main problem is ensuring that customers actually read the information.

E-mail is certainly cost-effective in terms of distribution, and could use the same content as leaflets and flyers. However, it is not clear exactly how many citizens have e-mail or whether they would actually read information distributed in this way. Junk e-mail is a significant problem so citizens may simply ignore this media.

In conclusion, the most effective advertising method is likely to be radio, because it can be targeted to potential tram customers at the appropriate time of day exactly when customers are using an alternative form of transport to the trams. Hopefully, potential customers will see the benefit of using trams as a way of avoiding traffic jams.

(d) Using credit card technology to pay for tram fees may have any or all of the following effects:

Benefits

No cash on tram. This will increase security for the tram staff as there will be no point in attempting to take money by force. There will also be other benefits such as no need for staff to count and bank money or time taken ensuring that fares collected equal the fares issued as noted by the ticket machines.

Entry to the trams should be quick because no money is collected for payment of fares or change given when the passenger does not have the correct fare. This will decrease stopping time for each tram and therefore decrease the overall journey time.

An accurate figure can be maintained showing the number of people on a tram at any one time. This will help Monitor customer journeys easily and identify where additional trams are needed and at which time of day.

Problems

The population of Erehwon is not used to using credit cards – therefore take-up of system may be slow. In fact the use of credit cards may present a barrier to people using the tram so the decision should be reviewed to ensure that it is appropriate.

Purchase of 'tram cards' may be difficult and inconvenient if people want to board the tram in a hurry. Purchasing from a local shop may not be an option in this case. The ability to purchase cards on the tram may be useful to encourage tram use.

A flat fee may be seen as unfair. Normal pricing for a journey is to pay for the distance travelled; as the distance increases then so does the fare. Maintaining a flat fee helps to ensure that the service is accessible to all users.

Answer 8

(a) An information centre is part of the overall IT support function. Its main aim is to support computer users specifically where those users have their own PCs and are attempting to write programs, spreadsheet macros or undertake other work that would normally be carried out by the IT department.

Key functions of an information centre may include:

- Providing of telephone support to assist users with queries
- Providing advice on which applications to develop and how to go about this
- Setting and enforcing hardware and software standards
- Monitoring of network traffic with the aim of reducing network bottlenecks.

Integration of business and technical staff implies that these groups will work closer together. An information centre may assist this process, as discussed below.

An information centre may be able to help in the integration of technical and business staff in the following ways.

Understanding of business needs

As technical staff will be providing detailed support to business staff, technical staff will have to understand in more detail how the business operates. In other words business staff will be asking technical staff for solutions to specific business problems. Integration will be improved where technical staff can start to be pro-active in this area, suggesting specific solutions to business problems.

Training

Part of the help desk function will be providing training for users on in-house and possibly third party software. Assuming that training sessions are classroom based then business and technical staff will actually meet each other. This will result in additional understanding of the requirements of each staff group and hopefully improve communication as contacts will be retained after training.

Call logging

The help desk should be maintaining a log of queries raised by business staff. Monitoring of this log will help technical staff be pro-active regarding help and advice to specific business staff requirements, for example issuing web pages on the support site for common or frequently asked questions. Being responsive to user needs in this way will help to raise the profile of technical staff and enable business staff to trust them more. Integration is therefore improved.

Diagnostic services

Technical staff will be able to use diagnostic software to 'see' the files and programs being worked on by business staff. Being able to talk through problems using this software will obviously increase communication between technical and business staff and make each staff group more aware of the needs of the other group.

The information centre may not necessarily assist with the integration of business and technical staff for the following reasons.

Skill sets

Technical staff may not have the necessary skill sets to run the help desk. This will be the case where technical staff come from the traditional background of the IT department being separate to the business departments. Technical staff will not have the appropriate listening or training skills and therefore will not be able to integrate effectively with business staff.

Incorrect attitudes

Either staff group may not have the necessary respect or time to understand how the other works. For example, business staff may see an information centre as a waste of time, especially where appropriate solutions are not forthcoming. Similarly, technical staff may see business staff as asking inappropriate or 'silly' questions, losing the respect of technical staff. The help desk will therefore tend to work against integration of the staff groups.

Company structure

The provision of a help desk centrally within a distributed company will tend to enforce the division between business and technical staff. Where help desk staff are only accessible by telephone or e-mail, they will tend to take on a 'faceless' personality making it difficult to interact with them. Provision of help desk within each location would be more appropriate.

(b) The IS, IT and IM strategies are normally set within an organisation to follow the overall business strategy. The IS strategy therefore considers what systems are required to support the business objectives; the IT strategy puts in place the appropriate hardware and software and the IM strategy deals with the storage and management of information collected.

While the focus of strategy development must be on the business, the information centre may make a contribution to this from the information collected about business users. For example: Logs of queries to the information centre will identify specific difficulties with the use of Information Systems or Technology. Amendments can be programmed to make those systems more user-friendly.

Similarly, the logs may identify new requirements of users. This will be particularly helpful where users are requesting specific changes to systems, especially where those changes will result in better client service. Amendments can be made to the IS and/or IT strategies to help provide that information to users.

Overall, IT provision within an organisation is expensive. Providing an information centre will encourage end-user computing which in turn helps users to prioritise their own development requirements. An information centre may therefore waive development costs, cutting the overall IT budgets.

Obtaining user input in the information centre will also assist the setting of the Information Management strategy. Where the information centre identifies user requirements, this will help to ensure that data is stored in ways in which it can be accessed quickly and efficiently to assist users.

The monitoring of network traffic by the information centre will identify where the IT strategy needs amendment to cope with higher volumes of data.

Monitoring of application development by users will help to ensure that applications follow company standards. Similarly, the centre may identify where those standards need changing or new standards are required as user requirements change.

Overall, the information centre has an important role of identifying and feeding user requirements into the strategy development process. This will help to ensure that systems provided by the organisation do actually meet user requirements.

Question 9

SK Consortium is an international PR and marketing agency. Its shares are listed on an international stock exchange. The company is based in London, but has offices throughout Europe, the Far East and India. Many members of staff are recruited locally. They are supplemented by members of staff based in corporate headquarters in London, but who work worldwide.

SK Consortium generally invoices in the customer's currency. For many years it followed a policy of not hedging currency risks, and has generally profited from this. The Finance Director, who was widely credited with successfully managing the treasury function, has retired. However, the 'no hedging' policy was not without its critics among major investors and financial analysts.

The SK Consortium Board is now concerned about currency volatility and the potential effect on its market value and wishes to evaluate different hedging mechanisms. The recently-appointed new Finance Director has suggested using either currency futures or forward contracts. She proposes to demonstrate to the directors how futures and forward contracts would have worked if a forthcoming transaction had been hedged. The details are as follows:

Receipt of US$875,000 is due on 1 June 2004. The company has known since the end of February 2004 that this receipt is to be expected.

Market information at 1 March 2004

Exchange rates US$/£		**US$ futures US$/£, contract size £62,500**			
			Price	*Initial margin*	*UK interest rate (% per annum)*
Spot	1.6132				
One month forward	1.6100	March	1.6022	£1,000	3.38
Three months forward	1.6038	June	1.5950	£1,500	3.41

Requirements

(a) Despite its success, the 'no hedging' policy was criticised. Discuss the basis for such criticism among investors and analysts and explain why and to what extent this policy, if continued, might affect the market value of the company's shares.

(8 marks)

(b) (i) Assume it is now 1 June 2004. The spot rate US$/£ is 1.6080 and the June 2004 currency futures rate is 1.6085. Calculate the net receipts in sterling that would have been expected on 1 March and today (1 June) under the two alternative hedging methods and comment on which would have been the most financially advantageous. Assume the profit (or variation) margin would be settled on the maturity or disposal of the futures contract.

(ii) Discuss the main features of these two hedging instruments and comment on their suitability for a company such as SK Consortium.

(17 marks)

Notes: Marks are distributed roughly equally between the two sections of requirement (b). A report structure is not required for this question.

(Total = 25 marks)

Tables

Present value table

Present value of 1.00 unit of currency, that is $(1 - r)^{-n}$ where r = interest rate; n = number of periods until payment or receipt.

Periods (n)	Interest rates (r)									
	1%	2%	3%	4%	5%	6%	7%	8%	9%	10%
1	0.990	0.980	0.971	0.962	0.952	0.943	0.935	0.926	0.917	0.909
2	0.980	0.961	0.943	0.925	0.907	0.890	0.873	0.857	0.842	0.826
3	0.971	0.942	0.915	0.889	0.864	0.840	0.816	0.794	0.772	0.751
4	0.961	0.924	0.888	0.855	0.823	0.792	0.763	0.735	0.708	0.683
5	0.951	0.906	0.863	0.822	0.784	0.747	0.713	0.681	0.650	0.621
6	0.942	0.888	0.837	0.790	0.746	0705	0.666	0.630	0.596	0.564
7	0.933	0.871	0.813	0.760	0.711	0.665	0.623	0.583	0.547	0.513
8	0.923	0.853	0.789	0.731	0.677	0.627	0.582	0.540	0.502	0.467
9	0.914	0.837	0.766	0.703	0.645	0.592	0.544	0.500	0.460	0.424
10	0.905	0.820	0.744	0.676	0.614	0.558	0.508	0.463	0.422	0.386
11	0.896	0.804	0.722	0.650	0.585	0.527	0.475	0.429	0.388	0.350
12	0.887	0.788	0.701	0.625	0.557	0.497	0.444	0.397	0.356	0.319
13	0.879	0.773	0.681	0.601	0.530	0.469	0.415	0.368	0.326	0.290
14	0.870	0.758	0.661	0.577	0.505	0.442	0.388	0.340	0.299	0.263
15	0.861	0.743	0.642	0.555	0.481	0.417	0.362	0.315	0.275	0.239
16	0.853	0.728	0.623	0.534	0.458	0.394	0.339	0.292	0.252	0.218
17	0.844	0.714	0.605	0.513	0.436	0.371	0.317	0.270	0.231	0.198
18	0.836	0.700	0.587	0.494	0.416	0.350	0.296	0.250	0.212	0.180
19	0.828	0.686	0.570	0.475	0.396	0.331	0.277	0.232	0.194	0.164
20	0.820	0.673	0.554	0.456	0.377	0.312	0.258	0.215	0.178	0.149

Periods (n)	Interest rates (r)									
	11%	12%	13%	14%	15%	16%	17%	18%	19%	20%
1	0.901	0.893	0.885	0.877	0.870	0.862	0.855	0.847	0.840	0.833
2	0.812	0.797	0.783	0.769	0.756	0.743	0.731	0.718	0.706	0.694
3	0.731	0.712	0.693	0.675	0.658	0.641	0.624	0.609	0.593	0.579
4	0.659	0.636	0.613	0.592	0.572	0.552	0.534	0.516	0.499	0.482
5	0.593	0.567	0.543	0.519	0.497	0.476	0.456	0.437	0.419	0.402
6	0.535	0.507	0.480	0.456	0.432	0.410	0.390	0.370	0.352	0.335
7	0.482	0.452	0.425	0.400	0.376	0.354	0.333	0.314	0.296	0.279
8	0.434	0.404	0.376	0.351	0.327	0.305	0.285	0.266	0.249	0.233
9	0.391	0.361	0.333	0.308	0.284	0.263	0.243	0.225	0.209	0.194
10	0.352	0.322	0.295	0.270	0.247	0.227	0.208	0.191	0.176	0.162
11	0.317	0.287	0.261	0.237	0.215	0.195	0.178	0.162	0.148	0.135
12	0.286	0.257	0.231	0.208	0.187	0.168	0.152	0.137	0.124	0.112
13	0.258	0.229	0.204	0.182	0.163	0.145	0.130	0.116	0.104	0.093
14	0.232	0.205	0.181	0.160	0.141	0.125	0.111	0.099	0.088	0.078
15	0.209	0.183	0.160	0.140	0.123	0.108	0.095	0.084	0.079	0.065
16	0.188	0.163	0.141	0.123	0.107	0.093	0.081	0.071	0.062	0.054
17	0.170	0.146	0.125	0.108	0.093	0.080	0.069	0.060	0.052	0.045
18	0.153	0.130	0.111	0.095	0.081	0.069	0.059	0.051	0.044	0.038
19	0.138	0.116	0.098	0.083	0.070	0.060	0.051	0.043	0.037	0.031
20	0.124	0.104	0.087	0.073	0.061	0.051	0.043	0.037	0.031	0.026

Cumulative present value of 1.00 unit of currency per annum, Receivable or Payable at the end of each year for n years $\frac{1-(1+r)^{-n}}{r}$

Periods (n)	Interest rates (r)									
	1%	2%	3%	4%	5%	6%	7%	8%	9%	10%
1	0.990	0.980	0.971	0.962	0.952	0.943	0.935	0.926	0.917	0.909
2	1.970	1.942	1.913	1.886	1.859	1.833	1.808	1.783	1.759	1.736
3	2.941	2.884	2.829	2.775	2.723	2.673	2.624	2.577	2.531	2.487
4	3.902	3.808	3.717	3.630	3.546	3.465	3.387	3.312	3.240	3.170
5	4.853	4.713	4.580	4.452	4.329	4.212	4.100	3.993	3.890	3.791
6	5.795	5.601	5.417	5.242	5.076	4.917	4.767	4.623	4.486	4.355
7	6.728	6.472	6.230	6.002	5.786	5.582	5.389	5.206	5.033	4.868
8	7.652	7.325	7.020	6.733	6.463	6.210	5.971	5.747	5.535	5.335
9	8.566	8.162	7.786	7.435	7.108	6.802	6.515	6.247	5.995	5.759
10	9.471	8.983	8.530	8.111	7.722	7.360	7.024	6.710	6.418	6.145
11	10.368	9.787	9.253	8.760	8.306	7.887	7.499	7.139	6.805	6.495
12	11.255	10.575	9.954	9.385	8.863	8.384	7.943	7.536	7.161	6.814
13	12.134	11.348	10.635	9.986	9.394	8.853	8.358	7.904	7.487	7.103
14	13.004	12.106	11.296	10.563	9.899	9.295	8.745	8.244	7.786	7.367
15	13.865	12.849	11.938	11.118	10.380	9.712	9.108	8.559	8.061	7.606
16	14.718	13.578	12.561	11.652	10.838	10.106	9.447	8.851	8.313	7.824
17	15.562	14.292	13.166	12.166	11.274	10.477	9.763	9.122	8.544	8.022
18	16.398	14.992	13.754	12.659	11.690	10.828	10.059	9.372	8.756	8.201
19	17.226	15.679	14.324	13.134	12.085	11.158	10.336	9.604	8.950	8.365
20	18.046	16.351	14.878	13.590	12.462	11.470	10.594	9.818	9.129	8.514

Periods (n)	Interest rates (r)									
	11%	12%	13%	14%	15%	16%	17%	18%	19%	20%
1	0.901	0.893	0.885	0.877	0.870	0.862	0.855	0.847	0.840	0.833
2	1.713	1.690	1.668	1.647	1.626	1.605	1.585	1.566	1.547	1.528
3	2.444	2.402	2.361	2.322	2.283	2.246	2.210	2.174	2.140	2.106
4	3.102	3.037	2.974	2.914	2.855	2.798	2.743	2.690	2.639	2.589
5	3.696	3.605	3.517	3.433	3.352	3.274	3.199	3.127	3.058	2.991
6	4.231	4.111	3.998	3.889	3.784	3.685	3.589	3.498	3.410	3.326
7	4.712	4.564	4.423	4.288	4.160	4.039	3.922	3.812	3.706	3.605
8	5.146	4.968	4.799	4.639	4.487	4.344	4.207	4.078	3.954	3.837
9	5.537	5.328	5.132	4.946	4.772	4.607	4.451	4.303	4.163	4.031
10	5.889	5.650	5.426	5.216	5.019	4.833	4.659	4.494	4.339	4.192
11	6.207	5.938	5.687	5.453	5.234	5.029	4.836	4.656	4.486	4.327
12	6.492	6.194	5.918	5.660	5.421	5.197	4.988	7.793	4.611	4.439
13	6.750	6.424	6.122	5.842	5.583	5.342	5.118	4.910	4.715	4.533
14	6.982	6.628	6.302	6.002	5.724	5.468	5.229	5.008	4.802	4.611
15	7.191	6.811	6.462	6.142	5.847	5.575	5.324	5.092	4.876	4.675
16	7.379	6.974	6.604	6.265	5.954	5.668	5.405	5.162	4.938	4.730
17	7.549	7.120	6.729	6.373	6.047	5.749	5.475	5.222	4.990	4.775
18	7.702	7.250	6.840	6.467	6.128	5.818	5.534	5.273	5.033	4.812
19	7.839	7.366	6.938	6.550	6.198	5.877	5.584	5.316	5.070	4.843
20	7.963	7.469	7.025	6.623	6.259	5.929	5.628	5.353	5.101	4.870

Formulae

Valuation models

(i) Irredeemable preference share, paying a constant annual dividend, d, in perpetuity, where P_0 is the ex-div value:

$$P_0 = \frac{d}{k_{pref}}$$

(ii) Ordinary (equity) share, paying a constant annual dividend, d, in perpetuity, where P_0 is the ex-div value:

$$P_0 = \frac{d}{k_e}$$

(iii) Ordinary (equity) share, paying an annual dividend, d, growing in perpetuity at a constant rate, g, where P_0 is the ex-div value:

$$P_0 = \frac{d_1}{k_e - g} \qquad \text{or} \qquad P_0 = \frac{d_0[1 + g]}{k_e - g}$$

(iv) Irredeemable (undated) debt, paying annual after-tax interest, $i[1 - t]$, in perpetuity, where P_0 is the ex-interest value:

$$P_0 = \frac{i[1 - t]}{k_{d\,\mathrm{net}}}$$

or, without tax: $$P_0 = \frac{i}{k_d}$$

(v) Total value of the geared firm, V_g (based on MM):

$$V_g = V_u + TB_c$$

(vi) Future value of S, of a sum X, invested for n periods, compounded at r% interest:

$$S = X[1 + r]^n$$

(vii) Present value of 1.00 payable or receivable in n years, discounted at r% per annum:

$$PV = \frac{1}{[1 + r]^n}$$

(viii) Present value of an annuity of 1.00 per annum, receivable or payable for n years, commencing in 1 year, discounted at r% per annum:

$$PV = \frac{1}{r}\left[1 - \frac{1}{[1 + r]^n}\right]$$

(ix) Present value of 1.00 per annum, payable or receivable in perpetuity, commencing in 1 year, discounted at r% per annum:

$$PV = \frac{1}{r}$$

(x) Present value of 1.00 per annum, receivable or payable, commencing in 1 year, growing in perpetuity at a constant rate of g% per annum, discounted at r% per annum:

$$PV = \frac{1}{r - g}$$

Cost of capital

(i) Cost of irredeemable preference capital, paying an annual dividend, d, in perpetuity, and having a current ex-div price P_0:

$$k_{\text{pref}} = \frac{d}{P_0}$$

(ii) Cost of irredeemable debt capital, paying annual net interest, $i[1-t]$, and having a current ex-interest price P_0:

$$k_{d\,\text{net}} = \frac{i[1-t]}{P_0}$$

(iii) Cost of ordinary (equity) share capital, paying an annual dividend, d, in perpetuity, and having a current ex-div price P_0:

$$k_{\text{e}} = \frac{d}{P_0}$$

(iv) Cost of ordinary (equity) share capital, having a current ex-div price, P_0, having just paid a dividend, d_0, with the dividend growing in perpetuity by a constant $g\%$ per annum:

$$k_{\text{e}} = \frac{d_1}{P_0} + g \qquad \text{or} \qquad k_{\text{e}} = \frac{d_0[1+g]}{P_0} + g$$

(v) Cost of ordinary (equity) share capital, using the CAPM:

$$k_{\text{e}} = R_f + [R_m - R_f]\beta$$

(vi) Cost of ordinary (equity) share capital in a geared firm (no tax):

$$k_{\text{eg}} = k_0 + [k_0 - k_d]\frac{V_D}{V_E}$$

(vii) Cost of ordinary (equity) share capital in a geared firm (with tax):

$$k_{\text{eg}} = k_{eu} + [k_{eu} - k_d]\frac{V_D[1-t]}{V_E}$$

(viii) Weighted average cost of capital, k_0:

$$k_0 = k_{\text{eg}}\left[\frac{V_E}{V_E + V_D}\right] + k_d\left[\frac{V_D}{V_E + V_D}\right]$$

(ix) Adjusted cost of capital (MM formula):

$$k_{\text{adj}} = k_{eu}[1 - tL] \qquad \text{or} \qquad r^* = r[1 - T^*L]$$

In the following formulae, β_{u} is used for an ungeared β and β_{g} is used for a geared β:

(x) β_{u} from β_{g}, taking β_{d} as zero (no tax):

$$\beta_{\text{u}} = \beta_{\text{g}}\left[\frac{V_E}{V_E + V_D}\right]$$

(xi) β_{u} from β_{g}, taking β_{d} as zero (with tax):

$$\beta_{\text{u}} = \beta_{\text{g}}\left[\frac{V_E}{V_E + V_D[1-t]}\right]$$

Other formulae

(i) Interest rate parity (international Fisher effect):

$$\text{Forward rate US\$/£} = \text{Spot US\$/£} \times \frac{1 + \text{nominal US interest rate}}{1 + \text{nominal UK interest rate}}$$

(ii) Purchasing power parity (law of one price):

$$\text{Forward rate US\$/£} = \text{Spot US\$/£} \times \frac{1 + \text{US inflation rate}}{1 + \text{UK inflation rate}}$$

(iii) Link between nominal (money) and real interest rates:

$$[1 + \text{nominal (money) rate}] = [1 + \text{real interest rate}][1 + \text{inflation rate}]$$

(iv) Equivalent annual cost:

$$\text{Equivalent annual cost} = \frac{PV \text{ of costs over } n \text{ years}}{n \text{ year annuity factor}}$$

(v) Theoretical ex-rights price:

$$\text{TERP} = \frac{1}{N + 1}[(N \times \text{cum rights price}) + \text{issue price}]$$

(vi) Value of a right:

$$\text{Value of a right} = \frac{\text{Rights on price} - \text{issue price}}{N + 1}$$

or

$$\frac{\text{Theoretical ex-rights price} - \text{issue price}}{N}$$

where N = number of rights required to buy one share.

Answer 9

(a) *Basis of criticism*

- Hedging is a risk reduction technique and as such has a real cost. These transaction costs are usually small relative to the transaction amounts involved.
- Risks of not hedging may be unacceptable to shareholders. In this case, this seems to be the situation for some investors and analysts. The investors clearly are unhappy with the level of risk and possible effect on market value of the shares. The criticism of the analysts is more difficult to explain, other than that they do not like volatility that might reflect poorly on their forecasting ability.
- The advantages of the company's current policy are that it saves the time and cost of hedging relatively small amounts. It seems sensible to hedge larger amounts, as it is then not taking risks with shareholders' money. The disadvantages are the time and costs involved, but, as noted above, these are relatively small compared with the risks.
- Therefore, not hedging is an option but carries risk. The company must determine its own risk profile and whether its policy is consistent with corporate objectives. However, unless the company has a stated objective of speculating on the foreign exchange markets, it has no right taking undue risks with shareholders' money.

Effect on company valuation

- None quantifiable on basis of cash flows, but the effect may be on the discount rate. If the market thinks the company's cash flows are more stable, then it may lower the discount rate thus increasing the value of future cash flows and the share price, all other things being equal.

(b) (i)

At spot on 1 March, the value of the contract is $\dfrac{\$875{,}000}{1.6132} = £542{,}400$

Receipts using a forward contract would be $\dfrac{\$875{,}000}{1.6038} = £545{,}579$

At spot on 1 June, the value of the contract would be $\dfrac{\$875{,}000}{1.6080} = £544{,}154$

At 1 March, the US$ was expected to strengthen against sterling. In the event, the US$ did not strengthen as much as expected, but entering into the contract was preferable to not hedging, although transaction costs would have to be considered.

Receipts using futures

Using June futures, the number of contracts needed is:

$$\frac{\$875{,}000}{1.5950} = \frac{\$548{,}589}{62{,}500} = 8.8 \approx 9$$

Initial margin payable is $9 \times £1{,}500 = £13{,}500$

On 1 June, close at 1.6080 = 544,154		(\$875,000/1.6080)
Variation margin	= +4,722	[(1.5950 − 1.6085) × 9 × 62,500]/1.608
Interest lost	= −115	(£13,500 × 0.0341 × 3/12)
Net receipts	= 548,761	

Comparison:

Forward contract	£545,579
Futures	£548,761
No hedge	£544,154

The most financially advantageous option, with the benefit of hindsight, would have been to hedge with futures as this would have yielded the highest net receipt.

(ii)

Feature	Currency futures	Currency forward contracts
Source	Exchange traded	Banks
Contract terms	Standard contract sizes and specific delivery dates	Your choice of contract size and maturity date
Price	Price transparency and more competitive than forward contracts	Prices vary, phone round for best quote
Liquidity	No problem, sell back to the market at any time	Fixed maturity contract
Counter-party risk	Practically zero as exposed to the exchange and does not take up bank credit lines	Greater exposure – and uses bank credit lines
Basic risk	Potential discrepancy between the cash market and the futures market	No such exposure
Administration	Complex system of margin calls and accounting	Simple to administer and account for
Main users	Banks, institutions and treasury departments of large corporates	Most treasury departments

Clearly SK Consortium is a large enough organisation with the necessary expertise to use either of these types of hedge, but forwards are much more straightforward to use and easier to operate. Futures, although used by large corporates, are predominately used by financial institutions, often speculatively. The element of risk attached to futures, although small, is something companies in the non-financial sector should consider as they will be risking shareholders' money on non-core operations.

Question 10

(a) Assume you are the Treasurer of AB plc, a large engineering company. You have forecast that the company will need to borrow £2 million by the end of September 2003 for at least 6 months. The need for finance will arise because the company has extended its credit terms to selected customers over the summer period. The company's bank currently charges customers such as AB plc 7.5% per annum interest for short-term unsecured borrowing. However, you believe interest rates will rise by at least 1.5 percentage points over the next 6 months. You are considering using one of three alternative methods to hedge the risk:

(i) forward rate agreements; or
(ii) interest rate futures; or
(iii) an interest rate guarantee (a short-term cap).

You can purchase an interest rate cap at 7% per annum for the duration of the loan to be guaranteed. You would have to pay a premium of 0.1% of the amount of the loan. As part of the arrangement, the company will agree to pay a 'floor' rate of 6% per annum.

Requirement

Discuss the features of each of the three alternative methods of hedging the interest rate risk and advise on how each might be useful to AB plc, taking all relevant and known information into account.

(12 marks)

(b) You are contacted by the company's bank and informed that another of the bank's clients, a smaller company in the same industry, is looking for a swap partner for a similar amount of borrowing for the same duration. This company, RO plc, would prefer variable rate finance whereas the bank knows that AB plc would prefer fixed rate. The borrowing rates applicable to AB plc and RO plc are as follows:

	Floating	*Fixed*
AB plc	LIBOR + 0.3%	7.5%
RO plc	LIBOR + 0.5%	8.5%

Requirements

(i) Comment briefly on why swaps may be used and recommend how the two companies here could co-operate in a swap arrangement to their mutual benefit. Support your recommendation with appropriate calculations.
(ii) Discuss the advantages and disadvantages of arranging a swap through a bank rather than negotiating directly with a counter-party.

(13 marks)

Note: A report format is NOT required in answering this question.

(Total = 25 marks)

Tables

Present value table

Present value of 1.00 unit of currency, that is $(1 + r)^{-n}$ where r = interest rate; n = number of periods until payment or receipt.

Periods (n)	Interest rates (r)									
	1%	2%	3%	4%	5%	6%	7%	8%	9%	10%
1	0.990	0.980	0.971	0.962	0.952	0.943	0.935	0.926	0.917	0.909
2	0.980	0.961	0.943	0.925	0.907	0.890	0.873	0.857	0.842	0.826
3	0.971	0.942	0.915	0.889	0.864	0.840	0.816	0.794	0.772	0.751
4	0.961	0.924	0.888	0.855	0.823	0.792	0.763	0.735	0.708	0.683
5	0.951	0.906	0.863	0.822	0.784	0.747	0.713	0.681	0.650	0.621
6	0.942	0.888	0.837	0.790	0.746	0.705	0.666	0.630	0.596	0.564
7	0.933	0.871	0.813	0.760	0.711	0.665	0.623	0.583	0.547	0.513
8	0.923	0.853	0.789	0.731	0.677	0.627	0.582	0.540	0.502	0.467
9	0.914	0.837	0.766	0.703	0.645	0.592	0.544	0.500	0.460	0.424
10	0.905	0.820	0.744	0.676	0.614	0.558	0.508	0.463	0.422	0.386
11	0.896	0.804	0.722	0.650	0.585	0.527	0.475	0.429	0.388	0.350
12	0.887	0.788	0.701	0.625	0.557	0.497	0.444	0.397	0.356	0.319
13	0.879	0.773	0.681	0.601	0.530	0.469	0.415	0.368	0.326	0.290
14	0.870	0.758	0.661	0.577	0.505	0.442	0.388	0.340	0.299	0.263
15	0.861	0.743	0.642	0.555	0.481	0.417	0.362	0.315	0.275	0.239
16	0.853	0.728	0.623	0.534	0.458	0.394	0.339	0.292	0.252	0.218
17	0.844	0.714	0.605	0.513	0.436	0.371	0.317	0.270	0.231	0.198
18	0.836	0.700	0.587	0.494	0.416	0.350	0.296	0.250	0.212	0.180
19	0.828	0.686	0.570	0.475	0.396	0.331	0.277	0.232	0.194	0.164
20	0.820	0.673	0.554	0.456	0.377	0.312	0.258	0.215	0.178	0.149

Periods (n)	Interest rates (r)									
	11%	12%	13%	14%	15%	16%	17%	18%	19%	20%
1	0.901	0.893	0.885	0.877	0.870	0.862	0.855	0.847	0.840	0.833
2	0.812	0.797	0.783	0.769	0.756	0.743	0.731	0.718	0.706	0.694
3	0.731	0.712	0.693	0.675	0.658	0.641	0.624	0.609	0.593	0.579
4	0.659	0.636	0.613	0.592	0.572	0.552	0.534	0.516	0.499	0.482
5	0.593	0.567	0.543	0.519	0.497	0.476	0.456	0.437	0.419	0.402
6	0.535	0.507	0.480	0.456	0.432	0.410	0.390	0.370	0.352	0.335
7	0.482	0.452	0.425	0.400	0.376	0.354	0.333	0.314	0.296	0.279
8	0.434	0.404	0.376	0.351	0.327	0.305	0.285	0.266	0.249	0.233
9	0.391	0.361	0.333	0.308	0.284	0.263	0.243	0.225	0.209	0.194
10	0.352	0.322	0.295	0.270	0.247	0.227	0.208	0.191	0.176	0.162
11	0.317	0.287	0.261	0.237	0.215	0.195	0.178	0.162	0.148	0.135
12	0.286	0.257	0.231	0.208	0.187	0.168	0.152	0.137	0.124	0.112
13	0.258	0.229	0.204	0.182	0.163	0.145	0.130	0.116	0.104	0.093
14	0.232	0.205	0.181	0.160	0.141	0.125	0.111	0.099	0.088	0.078
15	0.209	0.183	0.160	0.140	0.123	0.108	0.095	0.084	0.079	0.065
16	0.188	0.163	0.141	0.123	0.107	0.093	0.081	0.071	0.062	0.054
17	0.170	0.146	0.125	0.108	0.093	0.080	0.069	0.060	0.052	0.045
18	0.153	0.130	0.111	0.095	0.081	0.069	0.059	0.051	0.044	0.038
19	0.138	0.116	0.098	0.083	0.070	0.060	0.051	0.043	0.037	0.031
20	0.124	0.104	0.087	0.073	0.061	0.051	0.043	0.037	0.031	0.026

Cumulative present value of 1.00 unit of currency per annum, Receivable or Payable at the end of each year for n years $\frac{1-(1+r)^{-n}}{r}$

Periods	Interest rates (r)									
(n)	1%	2%	3%	4%	5%	6%	7%	8%	9%	10%
1	0.990	0.980	0.971	0.962	0.952	0.943	0.935	0.926	0.917	0.909
2	1.970	1.942	1.913	1.886	1.859	1.833	1.808	1.783	1.759	1.736
3	2.941	2.884	2.829	2.775	2.723	2.673	2.624	2.577	2.531	2.487
4	3.902	3.808	3.717	3.630	3.546	3.465	3.387	3.312	3.240	3.170
5	4.853	4.713	4.580	4.452	4.329	4.212	4.100	3.993	3.890	3.791
6	5.795	5.601	5.417	5.242	5.076	4.917	4.767	4.623	4.486	4.355
7	6.728	6.472	6.230	6.002	5.786	5.582	5.389	5.206	5.033	4.868
8	7.652	7.325	7.020	6.733	6.463	6.210	5.971	5.747	5.535	5.335
9	8.566	8.162	7.786	7.435	7.108	6.802	6.515	6.247	5.995	5.759
10	9.471	8.983	8.530	8.111	7.722	7.360	7.024	6.710	6.418	6.145
11	10.368	9.787	9.253	8.760	8.306	7.887	7.499	7.139	6.805	6.495
12	11.255	10.575	9.954	9.385	8.863	8.384	7.943	7.536	7.161	6.814
13	12.134	11.348	10.635	9.986	9.394	8.853	8.358	7.904	7.487	7.103
14	13.004	12.106	11.296	10.563	9.899	9.295	8.745	8.244	7.786	7.367
15	13.865	12.849	11.938	11.118	10.380	9.712	9.108	8.559	8.061	7.606
16	14.718	13.578	12.561	11.652	10.838	10.106	9.447	8.851	8.313	7.824
17	15.562	14.292	13.166	12.166	11.274	10.477	9.763	9.122	8.544	8.022
18	16.398	14.992	13.754	12.659	11.690	10.828	10.059	9.372	8.756	8.201
19	17.226	15.679	14.324	13.134	12.085	11.158	10.336	9.604	8.950	8.365
20	18.046	16.351	14.878	13.590	12.462	11.470	10.594	9.818	9.129	8.514

Periods	Interest rates (r)									
(n)	11%	12%	13%	14%	15%	16%	17%	18%	19%	20%
1	0.901	0.893	0.885	0.877	0.870	0.862	0.855	0.847	0.840	0.833
2	1.713	1.690	1.668	1.647	1.626	1.605	1.585	1.566	1.547	1.528
3	2.444	2.402	2.361	2.322	2.283	2.246	2.210	2.174	2.140	2.106
4	3.102	3.037	2.974	2.914	2.855	2.798	2.743	2.690	2.639	2.589
5	3.696	3.605	3.517	3.433	3.352	3.274	3.199	3.127	3.058	2.991
6	4.231	4.111	3.998	3.889	3.784	3.685	3.589	3.498	3.410	3.326
7	4.712	4.564	4.423	4.288	4.160	4.039	3.922	3.812	3.706	3.605
8	5.146	4.968	4.799	4.639	4.487	4.344	4.207	4.078	3.954	3.837
9	5.537	5.328	5.132	4.946	4.772	4.607	4.451	4.303	4.163	4.031
10	5.889	5.650	5.426	5.216	5.019	4.833	4.659	4.494	4.339	4.192
11	6.207	5.938	5.687	5.453	5.234	5.029	4.836	4.656	4.486	4.327
12	6.492	6.194	5.918	5.660	5.421	5.197	4.988	7.793	4.611	4.439
13	6.750	6.424	6.122	5.842	5.583	5.342	5.118	4.910	4.715	4.533
14	6.982	6.628	6.302	6.002	5.724	5.468	5.229	5.008	4.802	4.611
15	7.191	6.811	6.462	6.142	5.847	5.575	5.324	5.092	4.876	4.675
16	7.379	6.974	6.604	6.265	5.954	5.668	5.405	5.162	4.938	4.730
17	7.549	7.120	6.729	6.373	6.047	5.749	5.475	5.222	4.990	4.775
18	7.702	7.250	6.840	6.467	6.128	5.818	5.534	5.273	5.033	4.812
19	7.839	7.366	6.938	6.550	6.198	5.877	5.584	5.316	5.070	4.843
20	7.963	7.469	7.025	6.623	6.259	5.929	5.628	5.353	5.101	4.870

Formulae

Valuation models

(i) Irredeemable preference share, paying a constant annual dividend, d, in perpetuity, where P_0 is the ex-div value:

$$P_0 = \frac{d}{k_{\text{pref}}}$$

(ii) Ordinary (equity) share, paying a constant annual dividend, d, in perpetuity, where P_0 is the ex-div value:

$$P_0 = \frac{d}{k_e}$$

(iii) Ordinary (equity) share, paying an annual dividend, d, growing in perpetuity at a constant rate, g, where P_0 is the ex-div value:

$$P_0 = \frac{d_1}{k_e - g} \quad \text{or} \quad P_0 = \frac{d_0[1 + g]}{k_e - g}$$

(iv) Irredeemable (undated) debt, paying annual after-tax interest, $i[1 - t]$, in perpetuity, where P_0 is the ex-interest value:

$$P_0 = \frac{i[1 - t]}{k_{d\,\text{net}}}$$

or, without tax: $$P_0 = \frac{i}{k_d}$$

(v) Total value of the geared firm, V_g (based on MM):

$$V_g = V_u + DT_c$$

(vi) Future value of S, of a sum X, invested for n periods, compounded at r% interest:

$$S = X[1 + r]^n$$

(vii) Present value of £1 payable or receivable in n years, discounted at r% per annum:

$$PV = \frac{1}{[1 + r]^n}$$

(viii) Present value of an annuity of £1 per annum, receivable or payable for n years, commencing in 1 year, discounted at r% per annum:

$$PV = \frac{1}{r}\left[1 - \frac{1}{[1 + r]^n}\right]$$

(ix) Present value of £1 per annum, payable or receivable in perpetuity, commencing in 1 year, discounted at r% per annum:

$$PV = \frac{1}{r}$$

(x) Present value of £1 per annum, receivable or payable, commencing in 1 year, growing in perpetuity at a constant rate of g% per annum, discounted at r% per annum:

$$PV = \frac{1}{r - g}$$

Cost of capital

(i) Cost of irredeemable preference capital, paying an annual dividend, d, in perpetuity, and having a current ex-div price P_0:

$$k_{\text{pref}} = \frac{d}{P_0}$$

(ii) Cost of irredeemable debt capital, paying annual net interest, $i[1 - t]$, and having a current ex-interest price P_0:

$$k_{d\,\text{net}} = \frac{i[1 - t]}{P_0}$$

(iii) Cost of ordinary (equity) share capital, paying an annual dividend, d, in perpetuity, and having a current ex-div price P_0:

$$k_e = \frac{d}{P_0}$$

(iv) Cost of ordinary (equity) share capital, having a current ex-div price, P_0, having just paid a dividend, d_0, with the dividend growing in perpetuity by a constant g% per annum:

$$k_e = \frac{d_1}{P_0} + g \quad \text{or} \quad k_e = \frac{d_0[1 + g]}{P_0} + g$$

(v) Cost of ordinary (equity) share capital, using the CAPM:

$$k_e = R_f + [R_m - R_f]\beta$$

(vi) Cost of ordinary (equity) share capital in a geared firm (no tax):

$$k_{eg} = k_0 + [k_0 - k_d]\frac{V_D}{V_E}$$

(vii) Cost of ordinary (equity) share capital in a geared firm (with tax):

$$k_{eg} = k_{eu} + [k_{eu} - k_d]\frac{V_D[1 - t]}{V_E}$$

(viii) Weighted average cost of capital, k_0:

$$k_0 = k_{eg}\left[\frac{V_E}{V_E + V_D}\right] + k_d\left[\frac{V_D}{V_E + V_D}\right]$$

(ix) Adjusted cost of capital (MM formula):

$$k_{\text{adj}} = k_{eu}[1 - tL] \quad \text{or} \quad r^* = r[1 - T^*L]$$

In the following formulae, β_u is used for an ungeared β and β_g is used for a geared β:

(x) β_u from β_g, taking β_d as zero (no tax):

$$\beta_u = \beta_g\left[\frac{V_E}{V_E + V_D}\right]$$

(xi) β_u from β_g, taking β_d as zero (with tax):

$$\beta_u = \beta_g\left[\frac{V_E}{V_E + V_D[1 - t]}\right]$$

Other formulae

(i) Purchasing power parity (law of one price):

$$\text{Forward rate US\$/£} = \text{Spot US\$/£} \times \frac{1 + \text{US inflation rate}}{1 + \text{UK inflation rate}}$$

(ii) Interest rate parity (international Fisher effect):

$$\text{Forward rate US\$/£} = \text{Spot US\$/£} \times \frac{1 + \text{nominal US interest rate}}{1 + \text{nominal UK interest rate}}$$

(iii) Link between nominal (money) and real interest rates:

$$[1 + \text{nominal (money) rate}] = [1 + \text{real interest rate}][1 + \text{inflation rate}]$$

(iv) Equivalent annual cost:

$$\text{Equivalent annual cost} = \frac{PV \text{ of costs over } n \text{ years}}{n \text{ year annuity factor}}$$

(v) Theoretical ex-rights price:

$$\text{TERP} = \frac{1}{N+1}[(N \times \text{cum rights price}) + \text{issue price}]$$

(vi) Value of a right:

$$\text{Value of a right} = \frac{\text{Rights on price} - \text{issue price}}{N+1}$$

or

$$\frac{\text{Theoretical ex-rights price} - \text{issue price}}{N}$$

where N = number of rights required to buy one share.

Answer 10

(a)

(i) *Forward rate agreements (FRA)*

These types of agreement offer companies the facility to fix future interest rates on either borrowing or lending for a specific period. AB plc will be protected from the expected increase in interest rates. However, the company cannot then benefit from a fall in interest rates after the forward rate agreement has been entered into. There is no initial price or margin requirement, but the interest rate set for the FRA will reflect expectations of interest rate movements.

FRAs do not involve any actual lending or investment of the principal sum. FRAs are usually for at least US$1 million (or equivalent in other major currencies) and can be arranged for up to 2 or 3 years in the future. As AB plc wishes to fix borrowing costs, FRAs would be a suitable means of managing the interest-rate exposure. The actual borrowing of the £2 million would need to be arranged separately from the FRA.

(ii) *Interest-rate futures*

These are binding contracts between seller and buyer to make and take, respectively, delivery of a specified interest-rate commitment on an agreed date and at an agreed price. They can be used to protect against expected rises in interest rates by means of a 'short hedge', and are available for a maximum of 1 to 2 years. With a short hedge, futures contracts are sold now in the expectation that as interest rates rise the contract value will fall, and they can then be purchased at a lower price, generating a profit on the futures deal. This profit compensates for actual rises in interest rates experienced by companies that have borrowed funds from banks and elsewhere. If interest rates move in the opposite direction to that expected, a futures loss will occur but this will, to some extent, be offset by gains from cheaper interest costs in the cash markets.

Interest rate futures are 'standardised' forms of forward rate agreement. Standardisation will typically mean a set contract size, a specific settlement date and a specific interest period. This standardisation means interest futures are less flexible than FRAs and potentially less attractive to a company such as AB plc. Only a limited range of interest-rate futures contracts exist, but they all require a small initial deposit or margin.

(iii) *Interest rate guarantees*

These are short-term, interest rate options with a maximum maturity of 1 year. (Longer-term interest-rate options such as caps, collars and floors are also available.) The option guarantees that the interest rate will not rise above (alternatively, fall below) an agreed fixed level during a specified period commencing some time in the near future. The interest-rate protection for a borrower worried about interest rates is, therefore, similar to that given by a FRA.

However, there are major differences between interest-rate guarantees and FRAs. Interest-rate guarantees involve the payment of a premium to the seller of the guarantee, whether or not the option element of the guarantee is exercised.

No premium is payable with a FRA (although interest compensation may be payable, as described above). The second major difference is that interest-rate guarantees, while protecting against downside risk (such as an interest rate rise for AB plc), offer the option holder the opportunity to take full advantage of favourable interest-rate movements. For example, if interest rates fall, the guarantee is not used and the company borrows in the money market at the lower interest rate. Neither FRAs nor interest-rate futures allow the company to take full advantage of favourable interest-rate movements.

AB plc could use an interest-rate guarantee to protect against rising interest rates, but could still benefit if interest rates fall. However, the premium cost of interest-rate options is considered to be expensive by many companies.

The information in the question can be shown graphically as below:

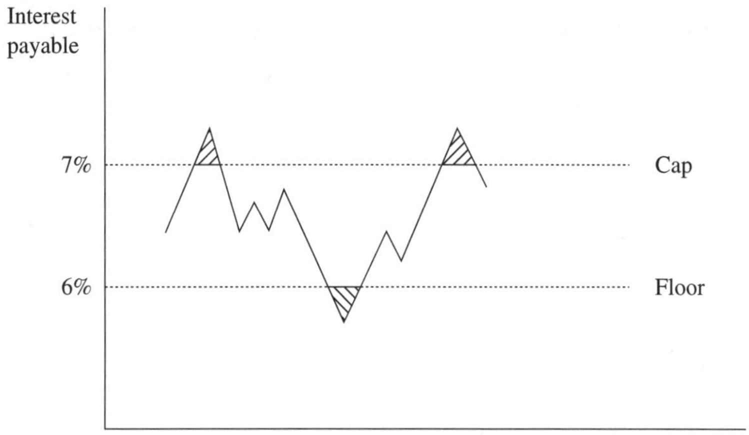

(b)

(i) An interest rate swap is simply the exchange of one stream of cash flows for another in the same currency. Companies' circumstances change and the type of financing taken out some years ago may be unsuitable for their requirements based on the expected cash flows from their current commitments. It is also possible that if a company is dealing in unusual currencies, the management of interest rate risk can be undertaken via a swap arrangement. Another reason for companies to involve themselves in swaps is when they have different views of how interest rates are going to move. Therefore, one company may consider it would be better off taking out a fixed interest loan, another company may prefer a floating rate loan. If two companies can be brought together each of them can borrow in the market in which they have a *comparative advantage* to the overall advantage of both of them.

In the circumstances of the question, AB plc is the larger company, which means it has a better credit rating than RO plc and hence it has preferential rates of interest. This provides an arbitrage opportunity that allows for a potential gain of 0.8% to be shared:

Difference in fixed rates	8.5% − 7.5% = 1.0%
Less: Difference in floating rates	0.5% − 0.3% = 0.2%
	0.8%

The bank has suggested a swap with a smaller company that would prefer a variable rate loan. However, although in absolute terms RO plc is paying more than AB plc in both markets, it is paying only 0.2% more in the floating rate market compared with 1% more in the fixed rate market. It therefore has a *comparative advantage* in the floating rate market. As this is the market in which it prefers to borrow, there is no incentive for a swap. If AB plc borrowed at fixed rate, which it prefers, and RO plc at variable, the situation would be:

No swap		*Swap*	
RO plc pays	LIBOR + 0.5%	RO plc takes fixed at	8.5%
AB plc pays fixed at	7.5%	AB plc takes variable at	LIBOR + 0.3%
Total	LIBOR + 8.0%	Total:	LIBOR + 8.8%

The question asks how the companies could co-operate in a swap to their mutual benefit. This would be possible if AB borrowed in the fixed market, RO borrowed in the variable market and they swapped interest payment responsibilities. A numerical example could be as follows, assuming any gain agreed is shared equally.

Assume:

(i) RO borrows in the variable rate market at LIBOR + 0.5% and pays AB 7.6% fixed.
(ii) AB borrows in the fixed rate market at 7.5% and pays RO LIBOR.

AB plc	%
Borrows at	7.5
Receives from RO plc	(7.6)
Pays to RO plc	LIBOR
Net cost	LIBOR − 0.1

This means AB plc is effectively borrowing at a variable rate, LIBOR − 0.1%, which is 0.4% less than it could do if it borrowed in this market on its own.

This means RO plc is effectively borrowing at a fixed rate of 8.1%, which is 0.4% less than it could do if it borrowed in this market on its own.

Given the greater bargaining power of AB plc, it might be able to negotiate a greater share of the gains than 50%. However, if AB plc genuinely thinks interest rates will rise by 1.5 percentage points over the next 6 months (a substantial rise) then it is unlikely to be persuaded to enter into a swap unless the terms are much more generous than are possible here. There are also the bank's fees to be taken into account that will reduce the gains available.

> *Examiner's Note:*
>
> Any attempt at quantifying the potential gain would have gained credit.

(ii) The advantages of using an intermediary, as opposed to setting up a swap arrangement directly with a counter party, can be summarised as follows:

- There is more flexibility and a significantly increased choice of maturity, currency and so on, when dealing with a bank. This would be especially advantageous when dealing with unusual currencies.

- The bank may have more idea of the credit risk of the organisation involved in the swap and may assume the credit risk, guaranteeing performance of the swap.
- The swap may be quicker to arrange and it may be possible to get it reversed by entering into a new swap transaction.

The main disadvantage is probably cost. Clearly, the bank would require commission or a fee for negotiating a swap and bringing the two parties together. This could be avoided if the company could make a direct contact.

Appendix A

Strategic Level

Management Accounting – Risk and Control Strategy (Paper P3)

The answers published here have been written by the Examiner and should provide a helpful guide for both tutors and students.

Published separately on the CIMA website (www.cimaglobal.com) from the end of February 2006 is a Post Examination Guide for this paper, which provides much valuable and complementary material including indicative mark information.

CIMA

Management Accounting Pillar

Strategic Level Paper

P3 – Management Accounting – Risk and Control Strategy

24 November 2005 – Thursday Morning Session

Instructions to candidates

You are allowed three hours to answer this question paper.
You are allowed 20 minutes reading time **before the examination begins** during which you should read the question paper, and if you wish, make annotations on the question paper. However, you will **not** be allowed, **under any circumstances**, to open the answer book and start writing or use your calculator during this reading time.
You are strongly advised to carefully read ALL the question requirements before attempting the question concerned (that is, all parts and/or sub-questions). The question requirements are contained in a dotted box.
Answer the ONE compulsory question in Section A on pages 169 and 170.
Answer TWO questions only from Section B on pages 171 to 174.
Maths Tables and Formulae are provided on pages 175 to 178.
Write your full examination number, paper number and the examination subject title in the spaces provided on the front of the examination answer book. Also write your contact ID and name in the space provided in the right hand margin and seal to close.
Tick the appropriate boxes on the front of the answer book to indicate which questions you have answered.

SECTION A – 50 MARKS

[the indicative time for answering this section is 90 minutes]

ANSWER THIS QUESTION

Question One

VCF is a small listed company that designs and installs high technology computer numerical control capital equipment used by multinational manufacturing companies. VCF is located in one Pacific country, but almost 90% of its sales are exported. VCF has sales offices in Europe, Asia, the Pacific, Africa, and North and South America and employs about 300 staff around the world.

VCF has annual sales of $200 million but the sales value of each piece of equipment sold is about $2 million so the sales volume is relatively low. Sales are always invoiced in the currency of the country where the equipment is being installed. The time between the order being taken and the final installation is usually several months. However, a deposit is taken when the order is placed and progress payments are made by the customer before shipment and upon delivery, with the final payment being made after installation of the equipment.

The company has international patents covering its technology and invests heavily in research and development (R&D, about 15% of sales) and marketing costs to develop export markets (about 25% of sales). VCF's manufacturing operations are completely outsourced in its home country and the cost of sales is about 20%. The balance of costs is for installation, servicing and administration, amounting to about 15% of sales. Within each of these cost classifications the major expenses (other than direct costs) are salaries for staff, all of whom are paid well above the industry average, rental of premises in each location and travel costs. Area managers are located in each sales office and have responsibility for achieving sales, installing equipment and maintaining high levels of after-sales service and customer satisfaction.

Although the head office is very small, most of the R&D staff are located in the home country, along with purchasing and logistics staff responsible for liaising with the outsource suppliers and a small accounting team that is primarily concerned with monthly management accounts and end of year financial statements.

VCF has a majority shareholding held by Jack Viktor, an enterpreneur who admits to taking high risks, both personally and in business. The Board of four is effectively controlled by Viktor who is both Chairman and Chief Executive. The three other directors were appointed by Viktor. They are his wife, who has a marketing role in the business, and two non-executive directors, one an occasional consultant to VCF and the other a long-time family friend. Board meetings are held quarterly and are informal affairs, largely led by Viktor's verbal review of sales activity.

Viktor is a dominating individual who exercises a high degree of personal control, often by-passing his area managers. Because the company is controlled by him, Viktor is not especially concerned with short-term profits but with the long term. He emphasises two objectives: sales growth to generate increased market share and cash flow; and investment in R&D to ensure the long-term survival of VCF by maintaining patent protection and a technological lead over its competitors.

Viktor is in daily contact with all his offices by telephone. He travels extensively around the world and has an excellent knowledge of VCF's competitors and customers. He uses a limited number of non-financial performance measures, primarily concerned with sales, market share, quality and customer satisfaction. Through his personal contact and his twin objectives, Viktor encourages a culture committed to growth, continual innovation, and high levels of customer satisfaction. This is reinforced by high salary levels, but Viktor readily dismisses those staff not committed to his objectives.

The company has experienced rapid growth over the last 10 years and is very profitable although cash flow is often tight. A high margin is achieved because VCF is able to charge its customers premium prices. The equipment sold by VCF enables faster production and better quality than its competitors can offer.

Viktor has little time for traditional accounting. Product costing is not seen as valuable because the cost of sales is relatively low and most costs incurred by VCF, particular R&D and export marketing costs, are incurred a long time in advance of sales being made. R&D costs are not capitalised in VCF's balance sheet.

Although budgets are used for expense control and monthly management accounts are produced, they have little relevance to Viktor who recognises the fluctuations in profit caused by the timing of sales of low volume but high value capital equipment. Viktor sees little value in comparing monthly profit figures against budgets because sales are erratic. However, Viktor depends heavily on a spreadsheet to manage VCF's cash flow by using sensitivity analysis against his sales and cash flow projections. Cash flow is a major business driver and is controlled tightly using the spreadsheet model.

The major risks facing VCF have been identified by Viktor as:

- competitor infringement of patents, which VCF always meets by instituting legal actions;
- adverse movements in the exchange rate between the home country and VCF's export markets, which VCF treats as an acceptable risk given that historically, gains and losses have balanced each other out;
- the reduction in demand for his equipment due to economic recession;
- a failure of continued R&D investment to maintain technological leadership; and
- a failure to control costs.

Viktor considers that the last three of these risks are addressed by his policy of outsourcing manufacture and continuous personal contact with staff, customers and competitors.

Required:

(a) Identify and evaluate the existing controls within VCF (including those applied by Viktor).

(20 marks)

(b) Write a report to the Board of VCF recommending improvements to the company's corporate governance, risk management strategy, and internal controls.
Note: You should use examples from the case to illustrate your answer.

(20 marks)

(c) Identify the exchange risks faced by VCF and recommend the methods that could be used to manage those risks.

(10 marks)

(Total for Question One = 50 marks)

SECTION B – 50 MARKS

[the indicative time for answering this section is 90 minutes]

ANSWER *TWO* QUESTIONS ONLY

? Question Two

As a CIMA member, you have recently been appointed as the Head of Internal Audit for SPQ, a multinational listed company that carries out a large volume of internet sales to customers who place their orders using their home or work computers. You report to the Chief Executive, although you work closely with the Finance Director. You have direct access to the Chair of the Audit Committee whenever you consider it necessary.

One of your internal audit teams has been conducting a review of IT security for a system which has been in operation for 18 months and which is integral to internet sales. The audit was included in the internal audit plan following a request by the Chief Accountant. Sample testing by the internal audit team has revealed several transactions over the last three months which have raised concerns about possible hacking or fraudulent access to the customer/order database. Each of these transactions has disappeared from the database after deliveries have been made, but without sales being recorded or funds collected from the customer. Each of the identified transactions was for a different customer and there seems to be no relationship between any of the transactions.

You have received the draft report from the Internal Audit Manager responsible for this audit which suggests serious weaknesses in the design of the system. You have discussed this informally with senior managers who have told you that such a report will be politically very unpopular with the Chief Executive as he was significantly involved in the design and approval of the new system and insisted it be implemented earlier than the IT department considered was advisable. No post-implementation review of the system has taken place.

You have been informally advised by several senior managers to lessen the criticism and work with the IT department to correct any deficiencies within the system and to produce a report to the Audit Committee that is less critical and merely identifies the need for some improvement. They suggest that these actions would avoid criticism of the Chief Executive by the Board of SPQ.

Required:

(a) Explain the role of internal audit in internal control and risk management. **(5 marks)**

(b) Analyse the potential risks faced by SPQ that have been exposed by the review of IT security and recommend controls that should be implemented to reduce them. **(8 marks)**

(c) Discuss the issues that need to be considered when planning an audit of activities and systems such as the one undertaken at SPQ. **(5 marks)**

(d) Explain the ethical principles you should apply as the Head of Internal Audit for SPQ when reporting the results of this internal review and how any ethical conflicts should be resolved. **(7 marks)**

(Total for Question Two = 25 marks)

? Question Three

A large doctors' practice, with six partners and two practice nurses has decided to increase its income by providing day surgery facilities. The existing building would be extended to provide room for the surgical unit and storage facilities for equipment and drugs. The aim is to offer patients the opportunity to have minor surgical procedures conducted by a doctor at their local practice, thus avoiding any unfamiliarity and possible delays to treatment that might result from referral to a hospital. Blood and samples taken during the surgery will be sent away to the local hospital for testing but the patient will get the results from their doctor at the practice. It is anticipated that the introduction of the day surgery facility will increase practice income by approximately 20 per cent.

Required:

(a) Identify the additional risks that the doctors' practice may expect to face as a consequence of the introduction of the new facility, and explain how a model such as CIMA's risk management cycle might be used to understand and control such risks. **(12 marks)**

(b) Explain the meaning of the term "risk appetite" and discuss who should take responsibility for defining that appetite in the context of the scenario outlined above. **(5 marks)**

(c) Critically discuss the role of systems based internal auditing in relation to the assessment of risk management procedures in any organisation. **(8 marks)**

(Total for Question Three = 25 marks)

Question Four

(a) LXN is a large book retailer in France and as a result of recent rapid sales growth has decided to expand by opening six new branches in the south of France. The estimated set up cost per branch is €250,000 and LXN wishes to raise the required funding (plus an additional 20 per cent for increased working capital requirements) via borrowing. The Treasurer at LXN is concerned about interest rate risk however, and is unsure about whether to opt for a fixed or floating rate loan. LXN's Board of Directors has indicated that it wishes to maximise the company's use of opportunities to hedge interest rate risk.

LXN currently has €2,000 million of assets and the following long-term debt in its balance sheet:

€15 million [(6% fixed rate) redeemable 2010]
£18 million [(Sterling LIBOR plus 3%) redeemable 2007]

All rates are quoted as an annual rate. The current exchange rate is €/£0.684.

Required:

Discuss the factors that should be taken into account by the Treasurer of LXN when deciding whether to raise fixed rate or floating rate debt for the expansion project and whether to hedge the resulting interest rate exposure.

(10 marks)

(b) LXN's Treasurer has negotiated a fixed rate of 6% or a variable rate of Euro LIBOR plus 1.5% for the required borrowing. In addition, a counterparty (MGV) has offered to convert any new fixed rate debt that LXN takes on into synthetic floating rate debt via a swap arrangement in which the two companies will share the quality spread differential equally.

MGV, the counterparty, can borrow at a fixed rate of 7.2% or at a variable rate of Euro LIBOR plus 2.5%.

Euro LIBOR is currently 5%. All rates are quoted as an annual rate.

Required:

(i) Briefly discuss the advantages and disadvantages of interest rate swaps as a tool for managing interest rate risk.

(5 marks)

(ii) Draw a diagram to illustrate how the transactions between LXN and MGV and the two lenders will operate if the swap is agreed.

(4 marks)

(iii) Calculate the interest rate terms payable by LXN. Evaluate the potential annual saving resulting from borrowing at a fixed rate and engaging in an interest rate swap, as against a straightforward floating rate loan.

(6 marks)

(Total for requirement (b) = 15 marks)

(Total for Question Four = 25 marks)

Question Five

Required:

(a) Identify the key reasons for the emergence of corporate governance regulations around the world.

(5 marks)

(b) Explain the core principles that underpin corporate governance regulations.

(10 marks)

(c) Discuss the role and responsibilities of audit committees as laid down in the Combined Code.

(10 marks)

(Total for Question Five = 25 marks)

(Total for Section B = 50 marks)

Area Under the Normal Curve

This table gives the area under the normal curve between the mean and a point Z standard deviations above the mean. The corresponding area for deviations below the mean can be found by symmetry.

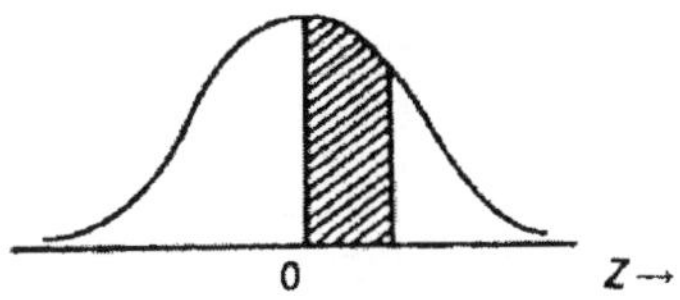

$Z = \frac{(X-\mu)}{\sigma}$	0.00	0.01	0.02	0.03	0.04	0.05	0.06	0.07	0.08	0.09
0.0	0.0000	0.0040	0.0080	0.0120	0.0159	0.0199	0.0239	0.0279	0.0319	0.0359
0.1	0.0398	0.0438	0.0478	0.0517	0.0557	0.0596	0.0636	0.0675	0.0714	0.0753
0.2	0.0793	0.0832	0.0871	0.0910	0.0948	0.0987	0.1026	0.1064	0.1103	0.1141
0.3	0.1179	0.1217	0.1255	0.1293	0.1331	0.1368	0.1406	0.1443	0.1480	0.1517
0.4	0.1554	0.1591	0.1628	0.1664	0.1700	0.1736	0.1772	0.1808	0.1844	0.1879
0.5	0.1915	0.1950	0.1985	0.2019	0.2054	0.2088	0.2123	0.2157	0.2190	0.2224
0.6	0.2257	0.2291	0.2324	0.2357	0.2389	0.2422	0.2454	0.2486	0.2518	0.2549
0.7	0.2580	0.2611	0.2642	0.2673	0.2704	0.2734	0.2764	0.2794	0.2823	0.2852
0.8	0.2881	0.2910	0.2939	0.2967	0.2995	0.3023	0.3051	0.3078	0.3106	0.3133
0.9	0.3159	0.3186	0.3212	0.3238	0.3264	0.3289	0.3315	0.3340	0.3365	0.3389
1.0	0.3413	0.3438	0.3461	0.3485	0.3508	0.3531	0.3554	0.3577	0.3599	0.3621
1.1	0.3643	0.3665	0.3686	0.3708	0.3729	0.3749	0.3770	0.3790	0.3810	0.3830
1.2	0.3849	0.3869	0.3888	0.3907	0.3925	0.3944	0.3962	0.3980	0.3997	0.4015
1.3	0.4032	0.4049	0.4066	0.4082	0.4099	0.4115	0.4131	0.4147	0.4162	0.4177
1.4	0.4192	0.4207	0.4222	0.4236	0.4251	0.4265	0.4279	0.4292	0.4306	0.4319
1.5	0.4332	0.4345	0.4357	0.4370	0.4382	0.4394	0.4406	0.4418	0.4430	0.4441
1.6	0.4452	0.4463	0.4474	0.4485	0.4495	0.4505	0.4515	0.4525	0.4535	0.4545
1.7	0.4554	0.4564	0.4573	0.4582	0.4591	0.4599	0.4608	0.4616	0.4625	0.4633
1.8	0.4641	0.4649	0.4656	0.4664	0.4671	0.4678	0.4686	0.4693	0.4699	0.4706
1.9	0.4713	0.4719	0.4726	0.4732	0.4738	0.4744	0.4750	0.4756	0.4762	0.4767
2.0	0.4772	0.4778	0.4783	0.4788	0.4793	0.4798	0.4803	0.4808	0.4812	0.4817
2.1	0.4821	0.4826	0.4830	0.4834	0.4838	0.4842	0.4846	0.4850	0.4854	0.4857
2.2	0.4861	0.4865	0.4868	0.4871	0.4875	0.4878	0.4881	0.4884	0.4887	0.4890
2.3	0.4893	0.4896	0.4898	0.4901	0.4904	0.4906	0.4909	0.4911	0.4913	0.4916
2.4	0.4918	0.4920	0.4922	0.4925	0.4927	0.4929	0.4931	0.4932	0.4934	0.4936
2.5	0.4938	0.4940	0.4941	0.4943	0.4945	0.4946	0.4948	0.4949	0.4951	0.4952
2.6	0.4953	0.4955	0.4956	0.4957	0.4959	0.4960	0.4961	0.4962	0.4963	0.4964
2.7	0.4965	0.4966	0.4967	0.4968	0.4969	0.4970	0.4971	0.4972	0.4973	0.4974
2.8	0.4974	0.4975	0.4976	0.4977	0.4977	0.4978	0.4979	0.4980	0.4980	0.4981
2.9	0.4981	0.4982	0.4983	0.4983	0.4984	0.4984	0.4985	0.4985	0.4986	0.4986
3.0	0.49865	0.4987	0.4987	0.4988	0.4988	0.4989	0.4989	0.4989	0.4990	0.4990
3.1	0.49903	0.4991	0.4991	0.4991	0.4992	0.4992	0.4992	0.4992	0.4993	0.4993
3.2	0.49931	0.4993	0.4994	0.4994	0.4994	0.4994	0.4994	0.4995	0.4995	0.4995
3.3	0.49952	0.4995	0.4995	0.4996	0.4996	0.4996	0.4996	0.4996	0.4996	0.4997
3.4	0.49966	0.4997	0.4997	0.4997	0.4997	0.4997	0.4997	0.4997	0.4997	0.4998
3.5	0.49977									

PRESENT VALUE TABLE

Present value of $1, that is $(1 + r)^{-n}$ where r = interest rate; n = number of periods until payment or receipt.

Periods (n)	Interest rates (r)									
	1%	2%	3%	4%	5%	6%	7%	8%	9%	10%
1	0.990	0.980	0.971	0.962	0.952	0.943	0.935	0.926	0.917	0.909
2	0.980	0.961	0.943	0.925	0.907	0.890	0.873	0.857	0.842	0.826
3	0.971	0.942	0.915	0.889	0.864	0.840	0.816	0.794	0.772	0.751
4	0.961	0.924	0.888	0.855	0.823	0.792	0.763	0.735	0.708	0.683
5	0.951	0.906	0.863	0.822	0.784	0.747	0.713	0.681	0.650	0.621
6	0.942	0.888	0.837	0.790	0.746	0.705	0.666	0.630	0.596	0.564
7	0.933	0.871	0.813	0.760	0.711	0.665	0.623	0.583	0.547	0.513
8	0.923	0.853	0.789	0.731	0.677	0.627	0.582	0.540	0.502	0.467
9	0.914	0.837	0.766	0.703	0.645	0.592	0.544	0.500	0.460	0.424
10	0.905	0.820	0.744	0.676	0.614	0.558	0.508	0.463	0.422	0.386
11	0.896	0.804	0.722	0.650	0.585	0.527	0.475	0.429	0.388	0.350
12	0.887	0.788	0.701	0.625	0.557	0.497	0.444	0.397	0.356	0.319
13	0.879	0.773	0.681	0.601	0.530	0.469	0.415	0.368	0.326	0.290
14	0.870	0.758	0.661	0.577	0.505	0.442	0.388	0.340	0.299	0.263
15	0.861	0.743	0.642	0.555	0.481	0.417	0.362	0.315	0.275	0.239
16	0.853	0.728	0.623	0.534	0.458	0.394	0.339	0.292	0.252	0.218
17	0.844	0.714	0.605	0.513	0.436	0.371	0.317	0.270	0.231	0.198
18	0.836	0.700	0.587	0.494	0.416	0.350	0.296	0.250	0.212	0.180
19	0.828	0.686	0.570	0.475	0.396	0.331	0.277	0.232	0.194	0.164
20	0.820	0.673	0.554	0.456	0.377	0.312	0.258	0.215	0.178	0.149

Periods (n)	Interest rates (r)									
	11%	12%	13%	14%	15%	16%	17%	18%	19%	20%
1	0.901	0.893	0.885	0.877	0.870	0.862	0.855	0.847	0.840	0.833
2	0.812	0.797	0.783	0.769	0.756	0.743	0.731	0.718	0.706	0.694
3	0.731	0.712	0.693	0.675	0.658	0.641	0.624	0.609	0.593	0.579
4	0.659	0.636	0.613	0.592	0.572	0.552	0.534	0.516	0.499	0.482
5	0.593	0.567	0.543	0.519	0.497	0.476	0.456	0.437	0.419	0.402
6	0.535	0.507	0.480	0.456	0.432	0.410	0.390	0.370	0.352	0.335
7	0.482	0.452	0.425	0.400	0.376	0.354	0.333	0.314	0.296	0.279
8	0.434	0.404	0.376	0.351	0.327	0.305	0.285	0.266	0.249	0.233
9	0.391	0.361	0.333	0.308	0.284	0.263	0.243	0.225	0.209	0.194
10	0.352	0.322	0.295	0.270	0.247	0.227	0.208	0.191	0.176	0.162
11	0.317	0.287	0.261	0.237	0.215	0.195	0.178	0.162	0.148	0.135
12	0.286	0.257	0.231	0.208	0.187	0.168	0.152	0.137	0.124	0.112
13	0.258	0.229	0.204	0.182	0.163	0.145	0.130	0.116	0.104	0.093
14	0.232	0.205	0.181	0.160	0.141	0.125	0.111	0.099	0.088	0.078
15	0.209	0.183	0.160	0.140	0.123	0.108	0.095	0.084	0.079	0.065
16	0.188	0.163	0.141	0.123	0.107	0.093	0.081	0.071	0.062	0.054
17	0.170	0.146	0.125	0.108	0.093	0.080	0.069	0.060	0.052	0.045
18	0.153	0.130	0.111	0.095	0.081	0.069	0.059	0.051	0.044	0.038
19	0.138	0.116	0.098	0.083	0.070	0.060	0.051	0.043	0.037	0.031
20	0.124	0.104	0.087	0.073	0.061	0.051	0.043	0.037	0.031	0.026

Cumulative present value of $1 per annum, Receivable or Payable at the end of each year for n years $\frac{1-(1+r)^{-n}}{r}$

Periods (n)	Interest rates (r)									
	1%	2%	3%	4%	5%	6%	7%	8%	9%	10%
1	0.990	0.980	0.971	0.962	0.952	0.943	0.935	0.926	0.917	0.909
2	1.970	1.942	1.913	1.886	1.859	1.833	1.808	1.783	1.759	1.736
3	2.941	2.884	2.829	2.775	2.723	2.673	2.624	2.577	2.531	2.487
4	3.902	3.808	3.717	3.630	3.546	3.465	3.387	3.312	3.240	3.170
5	4.853	4.713	4.580	4.452	4.329	4.212	4.100	3.993	3.890	3.791
6	5.795	5.601	5.417	5.242	5.076	4.917	4.767	4.623	4.486	4.355
7	6.728	6.472	6.230	6.002	5.786	5.582	5.389	5.206	5.033	4.868
8	7.652	7.325	7.020	6.733	6.463	6.210	5.971	5.747	5.535	5.335
9	8.566	8.162	7.786	7.435	7.108	6.802	6.515	6.247	5.995	5.759
10	9.471	8.983	8.530	8.111	7.722	7.360	7.024	6.710	6.418	6.145
11	10.368	9.787	9.253	8.760	8.306	7.887	7.499	7.139	6.805	6.495
12	11.255	10.575	9.954	9.385	8.863	8.384	7.943	7.536	7.161	6.814
13	12.134	11.348	10.635	9.986	9.394	8.853	8.358	7.904	7.487	7.103
14	13.004	12.106	11.296	10.563	9.899	9.295	8.745	8.244	7.786	7.367
15	13.865	12.849	11.938	11.118	10.380	9.712	9.108	8.559	8.061	7.606
16	14.718	13.578	12.561	11.652	10.838	10.106	9.447	8.851	8.313	7.824
17	15.562	14.292	13.166	12.166	11.274	10.477	9.763	9.122	8.544	8.022
18	16.398	14.992	13.754	12.659	11.690	10.828	10.059	9.372	8.756	8.201
19	17.226	15.679	14.324	13.134	12.085	11.158	10.336	9.604	8.950	8.365
20	18.046	16.351	14.878	13.590	12.462	11.470	10.594	9.818	9.129	8.514

Periods (n)	Interest rates (r)									
	11%	12%	13%	14%	15%	16%	17%	18%	19%	20%
1	0.901	0.893	0.885	0.877	0.870	0.862	0.855	0.847	0.840	0.833
2	1.713	1.690	1.668	1.647	1.626	1.605	1.585	1.566	1.547	1.528
3	2.444	2.402	2.361	2.322	2.283	2.246	2.210	2.174	2.140	2.106
4	3.102	3.037	2.974	2.914	2.855	2.798	2.743	2.690	2.639	2.589
5	3.696	3.605	3.517	3.433	3.352	3.274	3.199	3.127	3.058	2.991
6	4.231	4.111	3.998	3.889	3.784	3.685	3.589	3.498	3.410	3.326
7	4.712	4.564	4.423	4.288	4.160	4.039	3.922	3.812	3.706	3.605
8	5.146	4.968	4.799	4.639	4.487	4.344	4.207	4.078	3.954	3.837
9	5.537	5.328	5.132	4.946	4.772	4.607	4.451	4.303	4.163	4.031
10	5.889	5.650	5.426	5.216	5.019	4.833	4.659	4.494	4.339	4.192
11	6.207	5.938	5.687	5.453	5.234	5.029	4.836	4.656	4.486	4.327
12	6.492	6.194	5.918	5.660	5.421	5.197	4.988	7.793	4.611	4.439
13	6.750	6.424	6.122	5.842	5.583	5.342	5.118	4.910	4.715	4.533
14	6.982	6.628	6.302	6.002	5.724	5.468	5.229	5.008	4.802	4.611
15	7.191	6.811	6.462	6.142	5.847	5.575	5.324	5.092	4.876	4.675
16	7.379	6.974	6.604	6.265	5.954	5.668	5.405	5.162	4.938	4.730
17	7.549	7.120	6.729	6.373	6.047	5.749	5.475	5.222	4.990	4.775
18	7.702	7.250	6.840	6.467	6.128	5.818	5.534	5.273	5.033	4.812
19	7.839	7.366	6.938	6.550	6.198	5.877	5.584	5.316	5.070	4.843
20	7.963	7.469	7.025	6.623	6.259	5.929	5.628	5.353	5.101	4.870

FORMULAE

Annuity

Present value of an annuity of £1 per annum receivable or payable for n years, commencing in one year, discounted at r% per annum:

$$PV = \frac{1}{r}\left[1 - \frac{1}{[1 + r]^n}\right]$$

Perpetuity

Present value of £1 per annum, payable or receivable in perpetuity, commencing in one year, discounted at r% per annum:

$$PV = \frac{1}{r}$$

Growing Perpetuity

Present value of £1 per annum, receivable or payable, commencing in one year, growing in perpetuity at a constant rate of g% per annum, discounted at r% per annum:

$$PV = \frac{1}{r - g}$$

The Examiners for Management Accounting – Risk and Control Strategy offer to future candidates and to tutors using this booklet for study purposes, the following background and guidance on the questions included in this examination paper.

Section A – Question One – Compulsory

Question One is designed to test the candidate's ability to identify and evaluate a range of internal controls, including those that are financial and non-financial, qualitative as well as quantitative. The question further tests the candidate's ability to recommend improvements to corporate governance, risk management strategy and internal controls. This requires the candidate to apply knowledge of best practice in these areas to the facts of the case. The syllabus topics being tested are widespread, covering A (i), (iii) & (iv), B (iv), (v) and (vii), C (v) and (vi), D (i), (ii) and (vi). The question meets the learning outcomes by providing a case study of a small multinational distribution organisation that is controlled by a dominant individual. Candidates are expected to apply their understanding of management control, risk and internal controls to this case.

Section B – answer two of four questions

Question Two is designed to test the candidate's ability to explain the role of internal audit and to analyse and discuss the risks exposed by the internal audit of security in a newly implemented computer system. The question further tests the candidate's ability to apply CIMA's ethical guidelines to the case. The syllabus topics being tested are mainly B (i) and (iii), C (ii), (iv) & (vii), E (iv) & (v). The question meets the learning outcomes by providing a scenario in which the Head of Internal Audit has to address the risks of an inadequately designed IT system in which there are ethical issues surrounding how these risks and weaknesses are reported. Candidates are expected to apply their understanding of risks, internal control, internal audit and ethics to the scenario.

Question Three is designed to test the candidate's ability to identify risks within a particular context, explain possible tools for their control, and discuss the appropriateness of systems based internal audits for monitoring risk controls. The syllabus topics being tested are mainly B (Risk and Internal Control) and C (ii) and (iv) on internal audit. The learning outcomes are achieved by the creation of a mini scenario of a doctors' practice that is expanding into a new area of work that carries different risks. Candidates are thus required to apply their knowledge of risk identification, risk management and internal audit to a specific case.

Question Four tests a candidate's understanding of the tools that may be used to manage interest rate risk. Within the context of a scenario that contains information on a company's existing capital structure, the first part of the question requires discussion of the relative merits of using fixed or variable rate borrowing to fund an expansion project. The syllabus topic being tested is D (i) (Management of Financial Risk). The second part of the question, which also carried more marks, tests understanding of the use of swaps to manage interest rate risk. The syllabus topics being tested are D (ii) and (iii). The separate elements of the sub-question on interest rate swaps test both theoretical and application skills, including computation.

Question Five is a straightforward test of knowledge of corporate governance regulations and falls into syllabus section B (vii) on risk and internal control. Parts a and b of the question are phrased in a generic style that tests overall understanding of the reasons for the development of governance regulations and requires discussion of their link to risk management. Part (c) requires more detailed understanding of the UK regulations as laid down in the Combined Code with specific reference to the role of the audit committee.

The Examiner's Answers

The answers that follow are fuller and more comprehensive than would have been expected from a well-prepared candidate. They have been written in this way to aid teaching, study and revision for tutors and candidates alike.

SECTION A

Question One

Summary of financial information (contextual, useful but not required in solution).

A summary P&L (in $million) shows that

Sales	*100 units each year*	*$200*
Cost of sales	20%	40
Gross profit	80%	160
R&D	15%	30
Export marketing	25%	50
Management & admin	15%	30
Profit	25%	50

(a) **Financial controls**

Costing: as cost of sales represents only 20% of selling price, and other costs are period costs, often incurred more than a year in advance of sales taking place, it can be understood that product costing is not especially helpful. Indeed, lean accounting suggests that using techniques that do not add value is to be avoided.

Flexible budgeting is unlikely to be helpful in reconciling actual and target performance due to the high proportion of fixed, period costs. However, even 20% of sales is significant and there ought to be a comparison between standard cost and actual cost charged by the outsource supplier to ensure that variances are identified and investigated and, if necessary, corrected or at least used to modify the selling price.

Budgets: These are used by VCF in a limited manner. Budgets can be used for feed forward and feedback purposes. Viktor uses budgets for feed forward although this is limited to cash forecasting, and for feedback purposes in relation to expense control. This use could be expanded to integrate sales forecasts for cash purposes with budgets for control purposes so that area managers are held responsible for achieving sales targets as well as controlling costs, and so have profit responsibility. The cash forecast used by Viktor would then be integrated with profit reporting.

However, the "Beyond Budgeting" movement has recognised the limitations of traditional budgeting and recommends a more adaptive method of managing through targets linked to stretch goals and a more decentralised management style (contrasted with the centralisation of VCF through Viktor).

Quantitative controls

The Balanced Scorecard recognises the need for non-financial measures around customers, processes and innovation. VCF appears to use a small number of non-financial measures: sales, market share, quality and customer satisfaction. Three of these are customer measures. Given the importance of export sales, measures could also be expanded around the relative effectiveness of generating sales per head or per dollar spent in each area (country) with benchmarking of managers against each other. Quality is the only process measure and, given the long lead time, cycle time between order and installation may be a useful measure as well as rework, customer complaints, installation problems and so on. Given the importance of employees to VCF, measures should be implemented to expand on the relatively simplistic percentage of sales spent on R&D. These could include employee retention, training costs and employee satisfaction/morale.

Qualitative controls

There is little mention in the case of the qualitative controls that VCF could adopt. These include legislation and stock exchange listing requirements in the home country (which may or may not be rigorous); formal structures; rules, policies and procedures; and personnel controls such as recruitment, training and appraisal. Outsourcing manufacture does provide some control over costs and VCF may need to evaluate its supply chain including engaging in regular competitive tendering. There are area managers who control each geographic region and incentives are high, given the payment of above-average salaries and Viktor's dismissal of uncommitted employees. Viktor may get better results if he works more through his area managers than bypassing them and dealing directly with staff as this is likely to reduce the motivation of area managers and cause confusion in the minds of staff over the priorities they should pursue. Given Viktor's involvement and control over rewards, staff may be likely to bypass area managers and deal directly with Viktor. There is also a need to evaluate the effectiveness of the board of directors as governance processes within VCF appear to be weak, due to Viktor dominating the board.

Non-cybernetic methods

VCF does not make extensive use of cybernetic controls but seems to rely heavily on the informal, intuitive or judgemental controls applied by Viktor. Viktor is a dominating individual and clearly uses his power to control, either through telephone contact or via extensive travel. He does not rely extensively on traditional financial reports or non-financial reports but is heavily focused on sales growth and R&D. This is not an economic-rational or shareholder value approach but an approach rooted in a non-rational paradigm of culture rooted in personal power. While this is an important form of control, Viktor needs to balance his use of cybernetic and non-cybernetic forms of control. The limitation of non-cybernetic controls is that they can alter depending on the mood of Viktor and be unclear or ambiguous to employees. This personal control makes VCF very dependent on Viktor. If Viktor has a major illness or dies, it may be very difficult to replace him in the short term and this may lead to uncertainty among his managers as to who is in control and what priorities should be followed.

(b) To: Board of VCF

From: A Candidate

Date: 24 November 2005

Subject: Recommended Improvements

I have examined the information provided and I am outlining below my recommendations for improvement to each of corporate governance, risk management strategy and internal controls within VCF.

Corporate governance

As a small listed company, VCF needs to comply with most corporate governance requirements and the responsibility for compliance rests with the Board, not just with Viktor. Viktor operates as both Chairman and Chief Executive and it seems unlikely from the information given that the non-executives are independent as his wife, a long time family friend and an occasional consultant are his appointees to the Board. Therefore, it is unlikely that the board is effective in terms of the Combined Code, given its likely dominance by Viktor. Therefore VCF does not comply with the *Combined Code on Corporate Governance* and is required to explain its reasons in its Annual Report, under the "comply or explain" principle. In particular, the role of non-executive directors should be to have an enquiring mind, exercise independent judgement and show to the management (in this case, Viktor) that they are able to bring their knowledge and experience to bear and make a contribution to the effective governance of the business. Non-executive directors are expected to be independent. Under the Combined Code, none of the non-executive directors are likely to be considered as independent as his wife and the family friends have close family ties, while the consultant has a material business relationship with VCF. The Higgs Report identified the role of non-executive directors as to: challenge and develop proposals on strategy; scrutinise performance; satisfy themselves that financial information and risk management is robust; and determine appropriate levels of remuneration for executive directors and should be involved in appointing and removing executive directors, including succession planning (this latter point is very important in relation to Viktor).

The Board needs to meet more regularly and on a more formal basis and cover a broader spectrum of topics than sales. The Board also needs to exert a more independent stance from Viktor, perhaps seeking more independent members and appointing an independent Chairman who is not the Chief Executive.

Risk management strategy

VCF's risks have been identified in the question as patent infringement, exchange rate risk, economic downturns, failure of R&D, and failure of cost control. VCF's risk management strategies are identified in the question: legal action against competitors who infringe patents, acceptance of exchange rate risk; outsourcing manufacture, personal involvement with R&D, customers and competitors [*this information is given in the question*].

Risk management strategy incorporates the risk profile of the organisation, the risk assessment and evaluation process, and preferred options for risk treatment, responsibility and reporting processes. VCF appears to be a risk-taking organisation, as this is Viktor's personal style. There is no evidence of any formal risk assessment and evaluation process, in fact the risks identified in the case "have been identified by Viktor".

Internal controls

The Board has a responsibility to review internal controls. This is not limited to financial controls. The Board needs to take into account the significant risks faced by the company and the effectiveness of internal controls in managing those risks. There are serious difficulties with the risk management strategies adopted by VCF.

The risk management methods adopted in VCF rely heavily on the judgement of Viktor personally. Personal involvement is not an effective form of control that would assure an independent board, in fact, the death or illness of Viktor would likely place the company in serious jeopardy as he has such a key role in management control.

The Board should identify the necessary actions that are being taken to remedy weaknesses in internal control. In the absence of this, given Viktor's dominating position, the Board will have considerable difficulty in making its annual statement that there is an ongoing process for identifying, evaluating and managing the significant risks facing the company.

There are a number of areas in which internal control should be evident: budget versus actual reporting on a responsibility centre level; project and product profitability calculations, both before and after equipment is installed; management of the supply chain, especially in relation to the outsourcing of manufacture; and more routine internal control issues such as safeguarding assets, authorisation of expenditure, and so on.

Recommendations for improvement

Legal action taken in defence of patents can be very expensive and time consuming and may eventually be unsuccessful, although not taking legal action will seriously affect VCF's competitive advantage. Board approval should be sought prior to legal action being taken in respect of patent infringements.

Acceptance of exchange rate risk carries a significant potential cost to VCF, even though past experience suggests gains and losses are equal. This risk is offset to some degree by the phased payments made by customers. The Board should approve a corporate policy for exchange risks and implement appropriate hedging techniques to alleviate the risk.

Changes in governmental regulation, technological change or an economic downturn may seriously affect VCF and even threaten its survival, particularly as it is very sensitive to cash flow, despite the cash flow model used by Viktor. Outsourcing manufacture is a good way of protecting against downturn as VCF does not have the problem of maintaining utilisation of its production capacity, but it does have significant $110 million period costs (see above) although R&D and export marketing could be reduced in the short term. Given VCF's admitted cash flow limitations, a downturn could result in having to make staff redundant, losing the skill base that is so important to the company. VCF appears to be concentrated in manufacturing industry and there is no evidence of any portfolio approach. One way of managing the risk is by a diversification strategy to spread the risk over a portfolio of products or markets. The Board needs to monitor sales, expense and cash flow projections and hold management accountable for performance and for management's response to changing business conditions.

Personal involvement is a risky strategy as it relies on a single person, Viktor, to recognise and react to economic downturns. Potential failures of R&D and cost control are also subject to Viktor's personal actions. Improved control may be possible by improved reporting systems and delegation to other managers, especially in relation to cost control. Targets may be set for anticipated innovations and new patents. The Board should set financial and non-financial targets and monitor performance against those targets.

I trust that these recommendations meet with your approval, but please contact me if you require any further information.

Signed

A Candidate

(c) Monitoring of exchange rate trends is an important element of managing exchange risks. It is not clear whether VCF uses spot rates to convert foreign exchange into the home currency or whether forward rates are used. Although deposits and progress payments are made, all foreign currencies are remitted to the home country so the exchange risk to VCF is very high. In some of the countries in which sales are made, inflation may be high, so exacerbating the exchange risk. As the manufacture of equipment is outsourced in the home country, there is no ability to offset risk by matching sales with payments.

Exchange risk for VCF is a transaction risk. Sales are $200 million. 90% are export, so $180 million of sales involves some currency risk. A devaluation of the currency in which the sale is made (as the sale is invoiced in that country's currency) or a revaluation of the home currency would result in less income to VCF. For example, a revaluation of the home country's currency by 10% would result in a profit reduction of $18 million ($180 × 10%) which equates to 36% of the annual profit of $50 million (see above).

However, VCF also faces economic risk if long-term currency devaluations occur as profits will be affected. This risk could be avoided by invoicing in the home currency, although this may be a competitive disadvantage as the risk is effectively passed off to the customer.

Exchange rate risk could also be mitigated by outsourcing production from outside the home country to one or more of the customer countries where production may be less expensive and where offsetting of exchange risks could occur. A similar method of mitigating risk would be to borrow from one or more customer country.

As there is a long lead time, there is an opportunity to hedge exchange rates. Hedging protects assets against unfavourable movements in the underlying while retaining the ability to benefit from favourable movements. The instruments bought as a hedge tend to have opposite-value movements to the underlying and are used to transfer risk. A forward contract is an agreement to undertake an exchange at a future date at a set price. This minimises the uncertainty of price fluctuations for both parties. The main forward markets are for foreign exchange.

SECTION B

Question Two

(a) Internal audit is the independent and objective assurance activity that systematically evaluates the effectiveness of risk management, control and governance processes. The core role of internal audit is to provide assurance that the main business risks are being managed and that internal controls are operating effectively.

Internal auditors will not just focus on financial control but on risk management and broader internal control systems. Internal auditors should focus on matters of high risk and, where significant control deficiencies have been found, identify actions taken to address them.

Internal auditors assess how risks are identified, analysed and managed and give independent advice on how to embed risk management practices into business activities. Internal auditors need to make judgements about the measures that can be taken against risk: transferring the risk; reducing the likelihood of risk; reducing exposure to risk; detecting occurrences; and recovering from occurrences.

The role of the Head of Internal Audit is to develop an audit plan based on an assessment of significant risks, submit this to the audit committee for approval, implement the agreed plan and maintain a professional audit team to carry out the plan.

The Head of Internal Audit should be independent of the chief financial officer and should report to the audit committee of the Board by providing regular assessments of the adequacy and effectiveness of systems of risk management and internal control; reporting significant internal control issues and the potential for improving risk management and control; and providing information on the status and results of the annual audit plan and the adequacy of resources for internal audit.

(b) There seems to be a serious weakness in the design and/or operation of the present system. There may be a lack of controls over the information system as a whole, over specific applications such as the order entry system identified as the weakness here or over the network allowing customer access, or a combination of these. The most likely sources of the problem in this case are: poor systems development controls; poor network controls; or fraud by employees.

The potential risks faced by SPQ include: financial loss due to loss of customers; loss of orders; reputation loss; and fraud. The risk here may be only the one that has become evident. Broader risks that have not yet been identified may be a consequence of the failure of system development controls and the lack of proper testing and acceptance of the system by users; or failures in the operation of systems via the network leading to loss of other transactions.

Reducing the likelihood of risk is only possible through effective systems design and operating controls, and protection against fraud.

Systems development
Systems development controls should involve comprehensive system design and testing with sign-off by all parties before implementation. This involves being

satisfied that the system meets user requirements, functions satisfactorily, has adequate controls, and is auditable. Such a sign-off does not appear to have taken place in this case as the IT department advised against implementation and there has been no post-implementation review. Poor integrity controls can result in corruption of data within the system, and the absence of contingency controls can fail to identify lost transactions.

Network or operating controls
The risks faced by the company may be a consequence of poor security controls that fail to prevent unauthorised access, modification or destruction of data. Network controls avoid risks such as hacking, a computer virus/worm or accidental or deliberate customer alteration of data. There should be warning alarms in relation to attempted hacking. Preventive controls such as a firewall may also prevent unauthorised access. Examples of controls include data encryption, transaction authorisation, virus prevention, hacking detection, etc.

Reducing exposure to risk is possible through controls which, for example, ensure that all sales are delivered and funds are collected and that all transactions that enter the system are fully completed.

Computer audit techniques such as using test data or embedded audit facilities or audit interrogation software can be used to detect irregularities and can lead to recovery action if errors are quickly identified, enabling corrections to be effected.

Fraud
The problem may be evidence of employee fraud, with funds being diverted. Controls to overcome fraud risk include predictive controls such as effective screening of employees, training and supervision, the separation of duties, physical access controls, password access controls, etc. In addition, a culture needs to be fostered in which dishonesty is not tolerated and a fraud management strategy of prevention, identification and response is evident. Controls need to be put in place to reduce dishonesty and the opportunity and motive for fraud.

(c) **Problems with audit**
The reporting relationship of the Head of Internal Audit seems clear, as s/he has access to the chair of audit despite a reporting relationship to the Chief Executive.

One of the first problems is to identify the type of audit carried out. This seems to have been a transactions-based audit although the identification of missing transactions suggests elements of a systems-based audit. What is not known is why the chief accountant requested the audit. The chief accountant may have identified a risk and requested some internal audit work be carried out, hence there may be elements of a risk-based audit.

One issue to be considered in planning the audit is the extent to which the internal audit team was involved in the original design, testing and acceptance of the new system as this may compromise the audit team's objectivity in undertaking a review of that system. Another issue is whether the audit team assigned to this audit has the necessary skills and experience to carry out the audit, particularly as to whether the team is able to identify the weaknesses involved in the IT system and the extent to which it can assess whether the transactions involve deliberate fraud or hacking or accidental data corruption caused by design faults or human error.

What it is important to recognise here is that there has been "sample testing" that has revealed "several" transactions. It is unclear whether this sample was a statistically valid one or based on some other criteria. It is therefore difficult to generalise from these audit findings to the population of transactions. The audit plan for the review of IT security already carried out needs to be reviewed to ascertain how effectively the audit was carried out and in order to gauge the potential scale of the problem.

The audit has resulted in a draft report about "serious weaknesses" and this requires some investigation: Is there sufficient evidence to draw this conclusion? Is further testing called for? If further testing is required or there are weaknesses in the audit approach, then a more appropriate course of action may be to request a change to the internal audit plan to undertake further work to obtain more evidence in order to determine the extent of the problem. If however, the evidence does in fact reveal serious weaknesses, these need to be brought to the attention of the audit committee.

(d) The fundamental principles that relate to the work of accountants as internal auditors are integrity (acting honestly and avoiding misleading statements); objectivity (impartiality and freedom from conflicts of interest); professional competence and due care; confidentiality; professional behaviour and the avoidance of conduct that might bring discredit to CIMA; and technical competence (the presentation of information fully, honestly and professionally).

Most of these principles apply in the present case. If the evidence justifies it, integrity and objectivity require that it be brought to the audit committee's attention. However, professional and technical competence requires that the Head of Internal Audit be confident in the audit findings before doing so.

CIMA's *Ethical Guidelines* describe the process for resolving ethical conflicts. Accountants working in organisations may encounter situations which give rise to conflicts of interest, ranging from fraud and illegal activities to relatively minor situations. An ethical conflict is not the same as an honest difference of opinion.

CIMA members should be constantly conscious of, and be alert to factors which give rise to conflicts of interest. In the present case, the ethical conflict is the real or perceived pressure placed on the Head of Internal Audit not to embarrass the Chief Executive. There is also the question of divided loyalty to the Chief Executive, to the audit committee, and to the Head of Internal Audit's professional responsibilities as a CIMA member.

Although it has not been suggested to the Head of Internal Audit that the matter not be reported, there is a suggestion that the report be softened and that work carry on behind the scenes to improve the system.

However, it is important that a draft report be produced and submitted for comment before it is sent to the audit committee. This presents the opportunity for other views to be aired. One course of action may be to discuss the matter with the Finance

Director to determine his/her view and with the Chief Executive to determine that person's reactions to the draft audit report.

When faced with ethical conflicts, members should

- Follow the organisation's grievance procedure;
- Discuss the matter with the member's superior and successive levels of management, always with the member's superior's knowledge (unless that person is involved).

Discussion with an objective adviser or the professional body may be useful to clarify the issues involved and alternative courses of action that are available, without breaching any duty of confidentiality. Throughout, the member should maintain a detailed record of the problem and the steps taken to resolve it.

If an ethical conflict still exists after fully exhausting all levels of internal review, the member may have no recourse on significant matters other than to resign and report the matter to the organisation. Except when seeking advice from CIMA or when legally required to do so, communication of information regarding the problem to persons outside the employing organisation is not considered appropriate.

Question Three

(a) The additional risks that might be incurred as a result of the introduction of a day surgery unit may include any/all of the following:

Security
The new unit will presumably require the purchase and storage of additional equipment and drugs such as anaesthetics. In addition, if the unit is on the same premises as the current practice then it will be important to restrict access to the day surgery unit, in order to protect both patients and staff. Both of these changes imply increased security risks.

Staffing
A new staffing plan will need to be drafted that ensures adequate coverage of both aspects of the practice's activities. The skill profile of the day surgery staff may differ from that of existing staff and this may create problems for both recruitment and retention. Additionally, care will have to be taken to ensure that job comparability is fully reflected in the relative salary scales or there may be employee dissatisfaction.

Financial
The new unit will inevitably require some capital investment in new equipment and facilities, as well as in additional staffing and training. One possible risk is that the return on the investment will not match that currently being earned within the main practice, and any decision to go ahead with the new facilities should only be made after careful evaluation of the cash flow forecast arising from the proposal. There is also likely to be an increased cost for insurance.

In extending the service provision, the doctors may be "diversifying" their business risk, but this may also increase the financial burden if the investment is to be funded by borrowing. Furthermore, the practice is run as a partnership, and therefore if one of the doctors wishes to leave, it will be necessary for the others to have the cash to buy him/her out. If all the cash is tied up in the new surgery then this may be difficult.

Litigation

There is always a risk that a doctor may be sued for poor diagnosis or care of a patient. In the case of a general medical practice, the likelihood of this is limited by the relative simplicity of many of the procedures conducted by the doctor and the referral of patients to a hospital for diagnosis of more complex problems. Even simple day surgery procedures add complexity to the service provision, and if the doctors are inexperienced or have limited training there is a risk that they may make errors that would not occur in a regular hospital environment. As a result of the new facility there is therefore an increased risk of litigation against the individual doctors.

Contamination

The introduction of a surgery facility will lead to the generation of possible contaminated waste, the disposal of which is subject to strict regulation. Staff will need to be trained in the relevant procedures for dealing with such waste, and in minimising the risk of cross contamination of staff/patients and the avoidance of infections arising from handling such materials.

Operational

Operational risk arises out of the possibility that procedures will not be correctly documented or followed and financial, legal or other penalties are incurred as a consequence. The introduction of a whole new facility and associated new procedures therefore increases the potential operational risk exposure of the practice. For example, staff may incorrectly file patient records, make errors in timetabling surgical procedures or fail to order vital supplies. Additional control systems will therefore need to be established to minimise the risk of operational errors. Government regulations will also need to be complied with.

CIMA's "Risk Management: Guide to Good Practice" report argues that risk management should be a proactive process that is an integral part of strategic management – it should not simply take the form of a response to crises. This perspective on risk management is summarised in CIMA's risk management cycle, which is illustrated below:

NOTE: Candidates may use an alternative model, with marks being awarded for the principles rather than the detail of anyone model.

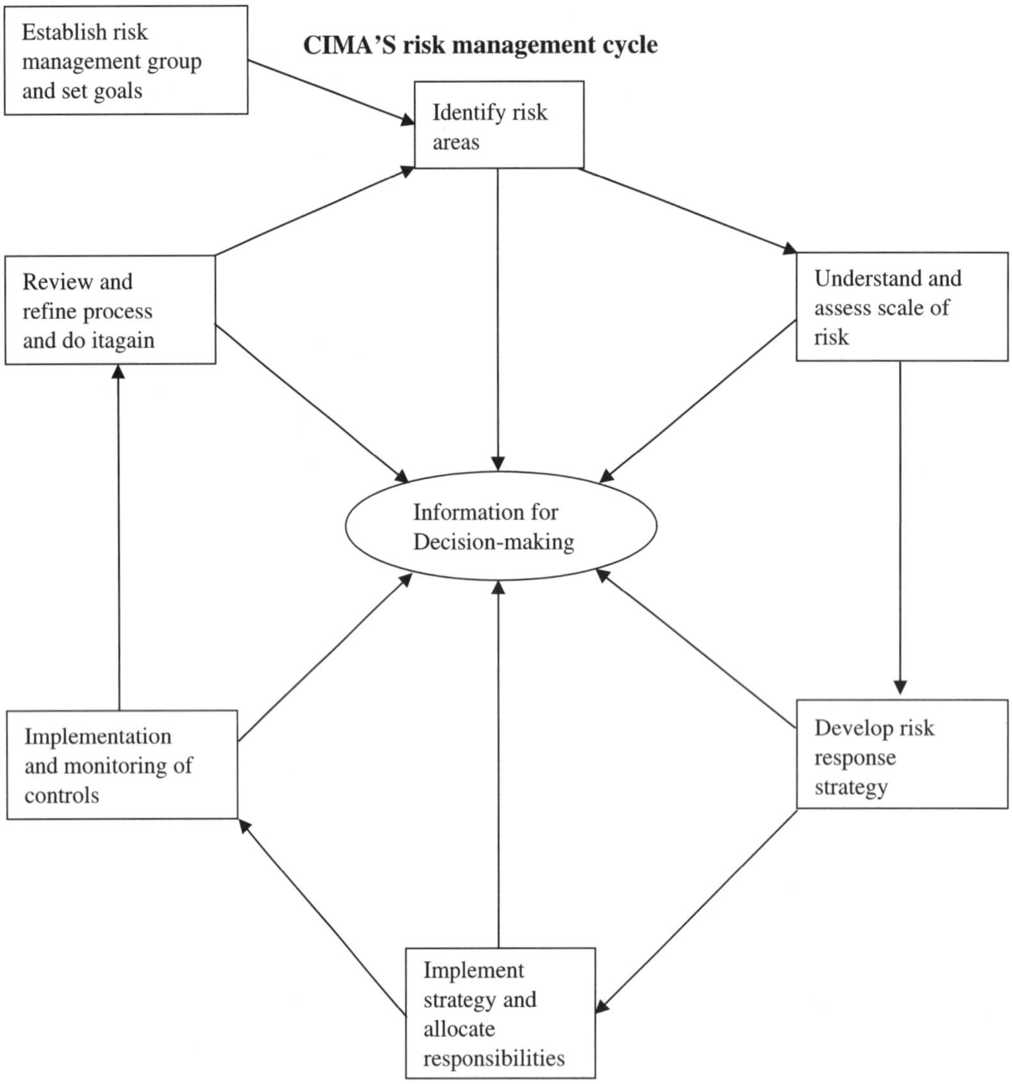

The cycle forms a control loop via a risk management process that begins with the establishment of a risk management group and the specification of goals, for example risk appetites for specific risk areas. The series of stages depicted in the cycle serves to ensure that an organisation more clearly understands the sources of the risks encountered in its business and the controls that might be used to manage them.

In relation to the scenario of the doctors' practice, a team would be established to identify potential risks and devise a strategy for ranking and controlling them, which would include allocation of responsibility for each risk category. For example, the practice nurses may be held responsible for establishing procedures to control the contamination and infection risks. Most importantly, the control process does not end with the allocation of responsibilities, but instead the control loop ensures post control reviews that ensure improvements in practice the next time around. In the doctors' practice, therefore, the risk management team would undertake regular reviews of the effectiveness of the risk control system and recommend changes as appropriate. Information is at the centre of the risk management cycle and there needs to be a continual review of the risks described above in terms of identifying and assessing the risk, developing a risk response, implementing and monitoring controls and reporting and risk review. This is an ongoing process in relation to existing and new risks.

(b) The term "risk appetite" refers to an organisation's willingness to take on risk in exchange for potentially higher returns. Psychologists take the view that attitude to risk is a matter of individual choice, and people may be risk taking entrepreneurs or one of those who prefers a lower income as an employee that is "guaranteed".

In the context of an organisation such as the medical practice portrayed in the question, the ultimate effects of the level of risk taken will be felt by the partners, and so it is their joint responsibility to define the practice's risk appetite. This may change over time as the membership of the partnership changes. Apart from taking an overall position in relation to their willingness to take on risks, the partners must also determine their risk appetite in relation to each specific risk type that is identified. For example, in relation to litigation, the doctors must decide the extent to whether they wish to purchase professional indemnity insurance to protect themselves against this risk, and the amount of insurance cover that is optimal. The insurance premiums will add to the costs of the practice, but will be offset by the additional revenue earned by the day surgery activities. Similarly, but in relation to a very different area of risk, security could be kept very tight via the employment of dedicated staff, but the partners must decide whether the level of risk warrants such expenditure. The risk appetite thus reflects the willingness to tolerate particular levels of risk, and the costs incurred in maintaining that risk profile.

Some broader consultation could also take place with senior staff, patient representatives to gauge their attitudes in relation to the proposal. This may be important to gauge the value of service improvements, additional opportunities for staff, and to better understand risks of failure of the service and so on.

(c) Risk management systems are different from normal operating systems in being concerned with appropriate planning for, and response to, uncertain developments that may occur. A systems-based approach is particularly appropriate because there will usually be few such developments. The term systems based internal auditing refers to the process whereby the audit is planned on the basis of validation of the effective functioning of operating, accounting or control systems rather than validation of the associated documentary records. It is common practice to use a risk based approach when planning an internal audit, so that the systems identified as being at highest risk are audited more frequently and in more depth than those which carry a lower level of risk.

In the case of a risk management system, the internal audit would focus on an assessment of the extent to which the defined risk management objectives were being met as a result of the established control systems. For example, if the declared objective was zero operational risk and hence zero operating errors, the audit would identify the procedures put in place to eliminate error, determine whether they were appropriate, and then test their operational effectiveness. Any faults or limitations in the system would then be reported and used in the redesign of the control system. The identification of faults may include comment on the practical viability of the declared objectives.

If an adverse event does occur, the organisation should undertake a detailed review, after the event, of both how the risk management system coped and also of the substantive event itself.

In essence a systems based audit thus checks whether objectives are being achieved or not, and comments on the factors that may be inhibiting that achievement. By focusing on the aspects of control that are subject to the greatest risk of failure, such an audit can be deemed to provide good assurance that system objectives are being achieved.

Question Four

(a) It is important to recognise that there is a very low level of existing gearing, and the scale of the proposed extra borrowing is fairly insignificant; 63% of the existing borrowing is floating rate and will be redeemed in two years; and the company's sensitivity to interest rate risk (its financial gearing) will be affected by its level of business risk and operational gearing.

In considering the factors that may be taken into account in deciding whether to raise fixed rate or variable rate debt, one of the key issues to consider is a company's attitude to risk, and its preferences for hedging any such risks either internally or externally. If an organisation is indifferent to financial risk then, regardless of interest rate trends, it will also be indifferent between fixed or variable rate borrowings. Equally, if it is sensitive to downside risk, but happy to accept upside risk then there may be a preference for variable over fixed rate borrowing in a world of falling interest rates. Similarly, if the overall preference is for cash flow certainty, then fixed rates may be preferred. Consequently, the first factor that may influence the decision is the risk preferences of the Board of Directors.

A second important consideration is the relative scale of the exposure. In the case of LXN the company is considering raising debt finance of €1.8 million, against assets of €2 billion and therefore, even taking into account the existing amount of long term debt, the exposure remains relatively insignificant. In other words, it probably does not matter whether the debt is of a fixed or variable rate nature, because of its small scale. Under such circumstances, the cost of hedging the exposure may outweigh the potential cost of remaining exposed to interest rate movements.

The question of whether to select one type of debt over another is dependent, in part, upon the treasurer's view of future interest rate movements. If he/she believes that interest rates are likely to rise, then locking into a fixed rate may be desirable; equally, if rates are expected to fall then a variable rate loan would be preferable. Furthermore, consideration must be given as to whether any anticipated changes in interest rates may also affect the level of activity in the underlying business. Where this might be the case, such as in an industry like construction, the higher interest rates leading to falling sales will mean that being locked in to fixed interest payments may not be desirable. It is unlikely, however, that the retail book market is interest rate sensitive.

The existing debt mix (fixed:variable) is also likely to influence the choice of how to fund new ventures. At current exchange rates, LXN has slightly more fixed rate borrowing than variable rate (€15 million versus €12.3 million respectively). Overdependence on either form of debt can increase exposure and hence incur additional hedging costs. In this instance, however, the additional borrowing is sufficiently small for this not to matter very much.

The absolute cost of the alternative forms of hedging is also important. If the exposure can be hedged internally via, for instance, the granting of matching credit facilities against revenue streams, then the hedging cost would be close to zero. LXN does not appear to have the opportunity to take advantage of such internal hedging and so if the hedging is arranged externally via, for example, the purchase of a forward-rate agreement or a broker arranged swap, then costs will be incurred and the scale of such costs may influence the borrowing decision. The limited availability of hedging options may thus affect the specific borrowing choice.

(b) (i) Interest rate swaps are a useful tool for the management of interest rate risk because they allow a company to switch between fixed and variable rate loans, and therefore take a position on the future direction of interest rates. For example, a company may believe that interest rates have "bottomed out" and hence choose to swap its variable rate loans for fixed rate ones set at the current low interest rate level. In making this swap, the company is affirming its belief that future rates will rise, that is, taking a position.

In many but not all cases, swaps are used to obtain funding at a lower rate than that available elsewhere, but they can also be used beneficially to manage future cash flow patterns. If, for example, a company is operating in a market where its incoming cash flows are uncertain, it may wish to use a swap to ensure that it has fixed rate commitments that are wholly predictable. In so doing, it minimises uncertainty of outgoings even if it cannot eliminate the uncertainty re incoming cash.

Interest rate swaps may also be used to manage interest rate risk in respect of investments rather than borrowings. In such cases a swap may be useful in enhancing the returns via speculation on interest rate movements, for example swapping a variable rate for a fixed rate investment in the belief that interest rates will fall.

Over and above cost, an advantage of interest rate swaps over simply borrowing appropriately in the first place, is that they allow the organisation to change its borrowing profile without having to renegotiate with lenders if circumstances change after the original borrowing.

(ii) Transactions if swap is agreed:

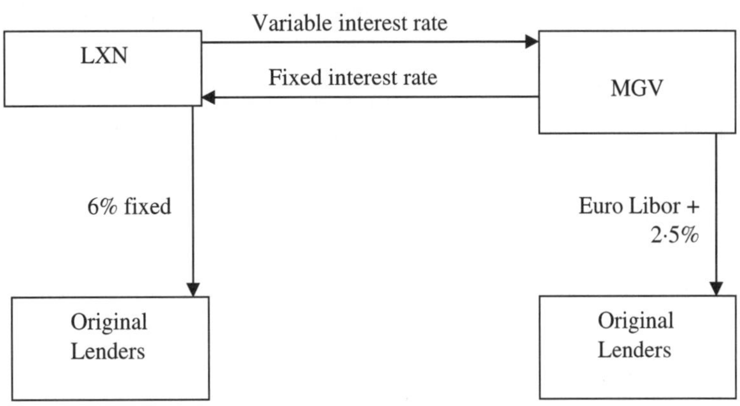

LXN swaps a fixed rate loan for a variable rate one based on Euro Libor.

(iii) Workings

LXN		MGV	
Borrows at	6%	Borrows at	Euro Libor + 2.5%
Receives from MGV	(6.4%)	Receives	(6.8%)
Pays to MGV	6.8%	Pays to LXN	6.4%
Net interest cost	Euro Libor + 1.4%	Net interest cost	7.1% fixed

The quality spread differential is 0.2% which is shared equally between the two parties. Variations in the workings are possible. The rates paid between the two parties will be open to negotiation. Therefore, the only certainties are the rates at which the two companies borrow from the market and the resulting net interest cost to each of them. The result is a net saving to both parties is 0.1% interest of the terms that they could otherwise have obtained, that is LXN pays 6.4% instead of 6.5% variable and MGV pays 7.1% fixed instead of 7.2%. On a loan of €1.8 million this generates a saving of €1,800 per year for LXN. This saving has to be offset against the additional risk arising from the swap because of the counterparty risk. LXN faces the risk that MGV will not make the cash payments on time, and any default losses would have to be covered. The credit risk can be minimised by seeking a credit rating on the counterparty before agreeing to a swap.

Question Five

(a) CIMA defines corporate governance as "the system by which companies are directed and controlled." This incorporates the role of the Board of Directors, and the relationship between the Board of Directors, shareholders and auditors.

Governance regulations have developed as a result of a series of corporate failures and recognition of the agency problem. Corporate failures can be deemed to reflect a lack of accountability to shareholders on the part of either the directors, auditors or both. If the board is able to make decisions that fail to take account of the interests of shareholders then there is scope for excessive risk taking that may result in failure. Governance therefore requires the establishment of procedures that enforce accountability via a process of monitoring the behaviour of the board and the associated internal control systems.

The governance regulations have therefore emerged as a response to corporate failures seen as arising from weak internal controls that have failed to protect the interests of shareholders and other stakeholders. Some governments have taken the view that the establishment of the necessary governance structures must be made a legal requirement, for example Sarbanes-Oxley. In other countries, such as the UK, legal regulation is more limited, but the stock markets require compliance with, in this case, the Cadbury Code.

(b) The general principles that underpin governance regulations around the world, including the Combined Code in the UK, the King Report in South Africa and the Sarbanes-Oxley Act in the USA are basically the same. They aim to achieve transparency and integrity in the relations between the board and the stakeholders in the company.

In the United Kingdom, the way in which these principles are put into effect is via recommendations of practice in the Combined Code which relate to:

- Directors;
- Directors' remuneration;
- Accountability and audit;
- Relations with shareholders;
- Institutional shareholders;
- Disclosure.

The Combined Code requires that the board of directors is made up of a mix of executive and non-executive directors who are collectively held responsible for the running of the business. The role of Chairman and Chief Executive should be held by different people. The procedures for appointment of directors should be transparent, and all new members of the board should receive training as appropriate. All members should be regularly submitted for re-election, and the full board should evaluate its work annually.

The code requires that the remuneration given to directors should be set independently, be transparent and also sufficient to motivate the appointment of suitably qualified staff. In the case of the executive directors, it is expected that a significant proportion of their remuneration should be linked to performance, for example via the use of stock options.

Accountability to shareholders is ensured within the Combined Code via requirements that the board should establish a sound system of internal controls and present a sound and understandable assessment of the company's position and prospects. In addition the relationship with external auditors should be appropriate and transparent.

Communication with shareholders should be encouraged via dialogue in the annual general meeting, but additional communication and dialogue is desirable to ensure that shareholders understand the corporate objectives. Similarly, a dialogue with institutional investors should be maintained that ensures a similar understanding of objectives.

The Combined Code suggests that the annual report should include a governance report which contains detailed information on how the board operates, frequency of meetings, the names of members of the board (including non-executives) and also its key associated committees, for example audit committee and remuneration committee. A description of the work of these committees together with how the board performance is evaluated should also be included.

In combination these core principles are intended to ensure that company directors are subject to independent oversight of their work, via both non-executive directors and auditors, and their remuneration is linked to corporate performance. As a result, the agency problem is minimised and board members are held clearly accountable to shareholders.

(c) The Combined Code requires that companies should establish an audit committee of two or three (depending on the company size) independent non-executive directors. The job of the audit committee, which should meet at least three times per year, is to serve as advisors to the board, with particular responsibility for reviewing the effectiveness of the internal control and audit system. In addition the committee works closely with external auditors in order to ensure the integrity of the financial statements and fulfillment of obligations on announcement of significant events to the stock exchange.

There are thus two key elements to the job of the audit committee – those relating to responsibilities in respect of internal control, and those concerning relations with the external auditors.

The audit committee is required to review the company's internal control and risk management systems, although it is becoming common practice for responsibility for the risk management review to be held by a separate risk committee that is a sub division of the board of directors. The committee's responsibilities include the appointment of the head of internal audit, and ensuring that there are sufficient resources and personnel to ensure the effective operation of the function. Additionally, the audit committee should take care to verify that there are no problems with access to information that may impede the workings of internal audit. Assurance on this point is achieved, at least in part, via meetings between the committee and head of internal audit, where issues of scope, access to information and so on may be raised. The head of internal audit will report directly to the head of the audit committee as well as the executive members of the Board of Directors.

The audit committee takes responsibility for reviewing the internal audit plan, and receiving regular reports on the results. The committee also reviews the response of executive management to the internal audit findings. For example, if controls in a specific area are found to be weak, the committee should ensure that management reacts to rectify the situation to their satisfaction. In so doing, they are fulfilling their role of monitoring the effectiveness of the internal audit and control function.

Another of the tasks of the audit committee is to recommend the appointment, re-appointment or removal of the external auditors. An important element of this role is the checking of the objectivity and independence of the auditors. This includes aspects such as the rotation of audit partners, the firm's quality controls to ensure avoidance of conflicts of interest, and the scale of any non-audit services carried out by the same firm. The board of directors, in conjunction with the audit committee, should also agree a policy on employment of former audit firm employees, particularly where they have been one time members of the external audit team. Compliance with ethical guidelines is important in relation to this issue.

At the start of the external audit, it is expected that the audit committee will meet with the audit team to review the scope of the intended audit and make recommendations for changes as required. Any issues arising during the course of the external audit, for example in relation to the use of judgment regarding the content of the financial statements, will be mediated by the committee acting as intermediary between the board and the external auditors. Similarly, where the auditors identify accounting errors, the committee takes responsibility for reviewing these and ensuring their explanation and elimination. Once the external audit is completed, the audit committee will review the effectiveness and completeness of the audit by checking it against the original audit plan and meeting with key accounting personnel who have been dealing with the auditors in their work. At the same time, the external auditor's management letter will be reviewed to ensure that recommendations to management have been acted upon as appropriate.

)rder Form

•r CIMA Official Study Materials for 2006 Exams

Title	Author	ISBN	ISBN 13	Price	Total
		CIMA Official Study Systems			
Management Accounting Fundamentals	Walker	0750667087	9780750667081	£33.00	
Financial Accounting Fundamentals	Lunt	0750667044	9780750667043	£33.00	
Business Mathematics	Peers	0750667052	9780750667050	£33.00	
Economics for Business	Adams	0750667060	9780750667067	£33.00	
Business Law	Sagar	0750667079	9780750667074	£33.00	
Performance Evaluation	Scarlett	0750667117	9780750667111	£33.00	
Decision Management	Wilks	0750667125	9780750667128	£33.00	
Risk and Control Strategy	Collier	0750667168	9780750667166	£33.00	
Organisational Management and Information Systems	Perry	0750667095	9780750667098	£33.00	
Integrated Management	Harris	0750667109	9780750667104	£33.00	
Business Strategy	Botten	0750667184	9780750667180	£33.00	
Financial Accounting and Tax Principles	Rolfe	0750667133	9780750667135	£33.00	
Financial Analysis	Gowthorpe	0750667141	9780750667142	£33.00	
Financial Strategy	Ogilvie	075066715X	9780750667159	£33.00	
TOP CIMA	Barnwell	0750667176	9780750667173	£33.00	
		CIMA Official Exam Practice Kits			
Management Accounting Fundamentals	Allan	0750665807	9780750665803	£14.99	
Financial Accounting Fundamentals	Allan	0750665831	9780750665834	£14.99	
Business Mathematics	Allan	0750665866	9780750665865	£14.99	
Economics for Business	Allan	075066584X	9780750665841	£14.99	
Business Law	Benton	0750665858	9780750665858	£14.99	
Performance Evaluation	Barnett	0750669322	9780750669320	£14.99	
Decision Management	Barnett	0750669292	9780750669290	£14.99	
Risk and Control Strategy	Robertson	0750669373	9780750669375	£14.99	
Organisational Management & Information Systems	Robertson	0750669306	9780750669306	£14.99	
Integrated Management	dalton	0750669314	9780750669313	£14.99	
Business Strategy	Allan	0750669365	9780750669368	£14.99	
Financial Accounting and Tax Principles	Patel	0750669330	9780750669337	£14.99	
Financial Analysis	Rodgers	0750669349	9780750669344	£14.99	
Financial Strategy	Allan	0750669357	9780750669351	£14.99	
TOPCIMA	Little	0750666277	9780750666275	£14.99	
		CIMA Revision Cards			
Management Accounting Fundamentals	Walker	0750664770	9780750664776	£6.99	
Financial Accounting Fundamentals	Holland	0750664762	9780750664769	£6.99	
Business Mathematics	Peers	0750664800	9780750664806	£6.99	
Economics for Business	Adams	0750664789	9780750664783	£6.99	
Business Law	Sagar	0750664797	9780750664790	£6.99	
Performance Evaluation	Scarlett	0750664819	9780750664813	£6.99	
Decision Management	Avis	0750664827	9780750664820	£6.99	
Risk and Control Strategy	Harris	0750664835	9780750664837	£6.99	
Organisational Management and Information Systems	Perry	0750664843	9780750664844	£6.99	
Integrated Management	Harris	0750664851	9780750664851	£6.99	
Business Strategy	Botten	075066486X	9780750664868	£6.99	
Financial Accounting and Tax Principles	Rolfe	0750664878	9780750664875	£6.99	
Financial Analysis	Gowthorpe	0750664886	9780750664882	£6.99	
Financial Strategy	Ogilvie	0750664894	9780750664899	£6.99	
				P+P (£)	2.95
				Total (£)	

ELSEVIER

CIMA PUBLISHING

Post this form to:
CIMA Publishing Customer Services
Elsevier
FREEPOST (OF 1639)
Linacre House, Jordan Hill
OXFORD, OX2 8DP, UK

Or FAX +44 (0)1865 474 010
Or PHONE +44 (0)1865 474 014

Email: cimaorders@elsevier.com

www.cimapublishing.com

Name: ______________________________

Organisation: ______________________________

Invoice Address: ______________________________
____
____

Postcode: ______________________________
Phone number: ______________________________
Email: ______________________________
Delivery Address if different:
FAO: ______________________________

Address: ______________________________
____
____

Postcode: ______________________________

Please note that all deliveries must be signed for

1. Cheques payable to Elsevier.
2. Please charge my:

Visa ☐ ☐ MasterCard
Amex ☐ ☐ Switch Issue No.______

Card No: ______________________________

Expiry Date: ______________________________
Cardholder Name: ______________________________
Signature: ______________________________

Date: ______________________________

CIMA Publishing is an imprint of Elsevier
Registered Office:
The Boulevard, Langford Lane, Kidlington, Oxford OX5 1GB, UK
Registered in England: 3099304, VAT 494 627212